The Charismatics and t

THE CHARISMATICS AND THE WORD OF GOD

A biblical and historical perspective on the
charismatic movement

VICTOR BUDGEN

 EVANGELICAL PRESS

EVANGELICAL PRESS
Faverdale North, Darlington, DL3 0PH, England

© Evangelical Press 1989
First published 1985
Second edition published 1989
Reprinted 2001

British Library Cataloguing in Publication Data

Budgen, Victor
  The Charismatics and the Word of God: a biblical and historical
  perspective on the charismatic movement.
  1. Gifts, Spiritual
  I. Title
  234'.12   BT 767.3

ISBN 0-85234-264-0

Printed and bound in Great Britain by The Bath Press, Bath

To Harry – in appreciation of a loyal
Christian friendship.

Contents

Preface

Yes, this is yet another book on the charismatic issue. As far as I know, one way in which it differs from other contemporary books is that it deals fairly extensively with various charismatic movements that have appeared in other centuries. Other books have casual allusions to them but, apart from recent treatments of Irving, little has been said about charismatic movements in the early church, in Luther's day and in that of the Wesleys, Whitefield and Jonathan Edwards. This book seeks to fill that gap.

But what matters supremely is how we interpret Scripture. Therefore the book begins by grappling with what the Bible says in certain key areas. What is prophecy? What is tongue-speaking? What does Paul teach about the cessation of the gifts? What are the marks of an apostle? It is hard to look simply at what Scripture says. There are so many modern claimants and contemporary testimonies. Before we realize what has happened, we have interpreted Scripture in the light of them. It has not in fact been Scripture alone which has determined the issue.

I can say that I have reached on scriptural grounds conclusions on these matters which now agitate so much of the church. Yet, for the most part, I felt myself to be in a very solitary position. For example, my view on prophecy, tongue-speaking and apostleship seemed to be held by few. Yet as I continued to read and study I found that I had countless companions from among the evangelical stalwarts of the past. Moreover, as they supported my own firm conclusion that this is a matter which is vital for the well-being of Christ's church, a matter on which it is wrong to be neutral, they seemed to be God's spokesmen of the past urging me to put this into print. Yet it must candidly be admitted that chapters 7 to 11, which deal with the historical material, may appear harder reading than the earlier and later chapters, especially if the reader is unfamiliar with the historical background. He can if he wishes omit these chapters on first reading or perhaps read just the last one (chapter 11) which deals with the Irvingite movement and with the beginnings of Pentecostalism at the turn of the century. It is hoped that those readers who do omit these chapters will go back to them, for it is rightly said that those who do not know their history are so often destined to repeat it. This is certainly happening today.

In this book most of the living authors quoted are not named in the main text. In this way it is hoped that the reader will be able to concentrate on the scriptural argument and not be side-tracked by personalities. The notes do provide the identity of the various spokesmen for those who wish to check. I have tried to draw on testimony from spokesmen from a wide variety of backgrounds and hope that I have not misquoted any of these or quoted them out of context. If I have done so, I apologize in advance. It has not been intentional. I have tried to play fair with all my sources.

New books have continued to appear since this book was first published. Much of the debate has been among evangelicals and has centred on the second prophecy of Agabus and the correct interpretation of 1 Corinthians 14:29 and 1 Thessalonians 5:19-21. These passages are discussed more fully in an appendix. In the appendix I have departed from my practice of not naming people in the text. The substance of the appendix first appeared in the magazine *Reformation Today* (Issues 101 and 102) and is used by kind permission of the editor.

As always, I am grateful for the help of my wife, Pauline, who has typed for hours so the book may be completed. I am also grateful to others who have helped in checking the manuscript and especially to my daughter, Elizabeth, who did the major part of this. Once again I must also express gratitude to the fellowship of Milnrow Evangelical Church, where most of the biblical material was originally given in a long series of studies. I am also grateful to Erroll Hulse for encouraging me to make the writing of this book a priority. I also wish to acknowledge indebtedness to Ian Bradley for providing helpful information for the material in the appendix.

My prayer is that all who read these pages may be increasingly motivated by the spirit of the prophet Isaiah: 'To the law and to the testimony! If they do not speak according to this word, they have no light of dawn' (Isa.8:20). And since it is from the Scripture alone that pure, unsullied light proceeds, it is with the scriptural testimony that we will begin.

Victor Budgen
April 1989

1.
Prophecy and the Old Testament

'Prophet – or dross' or 'How to discern the gift from the gimmick' were the titles which one popular youth magazine gave to a discussion of prophecy.[1] Accurate discernment in this realm is essential. Claimants to prophetic powers range from Jeanne Dixon, predicting only the day before Jacqueline Kennedy married Onassis that the lady in question had no thoughts of marriage, to a leading Pentecostal declaring in 1972, 'I prophesy that within the next twelve months the Berlin wall is coming down and there is going to be free access to all Iron Curtain countries including Russia.'[2] Christians will readily dismiss the former, especially when they know that she often uses a crystal ball and deck of cards given to her by a gypsy fortune-teller, although she has correctly predicted many things, such as the assassination of Jacqueline Kennedy's first husband, the President of the U.S.A. But what of the latter? He himself would claim that an earlier vision of 1958 was fulfilled in every detail. And yet the Berlin wall still stands as firm as ever. Is all prophecy, whether clearly pagan or supposedly Christian, a hit-and-miss affair, with striking successes and abysmal failures? How in fact do we discern the gift from the gimmick?

What then is prophecy? Is there any obscurity or vagueness in the biblical teaching on this matter? I submit that there is not. Although our task is to examine the New Testament gift of prophecy, we must start at the beginning. Prophecy is one of the great concepts of the Bible. It is much wider than the books which we normally think of as the prophetic books. The Jews described even books like Joshua and Judges and the books of Samuel and Kings as the 'former prophets', and the Lord Jesus Christ himself prefaced a quotation from the book of Psalms with, 'So was fulfilled what was spoken through the

prophet' (Matt. 13:35). In a sense the whole of Scripture is
prophetic. Nevertheless it would seem right to look more
narrowly at those figures who are clearly seen to be prophetic.
As we do this we shall draw out four essential characteristics of
true prophecy as described in God's Word.

Infallibility

The first characteristic is that *prophecy is God speaking. It is
infallible.* This emerges clearly in the first description of the
gift. Appropriately it was to Moses that the words were
spoken: 'Then the Lord said to Moses, "See, I have made you
like God to Pharaoh, and your brother Aaron will be your
prophet. You are to say everything I command you, and your
brother Aaron is to tell Pharaoh to let the Israelites go out of
his country"' (Exod. 7:1,2).

When we realize that the literal Hebrew says, 'I have made
you God to Pharaoh,' the point that it was God himself speaking emerges even more clearly. Moreover, nothing was to be
held back. Everything was to be told, for the voice behind the
words of the prophet was the voice from the throne. The whole
demeanour of Moses in the ensuing conflict with Pharaoh
illustrates this. Hesitancy and uncertainty were things of the
past as he stood up and proclaimed God's Word. Moreover,
Moses was the supreme forerunner of the Prophet who was to
come, namely Christ himself. After the feeding of the five
thousand many said, 'Surely this is the Prophet who is to come
into the world.' Peter saw Christ as the great Prophet foreseen
by Moses and like Moses himself (John 6:14; Acts 3:21-23).

Yet this mantle of infallibility as God's spokesman was not
only over Moses; it was over all true prophets. 'The word of
the Lord came to me, saying,' was the constant introductory
formula of Jeremiah (Jer. 1:4). 'An oracle: The word of the
Lord to Israel through Malachi,' is another typical beginning
(Mal. 1:1). This is the tone throughout all genuine prophecy.
'Perhaps' and 'maybe' are not in its vocabulary. Listen to the
contrasting language of an apocryphal book accepted by
Roman Catholics, but rightly rejected by biblical Christianity:
'I also will here make an end of my book. And if I have written
well and to the point in my story, this is what I myself desired;

but if meanly and indifferently, this is all I could attain unto' (2 Maccabees 15:37,38). Because it is obviously not God speaking, the contrast is glaring. The point does not need arguing.

The guidance of the Holy Spirit
Further indication of the infallibility of the prophets is to be found in the references to the Holy Spirit as the one who inspired them. The Holy Spirit never promotes error of any kind. In his first letter Peter states that when the prophets spoke of Christ's sufferings and subsequent glory it was by 'the Spirit of Christ in them', and in his second letter he declares, 'For prophecy never had its origin in the will of man, but men spoke from God as they were carried along by the Holy Spirit' (1 Peter 1:11; 2 Peter 1:21). This is borne out in the Old Testament by some seventeen passages where the Holy Spirit is directly linked with prophetic activity (Num. 11:29; 24:2; 1 Sam. 10:6,10; 19:20,23; 1 Kings: 22:24; 1 Chron. 12:18; 2 Chron. 15:1; 20:14; 24:20; Neh. 9:20; Joel 2:28,29; Micah 3:8; Zech. 7:12).

On the whole, (with occasional exceptions to be noted later) the prophets were holy men of fervent prayer. In the older translation of certain passages in Jeremiah it said that God rose up early to send his prophets (Jer. 7:13; 32:33). John Oman aptly commented, 'Naturally his prophets should follow his example.'[3] They were certainly men who got up to pray. A study of the life of Samuel, for example, would reveal that he was a man of regular prayer. So was Daniel, whose enemies seized on the very regularity of his devotional life as a pretext for apprehending him (1 Sam. 7:5; 8:6; 12:23; 15:11; Dan. 6:10-13). Jeremiah went away to pray before receiving clear guidance from God, as did Daniel and his friends (Jer. 42:4-7; Dan. 2:17-23). They were in touch with God and he could speak infallibly through them.

Of course, we realize that many deny this inerrancy. H.H. Rowley, the well-known liberal scholar and prolific writer on the Old Testament, expresses a widely held view of prophecy. 'That it was imperfect and fallible is not surprising, since it was mediated through imperfect and fallible men,' he concludes.[4] It has been put more picturesquely by another who holds this position: 'Our ignorance and imperfections hinder the reception and transmission of God's word. White light passing through, say, red glass is filtered so that only red light comes through; so what we see through the coloured glass is only part of the truth.'

It could be put quite differently. For example, people often refer to a 'curate's egg', meaning that something is a mixture of both good and bad points. Yet in the original *Punch* cartoon of 1895, a formidable bishop in gaiters says, 'I'm afraid you've got a bad egg, Mr Jones,' whereupon the timid curate replies, 'Oh, no, my Lord, I assure you! Parts of it are excellent!'[5] However diplomatic (or cowardly) the junior clergyman might have been, we all know what an egg is like when it is only good in part. It stinks! Prophecy which is only good in part is even worse. It is from the evil one himself.

'"Let the prophet who has a dream tell his dream, but let the one who has my word speak it faithfully. For what has straw to do with grain?" declares the Lord. "Is not my word like fire," declares the Lord, "and like a hammer that breaks a rock in pieces?"' (Jer. 23:28,29.) God's Word, like pure grain, provides wholesome food and it also burns into the conscience and breaks the hardest of hearts when he so wills. Luther expressed this in his typical flamboyant manner when he said that, in comparison with God's Word in the Bible, all other books were but waste paper.[6]

Supernaturalism

Secondly, we note the characteristic of *supernaturalism* in connection with true prophecy. In a period of dearth, the psalmist lamented: 'We are given no miraculous signs; no prophets are left, and none of us knows how long this will be' (Ps. 74:9). In his mind signs and prophecy went naturally and inevitably together. There is clear evidence for this viewpoint. In fact, the first actual use of the word 'prophet' in the Old Testament supports this. Abimelech, the King of Gerar, was directly informed by God that Abraham was 'a prophet' and would intercede on his behalf. When Abraham did this, God supernaturally intervened and healed Abimelech's wife and slave girls. At the time they were not able to bear children, since God himself had closed up their wombs (Gen. 20:7,17,18).

Next in the pages of Scripture we meet Moses, the prophet

par excellence. John Owen, the great Puritan expositor, said that, if the Jews were accurate in their calculations, the miracles performed by Moses exceeded all the rest recorded in the Old Testament.[7] Without seeking to submit all this to the test of the calculator, we must agree that the signs performed before Pharaoh, in particular, and on many later occasions were stupendous. Plague followed plague. The vast sea was mysteriously parted. A whole army was overthrown. Water flowed from the smitten rock. The very earth swallowed up the enemies and critics of Moses himself. Fittingly, at the end, Moses' body could not even be found. Indeed the Scripture would strongly support the contention of Owen by its epitaph: 'Since then no prophet has risen in Israel like Moses, whom the Lord knew face to face, who did all those miraculous signs and the wonders the Lord sent him to do in Egypt – to Pharaoh and to all his officials and to his whole land. For no one has ever shown the mighty power or performed the awesome deeds that Moses did in the sight of all Israel' (Deut: 34:10-12).

There was at least one other prophetic era in the Old Testament when signs were displayed in abundance. This was the period of Elijah and Elisha. Elijah raised the dead and saw the might of God manifested on Mount Carmel. Many miracles were performed by Elisha at the bidding of God: the leper Naaman was healed, a dead boy was raised, needy people were helped by various miraculous acts and even the very words of the King of Aram, spoken in the privacy of his bedroom, were known to the prophet. Gifts which Elisha had in profusion, other prophets displayed only occasionally. At the intercession of an unknown prophet, a rebellious king's hand was immediately restored (1 Kings 13:6). The blind prophet Ahijah knew that the disguised wife of Jeroboam was coming to see him before he even heard the sound of her steps (1 Kings 14:5). Daniel and his friends were preserved by the direct intervention of God, the one from the lions' den, the others from the fiery furnace (Dan 3;6).

The sign of prediction
However, it must be conceded that not all prophets performed miracles of the type we have just been considering, so can we legitimately say that all moved in the realm of the

supernatural and gave signs? The verse from Psalm 74 quoted earlier gives the clue, for the sign was particularly that of prediction. Because there were no miraculous signs no one knew how long the enemy would continue to oppress (Ps. 74:9). The very next verse shows the writer asking God, 'How long?' Similarly, when God spoke through Isaiah to the unbelieving King Ahaz, 'Ask the Lord your God for a sign, whether in the deepest depths or in the highest heights,' and the king surlily refused to ask for one, God's 'sign' was the great prediction of the virgin conception (Isa. 7:11-17). This was an event that was to take place some seven centuries later and was indeed a sign of one coming down from the highest of heights to the deepest of depths.

> He deigns in flesh to appear
> Widest extremes to join;
> To bring our vileness near,
> And make us all divine . . .[8]

Once again the biblical critics have strenuously sought to deny this aspect of prophecy. One of their leading spokesmen of former years, A.B. Davidson, gave away his case in so doing. He wrote, 'Prophecy is not identical with *prediction*. Prediction is the least element in it. I do not know that it is an essential element in it at all; though I should hesitate to affirm that it is not, because almost all, if not all, of the prophets in the remains which we possess of their literary activity do give predictions.'[9] Then well might he hesitate! In view of this what more need be said? He obviously could not find a prophet who did not predict, or he would have said so.

Therefore, although it has been repeated *ad nauseam*, that prophecy is 'not foretelling but forthtelling', such a view must be rebutted firmly. It reflects an outlook tinged with modernism. Prophecy is forthtelling, but it is also foretelling. Again and again it becomes what has been described as 'delayed miracle'. Prediction is a great sign. You cannot find a prophetic book in the Old Testament which does not give prediction. The birth of Isaac, the sojourn in Egypt, Saul's finding of the lost donkeys, the exact nature of the divided kingdom, the death of those who oppose God and even the very way they will die, the recovery of a good and penitent king from the brink of the grave, the rebellion of Absalom, the victory of Nebuchadnezzar, the precise manner of the punishment of false prophets are all set forth. Josiah and Cyrus were named in prophecy long before they were born. Detail after detail of the life and death and triumph of the coming Messiah was foretold by many prophets. There may be a conditional element sometimes. There may be surprising fulfilments. But there is much prediction.

Oddly enough, it is in the New Testament, in the letter of Jude, that we have a fascinating glimpse of the first recorded prophecy given by man. (God himself had already predicted the coming of Christ to defeat the serpent.) After describing false teachers, Jude writes, 'Enoch, the seventh from Adam, prophesied about these men: "See, the Lord is coming with thousands upon thousands of his holy ones to judge everyone, and to convict all the ungodly of all the ungodly acts they have done in the ungodly way, and of all the harsh words ungodly sinners have spoken against him"' (Jude 14,15). When Enoch spoke he made a prediction, speaking of the most distant of events – the second coming of Christ! Prediction is an essential element of prophecy. This was made plain from the outset in this remarkable manner.

Divine urgency

The third note characteristic of all true God-given prophecy is the note of *divine urgency*. How better can this be summarized than in the words of the prophet Amos?

> 'Surely the Sovereign Lord
>   does nothing
>   without revealing his plan
>   to his servants the prophets.
> The lion has roared –
>   who will not fear?
> The Sovereign Lord has spoken –
>   who can but prophesy?'   (Amos 3:7,8)

Sometimes prophets sought to escape from this burden. This was an impossible task, as Jeremiah found:

'But if I say, "I will not mention him
    or speak any more in his name,"
his word is in my heart like a burning fire,
    shut up in my bones.
I am weary of holding it in; indeed I cannot' (Jer. 20:9).

These statements showed that true prophets were under an overwhelming constraint. Amos, commanded by an angry priest to get back to his small-holding and shut up, simply reiterated his own sense of call and predicted unmitigated disaster in the priest's family, including the priest's own death. This was not going to happen in his own local community but in a foreign land (Amos 7:10-17). According to Viscount Mackintosh of Halifax, a north-country clergyman reproved a lay preacher for holding forth without qualifications. 'Qualifications!' retorted the preacher. 'What about you? Without your gown, you darena'; without your book, you couldna', and without your pay you wouldna'. As for me, I manage without all three.'[10] Without either seeking to establish the historicity of the lay preacher's reply or even to defend it totally, we can see that there is an echo of biblical truth. It was the false prophets who put on a special garment 'in order to deceive' (Zech. 13:4). It was the false prophets who continued to 'steal from one another words supposedly from me' (Jer. 23:30). It was the false prophets who could be described as those who 'tell fortunes for money' (Micah 3:11).

True prophets did not conceal the truth. They have been aptly described as 'the biggest bunch of Nosey Parkers in religious history'.[11] Not for them the deliberate face-saving ambiguities of the oracle of Delphi. Herodotus tells how Croesus consulted the oracle, asking what would be the outcome of his attacking Cyrus, whose power was growing rapidly. 'That he would destroy a great empire,' was the reply. But whether it would be the empire of Cyrus or Croesus was not specified! On this basis Croesus attacked and his empire was destroyed, but not so the reputation of the oracle. This was a simple example of prophetic 'Heads I win; tails you lose,' or, how to play safe and not lose face. This is not an unnecessary digression. It will be seen to be very relevant to our study of prophecy today. We emphasize that biblical prophecy is not of this ilk.

The great variety in prophecy

Prophecy was poured forth in a rich variety of forms. There are haunting parables, like that of Nathan, the weird symbolic acts of Ezekiel, the thunderbolts of Nahum, the broken-hearted wooing tenderness of Hosea, the criss-cross of question and answer between Malachi and his protesting hecklers, the terse, brief but definite statements of unnamed figures who loom mysteriously out of nowhere and vanish as melodramatically as they came. And if we need an imaginative mouthwash (and one assumes that God knows we do) there is all the cascading eloquence, poetic fervour and evangelical intensity of Isaiah. Not all the prophetic works may be literary masterpieces on the level of Isaiah, but they are all eminently readable. Enigmatic statements there may be. Tantalizing allusions there certainly are. Soaring mystic glimpses of heaven we occasionally meet. But there is never anything banal. If a story fit for a film-maker like Sam Goldwyn was a 'plot that starts with an earthquake and builds up to a climax', then Amos, despite being one of the most homespun and direct of the prophetic band, literally meets Goldwyn's requirements as a writer. The very first verse of his prophecy mentions a recent earthquake and the last chapter rises to raptures of gospel grandeur, as it depicts the spiritual earthquake in the coming of the penitent, believing Gentiles into the Christian church to be one people with the converted Jews.

In contrast to such spokesmen there were nearly always the opposing figures of the false prophets. As Egyptian magicians they imitated some of the actions of Moses. In massed array they confronted the lonely, courageous figures of Elijah and Micaiah. As a constant chorus with rapidly changing personnel, they taunted and jeered at Jeremiah. Nearly always they doled out religious syrup, insisting that there was to be peace when God had warned of judgement. They had a message that tickled the ear but bypassed man's heartfelt need. In commenting on our Lord's words about such men John Wesley pertinently declares, 'These are far above the rank of ordinary cut-throats; for they murder the souls of men.'[12] Furthermore, he shows that the context of Christ's words indicates that false prophets teach a broad way to heaven and deliberately avoid speaking plainly about judgement. True prophets regularly took this unpopular theme. A belief in the reality of judgement gave them their sense of urgency.

Therefore the prophets stand before us with all their heartfelt fervour and searing honesty. Jonah is the prime example. The most amazing miracle in the book of Jonah is not his being swallowed and released by the big fish, but his being penitent enough, honest enough and humble enough to record his resistance of God's will and, in particular, his absurd childish tantrums over the loss of a plant (he wanted to die because the shade had gone!) at the very moment when he was displaying callous indifference to the lost state of 'more than a hundred and twenty thousand people who cannot tell their right hand from their left' (Jonah 4:ll).

One modern writer, who pleads with fervour for the acceptance of certain modern prophecies on the evidence of many witnesses, cannot make up his mind as to whether Jonah is history or parable, despite the evidence of the Lord of glory, who distinctly said that it all happened.[13]

We recall the story of the occasion when Lord Kinsale was reading his Bible in the train. A stranger opposite him remarked, 'Excuse me, sir, but do you believe in that book you are reading?'

Kinsale: 'Oh, yes, I do indeed.'

Stranger: 'Well, I don't believe a word of it.'

Kinsale: 'I am sorry.'

Stranger: 'What about Jonah? Do you believe he recited a poem in the belly of the whale? Is that true?'

Kinsale: 'Well, when I get to paradise I will ask him.'

Stranger: 'Supposing he is not there?'

Kinsale: 'Then you can ask him!'[14]

Jonah, we may be sure, will be in heaven, but he also once had his feet very much on this earth and very happy he was to have them there again after being vomited up by the fish.

Testing

Fourthly, we must record that the prophets and prophecies always had to be *tested* in a stringent way. Any sign of falsity or inaccuracy, and they were to be put to death. '"But a prophet who presumes to speak in my name anything I have not commanded him to say, or a prophet who speaks in the name of other gods, must be put to death." You may say to yourselves, "How can we know when a message has not been spoken by the Lord?" If what a prophet proclaims in the name of the Lord does not take place or come true, that is a message the Lord has not spoken. That prophet has spoken presumptuously. Do not be afraid of him' (Deut. 18:20-22). The holy God who cannot lie is not to be misrepresented in any way. True prophets, fully aware of this, never shirked the test in any way, but rather welcomed it.

Even the announcement of a sign or wonder and its consequent fulfilment was not sufficient by itself to prove that a prophet was sent from God if the prophet gave teaching designed to lead them away from the living God who had redeemed them from Egypt (Deut. 13:1-5). It would seem to be in line with this that Jeremiah, after warning against false prophets who fail to give a real and deep diagnosis of the nature of sin and who 'dress the wound of my people as though it were not serious', declares,

> 'This is what the Lord says:
> "Stand at the crossroads and look;
> ask for the ancient paths,
> ask where the good way is, and walk in it,
> and you will find rest for your souls"' (Jer. 6:16).

The implications of all this must not be missed. The fact that a prophet is to be tested does not mean that what he says is a mixture even though he be a true prophet. The people were not being exhorted to sift the true from the false in the *message* and adhere to the true. They were rather being commanded to sift the true from the false among the *messengers* and to execute those who were emissaries of Satan. Elijah was right, in Old Testament terms, to order the execution of the prophets of Baal. Jeremiah was right when, as a spokesman of God, he proclaimed the imminent death of the false prophet Hananiah because he had preached 'rebellion against the Lord'. The passage pointedly concludes: 'In the seventh month of that same year, Hananiah the prophet died' (Jer. 28:17; see also Jer. 29:20-32).

It is in seemingly slight, devastatingly subtle, but

nevertheless fatal deviations from God's truth that Satan works through false spokesmen. Naegelsbach has fittingly said, 'Unmixed falsehood betrays itself too easily and is insipid. But falsehood mingled with truth is powerful error, and the beauty of truth serves to embellish and cover the ugliness of error.'[15] In tempting the first Adam, Satan began by casting doubt on the truth of God's word ('Did God really say . . .?'), then continued by wildly exaggerating the extent of the prohibition (from one to every tree in the garden) and finished by denying point-blank the command of God ('You will not surely die') (Gen. 3:1-4). Similarly, when Satan engaged in battle with the last Adam, enraged at hearing the Saviour say that 'Man does not live on bread alone, but on every word that comes from the mouth of God', he immediately counter-attacked by quoting a verse from Psalm 91 out of context, omitting a vital phrase from the quotation and ignoring the next verse, which reads,

> 'You will tread upon the lion and the cobra;
> you will trample the great lion and the serpent'
> (Psalm 91:13).

No doubt these were words which Satan would hardly wish to hear! False prophets always follow in the wake of their master by clouding, misquoting and then categorically denying God's truth. In Old Testament days the penalty for this was execution. It was as serious as that.

Further interesting features of prophecy

Needless to say there are many aspects of prophecy which are undoubtedly fascinating, often quite important and always worthy of study, but which are not of the same essential nature as the issues we have already discussed. Because today these things are often the ones emphasized instead of the essential marks, I must briefly allude to them.

Firstly, it does not matter whether we know precisely *how the prophets were inspired*. Sometimes we are told and often we are not. Moses, because of his pre-eminent place, enjoyed clearer revelations, seeing the form of the Lord and hearing a voice speaking (Num. 7:89; 12:6-8). Samuel also heard a voice (1 Sam. 3). To Jeremiah the word of the Lord frequently came. Dreams and visions were frequently employed and became almost the technical term for prophetic inspiration (Num. 12:6-8; Joel 2:28; Dan. 7:1 etc; Obad. 1). Sometimes there were angelic intermediaries (e.g. Zech. 2). Elisha even called for a musician on one occasion (2 Kings 3:15). The mode of inspiration cannot be reduced to one formula.

Secondly, the *length of the prophecy* is not the vital criteria. Obviously Isaiah is very long, while some prophets performed a ministry with just a sentence. But just as one or two sentences spoken from the Lord could expose the heart of Jehoshaphat's disobedience (2 Chron. 19:2,3), so one sentence from the false prophet Shemaiah could challenge all the inward spiritual resources of godly Nehemiah (Neh. 6:10). In this connection we assume that there were vocational prophets who prophesied regularly, while there were non-vocational prophets upon whom the Spirit came only occasionally (Num. 11:25).

Thirdly, it is clear that *some prophecies were canonical and some were not*. This simply means that some prophecies are recorded in detail in Scripture and others are either only alluded to or not even mentioned at all. Thus, although we know that Eldad and Medad prophesied, we know nothing whatsoever of the content of the message (Num. 11:27). Whereas the prophecy of Jonah to Nineveh is given in full, with all the various background details, consequent revival and widespread repentance, another sphere of his activity is only tantalizingly summarized: 'He (Amaziah) was the one who restored the boundaries of Israel from Lebo Hamath to the Sea of the Arabah, in accordance with the word of the Lord, the God of Israel, spoken through his servant Jonah son of Amittai, the prophet from Gath Hepher' (2 Kings 14:25). We do not know what story lies hidden behind these words. But we do know enough for our purposes. The prophecy was fulfilled. The non-canonical words were as infallible as the canonical.

Fourthly, and lastly, contrary to contemporary assumption, there is a sense in which, *in certain circumstances, the holiness of the prophet did not inhibit God from giving a pure message*. While I am convinced and have argued that overall the prophetic figures of the Bible were holy men, it still remains true that God was not dependent on the purity of the man for the purity of the message. As one of old said, 'God can make a straight line with a crooked stick'.[16] Saul is an example of this, as is the old compromising prophet mentioned in the strange story in 1 Kings 13 (1 Sam. 10:9-11; 19:23-25; 1 Kings 13:20-22). But the most glaring illustration of this is Balaam, who is constantly described as a rogue and charlatan by New Testament writers and yet who, impelled by God, gave forth certain glorious prophecies including one of the coming Messiah, 'I see him, but not now; I behold him, but not near. A star will come out of Jacob; a sceptre will rise out of Israel' (Num. 24:17; see 2 Peter 2:15,16; Rev. 2:14). At one point, when Balaam was embarking on a journey in disobedience to God, even the prophet's ass was made to speak and rebuke him. Someone has commented, 'When the prophet made an ass of himself, God made a prophet of the ass.' There is no limit to the power of God.

Therefore we acknowledge that, though Abraham had sinned and lied, he was still a prophet and God could instantly use him, though he was hardly a 'clean vessel' in the way the term is used today. Similarly, when Jonah reached Nineveh in a grumpy and disobedient mood, God still employed him to deliver a true and powerful message which brought revival to the whole city. (Is there any more strange picture in the whole Bible than that of the surly, uncompassionate evangelist disappointed at his own success?) These and other passages underline the fact that a sovereign God never fails to deliver his message intact and infallible, even through disobedient servants, hypocritical spokesmen and, for good measure, an ass!

2.
Prophecy in the New Testament and prophecy today

Infallibility of New Testament prophecy

In what ways, if any, does New Testament prophecy differ from Old Testament prophecy? Is the word employed in exactly the same way, or is it modified in any respect? Is it not significant that Old Testament prophecy signs off in its two final verses with a prediction? 'See I will send you the prophet Elijah before that great and dreadful day of the Lord comes. He will turn the hearts of the fathers to their children, and the hearts of the children to their fathers; or else I will come and strike the land with a curse' (Mal. 4:5,6). After an absence of prophecy for four centuries this prediction was fulfilled, for the New Testament makes it abundantly clear that John the Baptist was the Elijah who was to come (Luke 1:17; Matt. 11:13; 17:12). At once we are confronted with the fact that the key spokesmen in the two eras are seen as identical in their heaven-sent mission. The first great New Testament prophet was as much sent by God as any before him. Furthermore, the first recorded utterance to be described as prophecy in the New Testament is that of the father of John the Baptist. 'Filled with the Holy Spirit,' he specifically mentioned God's 'holy prophets of long ago' alongside his own son, who would be called 'a prophet of the Most High' (Luke 1:67,70,76). Moreover, if the references to prophecy and prophets in the Acts of the Apostles are counted, it will be found that allusions to spokesmen of former days outnumber references to contemporary prophets. There is not the slightest hint in any of these cases that the word was beginning to be used in any modified way.

The control of the Holy Spirit is everywhere emphasized in New Testament prophecy. It would seem true to say that there

is no important reference where the Holy Spirit is not
mentioned. On the Day of Pentecost Peter said twice that God
was going to 'pour out' his Spirit on people that they might
'prophesy' (Acts 2:17,18). Agabus made his first recorded
prophecy 'through the Spirit' and introduced the second by
the phrase, 'The Holy Spirit says,' (Acts 11:28; 21:11). The
opening verse of 1 Corinthians 14 states that prophecy is one of
the foremost of the *'pneumatikoi'* or gifts of the Spirit. The Holy
Spirit never puts his signature to any breath of error. It was
because they lied to the Holy Spirit that Ananias and Sapphira
were struck dead. This sad incident demonstrates his hatred of
all lying.

When God said through Peter that those inspired to
prophesy would 'see visions' and 'dream dreams', he was
using technical terms familiar to Jewish hearers and clearly
referring to infallible inspiration (Acts 2:17; see Joel 2:28;
Num. 12:6; Gen. 37:5-11; 40:5; 41:1-16; 1 Sam. 28:6; 1 Kings
3:5; 1 Chron. 17:3-15; 2 Chron. 32:32; Ps. 89:19; Isa. 1:1;
Obad. 1). Two references are particularly interesting. In one
we learn of the connection between visions and the Word of
God in very definite terms: 'The boy Samuel ministered before
the Lord under Eli. In those days the word of the Lord was
rare; there were not many visions' (1 Sam. 3:1). And in Ezekiel
we are told of the reality and sureness of these God-given
visions: 'The word of the Lord came to me: "Son of man, the
house of Israel is saying, 'The vision he sees is for many years
from now, and he prophesies about the distant future.' Therefore say to them, 'This is what the Sovereign Lord says: None
of my words will be delayed any longer: whatever I say will be
fulfilled, declares the Sovereign Lord'"' (Ezek. 12:26-28).

This, of course, does not merely mean that the prophets had
'spiritual hunches' or shrewdly put their finger on a problem
in a particular individual's life. God spoke directly to them.
Likewise, in New Testament days, God called to Ananias in a
'vision' and spoke to Peter during a 'trance' (in which his
mental faculties were not suspended). Peter's experience was
also called a 'vision' (Acts 9:10; 10:9-20). There are many
other examples of this. Also, when Ananias was being
prepared to confront Paul with words that would truly sum up
the apostle's forthcoming ministry, we simply read that 'The
Lord told him' (Acts 9:11; see also 22:12-16). When Peter was

being prepared for his ministry to Cornelius, the Gentile centurion, we learn that 'A voice told him' certain things (Acts 10:13-16).

As the sea began to rage during his journey to Rome, Paul made a purely human forecast. He warned, 'Men, I can see that our voyage is going to be disastrous and bring great loss to ship and cargo, and to our own lives also' (Acts 27:10). This was natural enough, but later Paul had to correct himself. He did it in this way: 'Last night an angel of the God whose I am and whom I serve stood beside me and said, "Do not be afraid, Paul. You must stand trial before Caesar; and God has graciously given you the lives of all who sail with you." So keep up your courage, men, for I have faith in God that it will happen just as he told me. Nevertheless we must run aground on some island' (Acts 27:23-26). When the ship did break to pieces on the coast of the island of Malta, of the 276 men on board 276 were saved. If 275 had been saved it would have been a truly remarkable incident, but a false prophecy.

Supernaturalism

Secondly, in our study of Old Testament prophets, we saw that they always moved in the realm of supernaturalism. (The reception of visions is part of this, of course.) The very use of the word 'prophecy' in the life and ministry of Jesus Christ illustrates that this aspect of the word loomed large in the mind of his contemporaries. It was after Christ had raised a young man from the dead that he was widely acclaimed as a 'great prophet'. It was the expectation of Simon the Pharisee that all true prophets would display discernment into people's characters. It was because of the feeding of the five thousand that many recognized Christ as *'the* prophet'. It was as Christ recounted her past marital entanglements to a bemused woman of Samaria that she instantly declared him to be a prophet. It was to a blindfolded and beaten Christ that mockers shouted, 'Prophesy to us, Christ. Who hit you?' (Luke 7:16,39; John 6:14; 4:15-19; Matt. 26:67,68.) It was expected that a prophet should manifest supernatural awareness, which might display itself in a variety of ways. No true prophet could be without this ability.

It hardly needs to be emphasized that many of the prophecies in the New Testament were given by the apostles themselves, especially in the writings which have come down to us. We have just considered a remarkable prediction of Paul. The ability of the apostles to heal, to discern spirits and to work miracles will be discussed later. This was a period of abundant miracle-working. But it is also important to notice that the two prophecies given by Agabus, a man outside the normal apostolic circle, reveal this supernaturalism in its most glaring and unmistakable form. In the first we are told that he predicted a 'severe famine' spreading throughout the entire Roman world. Luke then immediately adds, 'This happened during the reign of Claudius' (Acts 11:28). It would have been embarrassing if the famine had not come, since as soon as the prophecy was given, a widespread collection got under way. In the second instance, using the prophetic symbolism so familiar to readers of Jeremiah or Ezekiel, Agabus 'took Paul's belt, tied his own hands and feet with it and said, "The Holy Spirit says, 'In this way the Jews of Jerusalem will bind the owner of this belt and will hand him over to the Gentiles'"' (Acts 21:11). It would seem that others gave the same message (Acts 20:23). The remaining chapters of Acts show how exactly this was indeed fulfilled. True prophecy always is fulfilled.

This is because it is infallibly and supernaturally inspired by God. Therefore it is, according to Paul, when a 'revelation' comes that a man is enabled to prophesy (1 Cor. 14:30). This is a technical New Testament word. When the apostle is speaking of the way the New Testament writings were inspired it is to this term, in both its noun and verbal form *(apokaluptō, apokalupsis)*, along with its companion word 'mystery' *(mystērion)*, that the apostle repeatedly turns. This can very easily be checked by looking up Romans 16:25-27 (where the finished product is 'prophetic writings'), Ephesians 3:2-11 (where the apostle could now envisage them 'reading this') and Colossians 1:25-27 (where he is in process of giving them 'the word of God in its fulness'). The simple question is this: if 'revelations' and 'mysteries' were given for the purpose of writing the New Testament Scriptures, is the end result in any way less than fully inspired? Does the word 'revelation' change its meaning in any way when it is applied to a New Testament prophet? The answer is that it does not.

Divine urgency and need for testing

Thirdly, we said that there was a divine urgency in Old Testament prophecy. The note is unchanged in New Testament times. It may be Ananias or Agabus predicting the sufferings of Paul (Acts 9:16; 21:11). It may be an incensed Paul announcing the forthcoming blindness of Elymas, or a weeping apostle foreseeing wolves rising from the very ranks of the Ephesian congregation (Acts 13:11; 20:29-31). It may be Peter solemnly prophesying the death of Sapphira (Acts 5:9). In written form, it may be Paul predicting the coming glory of Christ the returning King, or Peter glimpsing the destruction and recreation of the universe, or John overwhelmed with the vision of the new heaven and the new earth (1 Thess. 4:13-18; 5:1-11; 2 Peter 3; Rev. 21;22). Always there is that same mark of divine urgency.

All of which leads us to the two passages which state that New Testament prophecy should be tested. 'Two or three prophets should speak, and the others should weigh carefully what is said' (1 Cor. 14:29). 'Do not put out the Spirit's fire; do not treat prophecies with contempt. Test everything. Hold on to the good. Avoid every kind of evil' (1 Thess. 5:19-22). Taken as they stand, with no background of Old Testament teaching or New Testament evidence, these passages could mean that prophecy is a mixture, partly good and partly bad. If this were so, it would be the task of the church to sort out the wheat from the chaff. But there is a background. 'A text without a context is a pretext.' (Taken by itself, Christ's reference to the Father as 'greater' than himself (John 14:28) could possibly mean that Christ was not God. It should not be taken by itself but interpreted in harmony with hundreds of other passages). Bearing in mind that although Old Testament prophecy was to be tested as stringently, yet there was only one kind of genuine prophecy – infallible and totally inspired by the Holy Spirit, these texts should be understood in the same way. This is confirmed by all of the evidence we have considered for the inspiration of the New Testament prophecy.

Therefore 1 Corinthians 14:29, which most likely means that the people weigh with a view to implementation (as in the collection for famine relief after the prophecy of Agabus),

could possibly mean that false prophecy (i.e. any prophecy
which has the slightest element of falsehood) is to be rejected
decisively and the false prophet dealt with. The last phrase of
1 Thessalonians 5:22 is rarely noted as it should be. It reads,
'Avoid every kind of evil.' (Many writers do not quote verse
22. They stop just before!) Any element of falsehood in a
prophecy means that God cannot be speaking. On the
contrary, it means that Satan is present. He is seeking to
infiltrate a church. Once more he is mounting his two-pronged
attack on the Christian. First of all, he is adopting the guise
whereby he 'masquerades as an angel of light', knowing that if
he appears through a very 'spiritual' medium, many will fail to
detect him, as Christians naturally desire not to be guilty of
resisting the Holy Spirit (2 Cor. 11:14). Secondly, he is
determined to spread large errors through small beginnings in
this way. 'A little yeast works through the whole batch of
dough,' warns the apostle Paul, as he contemplates the growth
of false teaching among the Galatians (Gal. 5:9; see Matt.
16:5-12).

There is, of course, the other side of this question and, just
as we took Balaam to illustrate the fact that God could get the
message right even though the instrument was thoroughly evil,
so we find that in the New Testament there is an even more
glaring example of this sovereign power of God. Caiaphas was
also a thoroughly evil man. As high priest he was a cynical
unbeliever, contemptuous towards the hangers-on around him
and a determined opponent of the Lord Jesus Christ, whose
death he desired above all else. Hardly a likely instrument for
one of the greatest prophecies in the Bible! Yet we read that
Caiaphas addressed the Sanhedrin as follows: 'You know
nothing at all! You do not realize that it is better for you that
one man die for the people than that the whole nation perish.'
Upon which John comments, 'He did not say this on his own,
but as high priest that year he prophesied that Jesus would die
for the Jewish nation, and not only for that nation but also for
the scattered children of God, to bring them together and
make them one' (John 11:49-52). God is never frustrated – he
can use the most evil instrument and deliver a perfect word.

Charismatic evasion of the main issue

Where do modern charismatics stand in all this? It hardly needs saying that almost to a man they refuse the first hurdle on the course. They simply remove completely the fence marked 'infallibility'. As far as they are concerned, no one need fall there! Because this is undoubtedly the central point in the whole discussion, we shall draw on a wide variety of charismatic testimony. The authors of a book chosen by a team of four reviewers in one magazine as the best and most balanced on the whole subject simply say, 'For although the prophet is the instrument of the Spirit of God he is not infallible, for he is still human and he may err.'[1] 'While prophecy is "revelation", that is, while it makes the mind or will of God clear, it must never be exalted to the level of biblical revelation,' they add later.[2]

An author who has written helpfully on many topics rhetorically asks, 'But does 1 Corinthians 14 imply this kind of infallible prophecy?'[3] His own answer is 'No' to this question, as he also refers to prophecy as a 'mixed phenomenon'. He argues thus particularly because of the verse exhorting us to test prophecy. Yet, on the same page where he says all these things, he also quotes with approval the definition of an itinerant evangelist who describes prophecy as 'a word in someone's mouth which they have not prepared, an immediate inspired utterance from God'. Are we then in a position when an 'immediate inspired utterance from God' can be a 'mixed phenomenon'? Where is all this leading us?

Another writer tells us that 'The purity of the prophecy will be proportional to the rent heart.'[4] A lady writer takes comfort from being told by elder statesmen in the movement that 'When we begin to prophesy there is nearly always a mixture of God's Spirit and our own thinking.'[5] A leading Methodist charismatic assumes that when we prophesy, 'Our brothers will correct in love.'[6] A man who is described as 'both a sociologist and a theologian' and as 'widely regarded as a modern-day prophet', acknowledging the fact that prophecy, in his view, is a mixed experience, cites the admission of John Woolman, the American Quaker who, 'not keeping to the Divine opening', said more than was required of him and went astray.[7] And from a writer whose books have been selling like hot cakes, we learn that 'A man may be strongly used in the prophetic office, and yet may be completely wrong from time to time.'[8] He goes on to say that such a person is not a false prophet. This is merely an illustration of the fact that we prophesy 'in part' (1 Cor. 13:9).

A Reformed writer has recently written a book of which one reviewer said, 'One feels that the current debate over the work of the Holy Spirit has been waiting for someone of his pedigree and stature to take up his pen.'[9] Yet what does this writer say about New Testament prophecy? Simply what all the others say. He feels that 1 Corinthians 14:29 shows that 'The potentially universal prophecy of the New Testament was less than infallible and irreformable and might need to be qualified, if not indeed corrected.'[10] He speaks of 'the derivative, noninfallible, noncanonical prophecy that continues in the church'.[11] Yet, oddly enough, this particular writer is still not too keen to identify what is happening today as 'the New Testament sign gift, now restored'.[12] Because of his acceptance of fallible prophecy it is difficult to see why he hesitates.

A 'Reformed charismatic', making the point that all prophecy was not canonical (this is not, as we have seen, at all the real point at issue) states: 'No, the congregations with their elders, etc., were to test the prophecy (1 Thess. 5:19-21) and were to sort out anything that was carnal or human – or even anything that was added to it by the (fallible and errant!) prophet himself.'[13] And a commentary on 1 Corinthians 12-14, with a commendatory foreword by a leading charismatic spokesman, goes even further and says, 'The wonderful and yet mysterious thing about prophecy is that the Holy Spirit, in all his perfection, combines with the human spirit in all its imperfection. One consequence of this, in our era and due to our weakness, is the fact that our prophesying is imperfect ("in part" 1 Cor. 13:9). It is also obvious that the value and purity of our prophecy is conditioned by the state of the human channel (cf Rom. 12:6).'[14]

Dishonouring to God
Not only is the Holy Spirit, the one who is 'the Spirit of truth', credited with falsehood in all this, but he who is likewise 'the Spirit of power' (John 16:13; Rom. 15:19) is charged with

being powerless to get the message right. Is God really dependent on the cleanness of the human channel or the extent to which the human heart is rent to get his message right? The insult to a sovereign God in all this must not be lost sight of. (It is particularly strange that people claiming to be 'Reformed' and to believe in God's sovereignty should adopt this view.) In some of the more orthodox writers one can, thank God, detect at least an undercurrent of unease. For example, one confesses his worry about the insistence that the prophecy 'must always be delivered in the first person as the direct words of God to the congregation or to an individual'.[15] Another warns, 'Beware the "I" prophecies.'[16] Unhappily others are far less inhibited.

A writer who has spoken at many conferences and written several books asserts quite categorically, 'In prophecy God speaks. It is as simple, and profound, and startling as that! What happens in the fellowship is that the word may suddenly be spoken by anyone present, and so, variously, a "Thus says the Lord" breaks forth in the fellowship. It is usually in the first person (though not always), such as "I am with you to bless you . . ." and has the directness of an "I-Thou" encounter . . . All of this – to repeat – is quite surprising and startling. Most of us, of course, were familiar with prophetic utterances as recorded in the Bible, and willing to accept it as the Word of God. Isaiah's or Jeremiah's "Thus says the Lord . . ." we were accustomed to, but to hear a Tom or a Mary today, in the twentieth century, speak the same way . . .'[17] He clearly equates the utterance of Tom and Mary as being on the same level as Isaiah and Jeremiah!

In similar vein, a Pentecostal can also compare his experience with the biblical prophets and declare with reference to one of his visions that 'I have never in my life ministered with more of the unction of the Holy Spirit . . . than I do here and now with the Spirit of God upon me and I prophesy . . .'[18] And one of the key figures in the movement, one who has been guilty of leading many into doctrinal compromise and who has even been nicknamed 'Mr Pentecost' (it is significant that within the movement a mere man can be given this title) has put together a book called *The Spirit bade me go*. He writes, 'It was my privilege to edit and prepare for publication in this form those revelations that I received from Him while ministering in conferences' and he goes on to speak of 'utterances made under the unction of the Spirit'.[19] A man and wife refused a request for a theological interpretation of their song, 'The King is Coming' in these words (the secretary was replying on their behalf): 'The song came quickly to them and they do not care to discuss the theology of it. In fact, they feel that to dissect the song would be tampering with the inspiration of the Holy Spirit who inspired the song.'[20] In all this we are obviously dealing with people who all feel that their words have been directly inspired by God.

Guide-lines for beginners

Others guide the beginner how to start his prophecy. One urges, 'Expect to prophesy. Ask Jesus to edify His Body on earth through you. As you have fellowship with the Lord and with your brothers and sisters in the Lord, you may find thoughts and words of inspiration coming into your mind that you have not heard, and did not compose. If they are according to Scripture, then share them with the Church. As with interpretation, you may just receive a few words, and as you start to speak, more may come. You may see a picture in your "mind's eye", and as you start to talk about that picture the words will come.'[21] 'It may well start through some mental picture coming to a member during a time of worship and silent adoration,' suggests another.[22] Acknowledging that prophecy is a mixture, he then pleads for loving encouragement to get the beginner started. 'Love will be welcoming towards embryonic prophecy. Love will be forgiving when mistakes are made,' and 'If love flows, if mistakes are expected and understood, if the tests outlined above are applied, the dangers inherent in this sensitive gift will be largely avoided, and its real blessings will become a very positive boon to the congregation.'[23] But is it really loving to get someone thinking they are a mouthpiece of God when they are not? After all it does say in chapter 13 of 1 Corinthians that 'Love . . . rejoices with the truth' (1 Cor. 13:6).

A 'prophetess' recounts her own experience. After first mentioning the existence of false prophecy she continues: 'How then can we know if a prophecy is from God or not? Someone might start off with "thus says the Lord" or "the

Lord says" (incidentally it is not necessary to start off like this but sometimes it helps the beginner to get going) and it sounds so authoritative as to be beyond contradiction.'[24] Being kind, we might call this 'spiritual kiddology'. If we are to be truthful and biblical, we must call it blasphemy. As a pastor, I must put the heaviest responsibility for this on the editors of the magazine who allowed it to be published and gave it their sanction. This kind of approach can only lead ultimately to much misery, pretence and deviation from scriptural truth.

Evasion of the issue of prediction

In the face of so much confusion, we are constantly being told that others are more balanced and cautious. So they are. They are very cautious in the matter of the supernatural, which was our second criteria of true prophecy. Listen to two of the leaders of the movement on the whole question of prediction in prophecy: 'Prophecy is a message from God, which is not necessarily anything to do with the future: a forth-telling, not primarily a foretelling.'[25] 'True prophecy is *forth*-telling, not *fore*telling.'[26] In this way Agabus and his ilk are safely wrapped in cotton wool and few seem to notice that the constant biblical note of supernatural foretelling is quietly relegated to the background.

Another writer is even more coy and canny on this issue of prediction. His words are 'Here we move on to more controversial ground, and the possibilities of abuse become greater.'[27] This could be put very differently. The conclusion might be that 'The possibilities of exposure become greater.' There is much more likelihood that here and there when the prophecy proves a dud someone with a bit of spiritual gumption is going to see, and even say, that the emperor has no clothes on. But, we ask, why is it controversial? Is not prediction a vital element in New Testament prophecy? Did not Agabus predict that a famine would take place? Did he not predict the imprisonment of Paul?

Others, at least in their definition of prophecy, are more true to the biblical pictures. Thus a leaflet issued by one charismatic group states, 'This gift is as the gift of old time prophecy – no different. It is still proclamation and prediction

. . . So it has to be admitted that the gift of prophecy is a psychic gift, rightly used, and that prophets have used detailed telepathic and even clairvoyant powers.'[28] This group has certainly practised what it preaches. In 1973 many young people in an area around one northern town were frightened when through their ministry a prophecy was given warning of a coming military take-over in England. Soon after this the magazine of the organization commented on the prophecy as follows: 'Believing as we do that time is limited for freedom of Christian action in our country – and that physical judgement is less than two years away – we desire to use every minute we can to bring others to Christ while we may.'[29] Here now is an excerpt from a prayer letter issued by the same group in 1975: 'In the January of 1973 a prophecy was given . . . which told of freedom to minister in 1973 and 1974, with the inference that the same freedom would not exist beyond 1974. We linked this at the time with Rev. David Gardner's "A Warning to the Nation" which he reiterated in the February of 1973. It seemed likely then – as indeed it still does – that freedom for everything would be lost to us through a military take-over or occupation of the land. Now that the two years have come and gone we can look back and marvel at the way in which that prophecy has been increasingly implemented, short of military action to date . . .'[30] They then go on to say that inflation and the high price of petrol have inhibited travel and in this way the prophecy has been fulfilled! Enough said?

Tragedies that ensue
Speaking candidly of the early days of the apostolic movement in Britain, an old experienced Christian writes, 'Domestic tragedies resulted from obedience to certain utterances of the "prophets" in the local assembly. Nevertheless, the fact remains that there is a genuine gift of prophecy . . .'[31] Is he really experienced enough? When will they ever learn? 'Soulish, carnal prophecies which lack anointing and direction can cause havoc in fellowships,' warns another.[32] How right he is! There is the case recorded (and no doubt many more that are not recorded) of the handsome young widower in the charismatic movement who was confronted by a lady claiming that the Holy Spirit had revealed in prophecy that they should marry. When the young man pointed out that another woman

had received the same prophecy, the first woman denounced the second as a false prophet![33] Another has told how 'Some claiming this gift in one Socialist country told Christians in a neighbouring Socialist country that the Lord had ordered the latter to leave their fatherland because of the persecution that was coming.' One can imagine the confusion this message caused.[34]

The tragic nature of all this has perhaps been clearly focused in the recent death of a leading charismatic. 'God "healing my cancer" Canon says,' was a heading in *The Times*. His obituary followed soon after this.[35] He was honest enough to record in his final book how various leaders predicted his recovery. 'I don't accept this cancer and I believe that God wants to heal you,' declared one pastor, while in what purported to be a 'prophetic word' a Roman Catholic charismatic announced that the cancer would not lead to death.[36] A reviewer rightly pointed out that not only were these false prophecies in the light of Deuteronomy 18:20-22, but also properly showed that 'To assure a dying man that he has been healed is to leave him in a turmoil of self-scrutiny and doubt!'[37] And yet because of the conditions of 'low visibility' in which much of the modern debate is conducted, the real questions were not asked in this review. What is the standing of the various prophets or prophetesses who made predictions of this nature? Have they been subject to any disciplinary procedure? And what of the 'gift of discernment'? The sick man had himself written a book of guide-lines on the gifts. Why did he not by discernment recognize the false prophets? If one who has written and spoken so often on this theme cannot detect them then how on earth (or in heaven) can genuine but very immature Christians of a few months' growth show discernment in these matters?

Moreover it is sad to find the long-awaited treatment of the subject by a Reformed writer so feeble under this heading. Here are his words: 'The authenticity of predictions must be tested by watching to see if they are fulfilled (Deut. 18:22). The only effect such predictions should ever have on anyone's conduct is to induce preparedness of mind for the possibility that they will be fulfilled, alongside of preparedness for the possibility that they will not!'[38] Could you have a better example of sitting on the fence than this? (In actual fact he

does go on to mention one prophecy made about his own stay
in Vancouver – it was false!) Has this writer never seen young
Christians alarmed, distressed, fearful or bewildered when
they are 'under' prophecies? Does he think that it is necessary
for them to be 'under' prophecies in this way? It is sad that so
many seem blithely unaware of the heartache, bewilderment
and near despair that can follow in the wake of such false
prophecies. I know at first-hand of the disturbance and worry
caused to some young Christians after the prophecy already
referred to about a military take-over. To sit on the fence in
matters like this is not only pastorally an uncomfortable
position; it may ultimately be the last refuge of the coward
before he topples off to his own hurt.

The cutting edge vanishes

With regard to genuine prophecies we also noted that these
were direct and urgent and there was often the clear note of
challenge and judgement. I have made quite a collection of
'prophecies' and must be selective. They all have the note of
the 'promise box' or 'blessed thoughts' calendar and are, not
to mince words, very much in the vein of the oracle of Delphi
or akin to fortune-telling. They are so couched that they could
hardly be wrong! Or at least some event could be found which
would correspond to something within them.

Thus a word of prophecy given at a renewal conference in
Edinburgh begins: 'O my people, I am going to bless this city.
My people, be encouraged tonight; for throughout this city I
have my own people. I tell you they are seeking me; even
tonight. I have my own people who are seeking me in tears and
are longing in their hearts for what I have shown you my
people.'[39] And then in the midst of what can only be described
as a lot of pseudo-biblical, repetitious verbiage we learn that
God is over the city and has called the people to be witnesses
in the place and that he is going to move with his Spirit.

A well-known magazine printed a prophecy which was
given at a conference, assuring us that it was 'of such high
calibre and spiritual import we felt it ought to be shared with a
wider circle of readers'. The prophecy begins: 'My children,
know that I am with you in everything you do. When you feel

inadequate and unable to meet the task I have set before you, then look to Me and I will supply the needed strength. When you learn to recognize where your strength lies then you will discover the secret of working for Me and with Me. I am your strength, your joy, your peace, your hope. Without Me, nothing you do will ever last eternally. My power working through you will bring to nought the things of time, and establish eternal values within your being.'[40] It then goes on to say in the familiar way that God's Spirit is going to move with joy. Comments one who has had some years of experience within the Pentecostal movement: 'This prophecy is typical of any given week by week in Charismatic groups or in Pentecostal churches.' Since he could not recall any nationwide movement of the Spirit in 1973 or since, he feels, rightly, that despite its seeming pleasantness and sheer inoffensiveness it was a 'false' prophecy.[41]

We noted the firm judgemental note in Old and New Testament prophecy. Warnings were probably as frequent as promises. Peter predicted the death of Sapphira and Paul the blinding of Elymas. Listen now to five modern proponents: 'The abuse of prophecy is to point the finger, to accuse or condemn.'[42] 'Prophecy should not strike a note of condemnation.'[43] 'The Bible consistently teaches that God's people need not fear. That is why I have reservations about teaching or prophecy that imparts fear to God's people.'[44] 'If in any way it is condemnatory ("there is therefore now no condemnation for those who are in Christ Jesus") or destructive or does not tie up with other prophecies etc. do not act upon it.'[45] 'Neither is it likely that either an interpretation or a prophecy which are condemnatory in content are of the Holy Spirit.'[46] Yet we learn that after Peter's fulfilled prophecy about Sapphira 'great fear seized the whole church'! (Acts 5:11.)

By contrast to all this, a Dales Bible Week speaker, author of a book on prophecy and self-styled prophet, asserts strongly that, among other things, his role was that of 'spiritual trouble-shooter'! He criticizes the woolly and nebulous prophecies which abound, saying, 'Prophecy is a revelation gift designed to make things clear and therefore specific. "I will bless you saith the Lord" may well be true, but it's not prophecy unless we are also told what blessing we can expect. Is it to be a £5 note or my aunt getting saved? Such prophecies need another prophecy to explain them.'[47] Yet now listen to one of the modern books: 'Any attempt to give highly specific instructions to the group, or to individuals in it, under the guise of prophecy, should be strenuously discouraged by the leaders of the meetings because of the problems which will almost invariably arise as a result.'[48] No forecasting of future careers or future marriage partners here!

The 'trouble-shooter' was very specific in a message he gave later to the leadership at the Dales Bible Week. After listeners had learned that the Lord Jesus Christ is really dependent on us for the timing of his second coming, they were then told that 'The corporate prophetic voice that God is raising up is the greatest thing that God has ever done.'[49] The mind boggles and the heart sinks. Greater than the incarnation? Greater than the atonement? Greater than the resurrection? One commentator aptly wrote, 'This is the height of delusion and would seem to fall into the category of the false prophets referred to by our Lord in Matthew 24, especially verses 4,5 and 24-28. They are falsely claiming that his coming is imminent and that they are especially associated with his coming. This is a recurrent feature of sects!'[50]

The testing of prophecy

Our fourth comment on prophecy was that it must be tested. Yet we made it clear that true prophecy would always stand the test. If there was any element of falsehood in the prophecy in Old Testament times, the prophet was to be executed. By analogy we would expect church discipline to be exercised on any false prophet today by any church which whole-heartedly adheres to the New Testament. Whether that discipline should be rebuke and warning, suspension from the Lord's Table or full excommunication, should be left to the discretion of the congregation which is aware of the facts. Yet we have already been confronted by the fact that there are innumerable false prophecies. I make bold to say that there are not innumerable acts of discipline – even of the mildest kind!

In face of the obvious banality and falsity of many prophecies, most charismatics, acknowledging as they do that prophecy is a 'mixed phenomenon', freely admit that prophecy does need sifting. As we have seen, some envisage elders or maturer Christians correcting the aspiring prophet or prophetess. Yet others would bring in at this point their concept of people who are endowed with the gift of discerning spirits. One expresses it like this: 'Foreign elements (from the vast realm of the subconscious) can find their way into prophetic utterance and cloud and distort it. One prophecy would be so similar to another as to be indistinguishable – and yet arise from a different spiritual source. In a case such as this, rational "testing" would not suffice . . . A foreign element in the midst of an inspired prophecy can only be detected charismatically, as one of the hearers is enlightened from above. This too could be called a prophetic gift – a specialized form of the Gift to diagnose imperfect prophecy.'[51]

There is an obvious question that needs to be put to those who think like this. Is there not a further need of a charismatically gifted person to detect whether the charismatically gifted person who is claiming to sift out the foreign element in the prophecy is truly charismatically gifted or not? What must not be lost sight of in all this is that despite appearances the final authority is no longer in Scripture. The final authority is in whichever charismatically gifted man happens to stand at the end of the line. The opportunity for Satan to have a field day is unlimited.

Of course, some do attempt to give other tests. In one book the reader is given no less than seven tests to check on whether prophecy is valid.[52] We look at some of them. One is that the prophet is humble. Was Jonah humble when he went to Nineveh? Another is that the church must be edified and built up, even though there is a disturbing element in the message. How does the reaction of the church to the news of Paul's imprisonment as announced by Agabus fit in here? As they began pleading with Paul, he had to say to them, 'Why are you weeping and breaking my heart?' (Acts 21:13) Instant edification all round in an unfamiliar form? Or did they not know how to apply these tests? Another test is that the prophet does not go on too long. Yet in Holy Scripture we are told with reference to two authentic prophets, 'Judas and Silas, who themselves were prophets, said much' (literally with much speech) 'to encourage and strengthen the brothers' (Acts 15:32). Yet another test is that the message must be spoken with love. Now, to be sure, love can be defined in many ways, but one wonders how Elymas felt when Paul, filled with the Holy Spirit, looked straight at him and said, 'You are a child of the devil and an enemy of everything that is right! You are full of all kinds of deceit and trickery. Will you never stop perverting the right ways of the Lord? Now the hand of the Lord is against you. You are going to be blind, and for a time you will be unable to see the light of the sun' (Acts 13:9-11). Yet we read that God instantly honoured this strong prophecy and that 'Immediately mist and darkness came over him, and he groped about, seeking someone to lead him by the hand' (Acts 13:11). These tests are mostly man-made, arbitrary and are largely camouflage for the fact that the major biblical test, the infallibility of the message, is roundly rejected.

Man-made tests

What is happening repeatedly is that young Christians (and many older ones) are accepting guide-lines on matters like this and failing to recognize that the 'lists' and 'tests' are purely man-made. Having forsaken thorough, careful biblical interpretation, they are prey to every charlatan. For example, some of the contradictions are so obvious and tragic that none but those who have been led astray could fail to recognize them. Here is a Dales Week speaker, being interviewed in a popular youth magazine and talking about the fact of inspiration. One moment he is stating that 'Physical feelings are a very unreliable guide to a forthcoming prophecy,' and, in the next breath, in response to a question about the 'anointing', he is asserting, 'Usually it consists of tingles down the spine, a wobbly hand (or knee, if sitting down) and a general feeling of exhilaration.'[53] No doubt for some months after this there were a crop of young folk torn between a desire to detect their knees going wobbly or to feel nothing at all! They would do better to read their Bibles more carefully.

'But we still have the test of the infallible word,' they say.[54] Many chime in here. All prophecy has to be tested by Scripture. It must be rejected if it is unscriptural. If someone forecasts the end of the world, some will know that this is contrary to biblical teaching and they must reject such a prophecy. If someone predicts that a young Christian should marry an unbeliever, most Christians will reject this because they know that we should not be mismated. But what if someone predicts that there will be a military take-over in two years? It is all very well saying that the events will prove whether it is right or wrong. For two years some susceptible souls will be 'under' such a prophecy. It is far from harmless and it cannot immediately be tested by Scripture. This is true to a degree of many other prophecies. Moreover, how is the toddler in the faith to sort all this out?

Anyone can see the confusion and the conflicting voices. The 'discernment' and assessment of one group is not accepted by another. Suspicions in these realms can be rife. While two authors argue that today the prophet is an 'expository preacher', others would say a resounding 'No' to this and allege that these writers have totally misunderstood the gift of prophecy.[55] But these two writers were chosen by a team of four reviewers as having written the best book on the subject! Most, realizing correctly that in Corinth prophecies came regularly, two or three a week at least, expect this to happen today and go merrily on, blithely ignoring the pile of banal, false and unfulfilled prophecies, as they gaily anticipate next week's hotch-potch. Some few, realizing that this will not do and that it reflects dishonour on the name of God, accept that prophecy is infallible and therefore cautiously expect two or three in their lifetime, usually by hearsay from Korea or Indonesia, with the consolation that those who lived in Covenanting Scotland usually got twice as many in their day. Thus one much-quoted modern writer, referring to the life of John Welsh (and presumably the prophecies with which he is credited), speaks of 'miracles performed in certain strange and extreme circumstances'.[56] It all sounds solid, cautious, balanced, Reformed (and all the other epithets we usually apply), whereas in actual fact it is simply face-saving and unscriptural. Either prophecy continues regularly or it has ceased.

In many ways the situation is rather like that of the Irish family who were always tumbling around and fighting among themselves. Let a hostile stranger appear in the midst and they would soon present a united front, only to return to the squabble as soon as the footsteps of the stranger had faded away. It may be that all groups would dismiss my challenge with a cursory, 'Oh, well, he does not believe that prophecy is freshly given to individuals today! He is resisting all the widespread evidence,' ignoring the fact that many charismatics would declare null and void the prophecies accepted in their own group.

Some argue that if there are large numbers claiming the gift of prophecy, surely the Lord would not permit a spirit of delusion to rest upon so many. The majority must be right. Micaiah stood a lonely figure against the massed ranks of the prophets who had given Ahab an 'encouraging' word. He was sure that it was a 'lying spirit' in the mouth of the false prophets. Others felt equally convinced that the Holy Spirit was on their side. 'Then Zedekiah son of Kenaanah went up and slapped Micaiah in the face. "Which way did the Spirit of the Lord go when he went from me to speak to you?" he asked' (1 Kings 22:24 see NIV footnote). Yet, as the account shows, the Holy Spirit was with the one man rather than the crowd. And it was the crowd who actually claimed to have the Holy Spirit. Are we sure that the same thing is not happening today?

3.
The gift of tongues

Tongue-speaking looms very large in this whole issue of the charismatic movement and the question of the gifts today. We are fortunate in having one whole chapter of the New Testament, 1 Corinthians 14, which deals extensively, thoroughly and finally with the whole issue. This chapter obviously bids us to careful study. This, strange though it may seem, is something which has hardly ever been done in our time. 'How can he say that,' gasps an astonished reader, 'when he must know of the plethora of books on the whole question of tongue-speaking?' Of course, there are shelves of books and booklets on tongues and tongue-speaking, but that is not necessarily the same thing as a systematic study of the Bible's teaching. Sadly we will find that, as with regard to prophecy, verse after verse of plain biblical teaching is ignored and in many cases replaced by the latest pronouncement of some charismatic leader. Descriptions of contemporary experience have become normative. It is a first-rate tragedy, but it has happened, with many being totally unaware of the satanic confidence trick.

As already stated, it is sheer myth to think that this is a subject that has been properly and exhaustively discussed. It must in honesty be said that some big names have given encouragement to this view. Thus, on the front cover of a book dealing with the gifts and written by an old Christian stalwart, one of the most revered Bible teachers of our day is quoted as saying, 'I think the way you have handled the question of "tongues" is quite perfect.'[1] I can in no wise agree with this staggering judgement. The discussion in the book is quite skimpy and question-begging. Another book by a leader respected in the north of England is rambling and discursive, draws on irrelevant analogies from all kinds of sources and

gives no proper exegesis at all.[2] I make bold to assert that no
charismatic book that I have consulted (and I have not
deliberately ignored any) actually goes through the passage
verse by verse. In fact it is more than significant that four
discussions by well-known authors all adopt exactly the same
technique. They employ their own question-and-answer
system.[3] This enables them to avoid grappling with the
passage in detail and also to avoid commenting at any length
on the opening verses of the chapter, where, not unnaturally,
we find that the gift is defined. Therefore, after a paragraph or
two where we will seek to define the meaning of the word
'tongue' we shall pursue a detailed analysis of the opening
twenty verses of the chapter.

Tongues are real languages

I must first of all record my strong preference for the
translation in the footnote of the New International Version
which renders 'tongue' as 'another language'. I prefer this for
the following reasons.

1. Exactly the same word *(glossa)* is used here in the Greek
as in the Pentecost account, where the hearers from different
regions indisputably heard a variety of genuine languages
spoken.

2. In verses 10 and 11 Paul refers to the multitude of
different languages, each of which has clear meaning.

3. Most conclusively of all, the quotation from Isaiah in
verse 21 takes us to the time when the people of God heard
what seemed to them the gibberish of the Assyrian language,
but which was nevertheless authentic speech. This is seen as a
parallel with the uncomprehending listener who hears a man
speaking in 'tongues'. It may sound like gibberish, but it is
authentic speech.

A leading charismatic incidentally confirms this
interpretation when he writes, 'The New Testament calls it
"language" – never "gibberish".'[4] So also another writer and
leader: 'His [Paul's] implication is not that they were speaking
gibberish or ecstatic speech, but in languages not known to
any of their fellow worshippers.'[5] In this writer's view the
manifestation of the gift at Corinth was essentially the same as

on the Day of Pentecost. Yet another leader says, 'They are neither gibberish nor "ecstatic utterances". They are straightforward languages.'[6] I agree with all this. This is important for our understanding of the passage.

Yet the almost universal charismatic/Pentecostal assumption is that the speaker himself did not understand what he was saying. From this I vigorously dissent. I believe that this is a view which is imposed upon the passage because of the current experiences of men. I furthermore believe that the passage itself gives repeated indications that the speaker in other languages did understand what he was in fact saying. In fact I believe that there are at least eight such indications! *I believe that this in itself is of tremendous significance, not only for the interpretation of one chapter of the Bible, but for our whole theology.*

The tongue-speaker understood the language

Firstly, we note that it does not say in verse 2 that the speaker did not understand what he was saying, although it does stress that others did not understand him. Moreover he spoke to God and did not just make sounds. The word is the normal word for coherent, logical speech. If he did not understand, it is most strange that the apostle does not mention it at this point. In this introductory verse we would have expected him to say this if it were so.

Moreover Acts 2, the foundational chapter in the New Testament on the gift of other languages, gives an impression of widespread intelligibility. At least this was the opinion of Matthew Henry, who wrote, 'We may suppose that they understood not only themselves but one another too.'[7] Much of the significance of Pentecost was that it was a resounding reversal of the curse of Babel, which had involved the confusion of languages. This aspect supports the interpretation of Matthew Henry very strikingly.

What is a 'mystery'?
Secondly, we pause and consider in some detail the word which nearly all, if not all the charismatic expositions, completely ignore – namely the word 'mysteries'. 'He utters mysteries with his spirit,' declares the apostle (v.2). Here Paul

is actually defining what the gift is, and all the books which are keen to promote what they believe this gift to be ignore him. How strange! Could it be that they wish to leave a vague impression that the speaker in another language was mystified because he did not understand and then pass on before anyone has time to query this?[8]

The word 'mystery', so frequently used in the New Testament, is clearly defined for us in three basic passages, namely Romans 16:25-27; Ephesians 3: 2-6 and Colossians l: 25-27. That we should be in no doubt about the meaning of this term God has defined it in identical fashion three times, for all the above passages contain the fivefold element in the import of the word. All tell us a 'mystery' (l) concerns the glory of the gospel, (2) which means the inclusion of the Gentiles, (3) which was a fact hidden and concealed in ages past, (4) but is 'now revealed' (Romans), 'has now been revealed' (Ephesians), 'is now disclosed' (Colossians) and (5) is in process of being set down in the word of 'prophetic writings'. *Far from being something hidden or concealed, a 'mystery' is a gloriously 'open secret' which we ourselves would never have discovered had not God revealed it.*

After dealing in a thorough-going way with the various usages of the word 'mystery'in the New Testament, Leonard Coppes says, 'In each instance "mystery" is truth made known . . . The uses of the word "mystery" in l Corinthians bear the same connotation. In l Corinthians 2:7 "mystery" is the gospel preached by the apostles (7), and made known to them by God's Spirit (10). It is divine verbal revelation.'[9] Unger sees this point and says,'The "mysteries" are New Testament revelations of truth now contained in the written Scriptures, then not yet available.'[10] Charles Hodge in his thorough discussion of this chapter says that '*Mysteries* means divine truths; things which God has revealed,' and adds, 'To make the word mean "things not understood by the hearer" is contrary to the usage of the word.'[11]

In a previous chapter we have discussed the connotation of infallibility that the word possesses along with its sister word 'revelation'. Why should God choose to give alongside prophecy and the gift of knowledge certain revelations of mysteries in other languages? Above all a mystery was particularly concerned with the spread of the gospel to the

Gentiles, implying the breaking down of the barrier between Jew and Gentile. It obviously fits in with the whole emphasis of Acts 2 and the universalism implied in Peter's quotation of the prophecy from Joel. It also ties in with God's gift of other languages to the Gentile household of Cornelius in order to convince Peter once and for all that the gospel was indeed for penitent believers of every race and nation.

What is edification?
Thirdly, we have the equation by Paul of the effect of prophecy upon the public gathering of believers and the effect of speaking in another language upon the individual. 'He who speaks in a tongue edifies himself, but he who prophesies edifies the church' (v.4). In both cases the result was edification – in the one case corporate and in the other private and personal. Prophecy was for 'strengthening, encouragement and comfort' (v.3). Obviously this took place in the normal biblical manner. Through clear teaching, their thoughts and then their whole beings were uplifted. We are not interpreting Scripture properly if we suddenly turn to Buddhist or mystic categories of thought when we think of the edification that the gift of other languages brought. Obviously it came to the individual with precisely the same effect as public prophecy to the congregation. The speaker understood and was strengthened, encouraged or comforted. The fifth verse underlines the correctness of this interpretation because the clear implication is that when the other language was interpreted for the benefit of the whole church, it was of the same value as prophecy. This also supports the argument that the other language was from the very first an infallible revelation.

The writer of the relevant section of Matthew Henry's commentary succinctly says at this point, 'What cannot be understood can never edify.'[12] So also Jamiesson, Fausset and Brown, who write that the speaker edifies himself, 'as he understands the meaning of what the particular "tongue" expresses'.[13] Says Hodge, 'They were edifying, and therefore intelligible to him who uttered them.'[14] With this Matthew Poole also agrees in his comment that 'Knowledge or understanding of the things that any man speaketh, is necessary to the improvement of them by their being a means to promote faith and love; for how shall what men say in the least promote, either my faith in God and Christ, or my love to Him, if I understand not what they say?'[15] If we accept this, the point is proven. But there is more evidence.

Importance of intelligibility

Fourthly, we note that the passage continues by stressing above all else the value of teaching, whether it be in the form of 'revelation or knowledge or prophecy or word of instruction' (v.6). Then the point that clarity and meaning are of paramount and basic importance is developed in verses 7-9. Even when we consider lifeless musical instruments, it is vital that the tune be recognized. Since there is a battle raging, we need to be able to recognize the correct signals. And so in verse 9, 'So it is with you. Unless you speak intelligible words with your tongue, how will anyone know what you are saying? You will just be speaking into the air.' The emphasis on intelligibility cannot be missed. Was not the 'other language' intelligible to the speaker? If it was not, the implication is that it was of no benefit, for it is not helpful when we hear a language that we do not understand because 'none of them is without meaning' (v.10). Such a speaker is a 'foreigner to me' (v.11). Is it therefore good that we ourselves privately listen to speech that is foreign to us? Again and again in the passage Paul asserts the value of meaningful language. Did not the speaker in other languages then employ language meaningful to himself? The implication is that he did.

Praying to interpret the tongue

For our fifth point we must deal in some detail with the two verses which are always quoted to prove that at first the language was not understood by the speaker. Thus we are faced with the question posed in verse 13, where we read, 'For this reason the man who speaks in a tongue should pray that he may interpret what he says.' Does this clearly imply, or even prove, that our argument is wrong and that in fact the language was not understood by the speaker until he prayed for a further gift of interpretation? This is indeed the widely held view.

What was the gift of another language? It was a 'mystery', an infallible utterance from God, and therefore needed to be conveyed with precision and total accuracy to a new group of hearers. At this point we need to discover the significance of the word 'interpret'. The author of the article on 'Tongues' in the *New Bible Dictionary* says, 'A definite linguistic form is suggested by the Greek words for "to interpret", which, elsewhere in the New Testament, except in Luke 24:27, always means "to translate"'.[16] 'The Greek word here for interpretation is *hermeneuo*, which means "translation",' says another writer. [17] What is especially interesting is that one of those writing in support of the use of the gift today also confirms this view. He states, 'The word is used in Luke 24:27 of Jesus "explaining the things concerning himself", and also in John 1:38,42; 9:7 and Acts 9:36 with the ordinary meaning of "translation". This would seem to contradict the extraordinary assertion that an interpreter of "tongues" need not understand the "language" himself, but is speaking out the words which God gives him. The natural meaning of "translate" in its general biblical usage seems to imply that the interpreter must have a direct understanding.' [18]

We have established that the most likely meaning of the word is 'translate', but it has already been argued that the speaker himself understood what was said. But we have also seen that the whole must then be conveyed to others with total accuracy. Presumably, particularly if the time speaking in another language were at all lengthy, the speaker would need to pray that every detail was faithfully translated, not one part of the infallible communication being omitted, distorted or even paraphrased. For this he needed to pray for another supernatural gift which did not imply that he had no understanding when the utterance was originally given.

A writer of old pointed out that although the speaker in other languages understood, he had not produced his words by an effort of the understanding, since they had been directly given by God. Yet he 'could have little, if any, greater advantage for interpretation, (supposing him not to possess the gift of interpretation,) than that which an Englishman who understands Latin would have for interpreting a Latin discourse after once hearing it. Now I would ask whether we should expect to hear from such a man a correct *interpretation* of the discourse he had just heard in Latin. No; it would be an almost unexampled effort of memory to give what could fairly be called an interpretation of it. Ask even a man who preaches

quite extempore to preach over again the sermon he has just
delivered, and how often would it be found that much of it had
escaped from his memory. How much more, then, would this
be the case, if the whole of the discourse had been uttered by
him in a tongue not his own, by the exercise of a peculiar
power given him by the Holy Spirit. It would not surely be at
all wonderful that he should be unable to give in another
language an interpretation of what he had thus spoken, or
retrace that which had not been produced by an effort of his
understanding.' [19] This is a helpful and relevant comment.

In verse 14 Paul affirms, 'For if I pray in another language,
my spirit prays, but my mind is unfruitful.' This again is
usually understood as though the speaker had some inward
glow, some bodily upbuilding although the mind was
bypassed. It was a kind of spiritual pick-me-up but did not
initially effect the understanding. As in the case of the word
'mystery', we must let Scripture interpret Scripture at this
point. How is the word 'spirit' used in Scripture? In actual fact
it is in this very letter that Paul gives the clearest definition of
the word. In chapter 2:11 he asks somewhat rhetorically, 'For
who among men knows the thoughts of a man except the
man's spirit within him?' And at once we are introduced to the
spirit of man as supremely a knowing faculty. [20]

Does the rest of Scripture bear this out? It certainly does.
'Immediately Jesus knew in his spirit that this was what they
were thinking in their hearts' (Mark 2:8). 'My spirit rejoices in
God my Saviour' (Luke 1:47). 'The spirit is willing, but the
body is weak' (Matt. 26:41). 'He was greatly distressed'
(literally, his spirit was provoked within him) 'to see that the
city was full of idols' (Acts 17:16). 'The unfading beauty of a
gentle and quiet spirit' (1 Peter 3:4). In these examples the
'spirit' of the men or women concerned was obviously an
understanding spirit. The word is not used of some deep inner
part of man which is not linked with the conscious mind. It is
used in exactly the opposite sense. So, unless we believe in the
view of soul-sleep after death, we must also interpret two other
references to the spirit as fully supporting the view that it is a
faculty which above all knows and apprehends. 'Father, into
your hands I commit my spirit,' said the expiring Saviour
(Luke 23:46). 'Lord Jesus, receive my spirit,' cried the dying
Stephen (Acts 7:59). It is the undying, conscious, knowing

part of man that is described by 'spirit'.

If, then, the spirit is supremely a knowing faculty, this fully supports the view that the speaker in other languages knew what he was saying. But we are still left with the phrase at the end of verse 14 where Paul says, 'but my mind is unfruitful,' and clearly from what we have just seen this in no way means that the mind was not involved. The context both before and immediately after verse 14 determines the meaning of the phrase. In verse 12 the Corinthians are told 'to try to excel in gifts that build up the church'. In verses 15-19 the need for others to understand so that they can say a legitimate and heart-felt 'Amen' is urged. In other words, the mind needs to be fruitful in the common biblical sense of bearing fruit for the benefit of others.

The writer of the relevant section of Matthew Henry's commentary, John Wesley, Charles Hodge and Matthew Poole all saw this as the obvious meaning. Here is the comment from Matthew Henry's commentary: 'His own mind might be devoutly engaged, *but his understanding would be unfruitful* (v.14), he would not be understood, nor therefore would others join with him in their devotions.' [21] On the phrase, 'my spirit prays,' John Wesley says, 'By the power of the Spirit I understand the words myself' and on the phrase 'but my mind is unfruitful,' he comments, 'The knowledge I have is no benefit to others.'[22] 'The words, therefore, must be understood to mean, "my understanding produces no fruit" i.e. it does not benefit others,' says Hodge. [23] Matthew Poole reminds us, 'Nor is it here said, my *understanding* is dark or blind, but *unfruitful*, that is, though myself understand, yet my knowledge bringeth forth no fruit to the advantage or good of others.' [24] Therefore nothing in verses 13 and 14 contradicts our basic proposition that the speaker himself understood what he was saying.

Singing in another language
Sixthly, verses 16-19 point to the same conclusion. How did the speaker in other languages know that he ought to sing? Did he not then know that the content of the other language was such as that of the lyrical, poetic exultation of the type of Philippians 2:5-11 or 1 Timothy 3:16? How did he know that he was giving thanks? Did he just have a general sense of euphoria? Perish

the thought! The 'Amen' that he was able to give was just as meaningful as the 'Amen' that others gave when the language was translated. Scripture gives no countenance to meaningless 'Amens'! Again in verse 19 Wesley comments on the phrase 'intelligible words': 'in a rational manner; so as not only to understand myself, but to be understood by others'. [25] Surely this is indeed the import of the apostle's words. He is still afffirming the unsurpassed virtue of intelligibility! He would even prefer to speak just 'five intelligible words to instruct others than ten thousand words in another language' (v.19).

The climax of the passage

Because Wesley displays such acute discernment in his interpretation of this passage he will introduce our seventh point for us. Wesley so clearly and ably sees the pivotal and climactic nature of verse 20, where we are told to be adults in our thinking and to stop thinking as children. He writes, 'Knowing religion was not designed to destroy any of our natural faculties, but to exalt and improve them, our reason in particular.' [26] This is, of course, the nub of the whole issue. We shall return to this point in our next chapter.

Speaking to himself
Eighthly, Paul commands that where there is no one with the gift of translation, 'The speaker should keep quiet in the church and speak to himself and God' (v.28). How do we speak to ourselves? Do we utter mumbo-jumbo? Do we just string together empty sounds? Of course not. The proper meaning of the words is that the speaker was addressing himself and understood what he said and that he was also speaking coherently and intelligibly to God himself.

Therefore in my view there are eight scriptural indications that the speaker in other languages in 1 Corinthians 14 understood what he was saying. This means that modern instances of this practice are spurious. At least in no instance that I have come across does the speaker claim to understand what he says. He may say that he knows the gist or has a 'general sense', but we have seen that the passage cannot support this generalizing meaning.

If we judge, as I will seek later to demonstrate, that the best interpretation of the previous chaper of 1 Corinthians is that the 'perfection' of verse 10 is indeed the completion of the canon of Scripture, then this is not a surprising conclusion. Clearly, if the infallible but partial revelatory gifts of prophecy, other languages and knowledge ceased at the coming of the complete revelation of God's truth, then there can be no authentic speaking in other languages in this sense today.

Of course, when this position is taken, immediately the accusation of incipient or concealed modernism is made. Thus one contributor to a Christian newspaper asserted that, if we believe that certain gifts have ceased, 'we have come close to reasoning like liberals, have argued like Catholics and entrenched ourselves behind a new dispensationalism'. (Quite a catalogue of charges!) He then elaborated on one of these three points: 'We have almost reasoned like liberals in that we have come perilously near to cutting out or "blue pencilling" two *entire chapters* of an apostolic epistle!' [27] The language and the concept are evidently catching for some time later we find a correspondent in the same paper arguing in the same context that 'To "blue pencil" chapters of the Word of God as "not for today" is what we accuse the liberals of . . .' [28]

This is a very grave accusation. It could, for instance, be argued that the dishonest furtive modernist in some ways is even worse than the open denier of Scripture. Yet while it is my conviction that every word of Scripture is not only inspired but also has its relevance for every age, let us remind ourselves that this is particularly so in countless instances where a passage apparently deals with a dated issue or with an incident which will only occasionally have an exact replica in the church today. For example, I have never resided in an area nor pastored in a church where incest has actually come up as a matter of church discipline, where one member has gone to law against another member, where 'food sacrificed to idols' has been a burning local issue, or where drunkenness at the Lord's Table has proved a real stumbling-block. All of these were actual issues in the Corinthian church (1 Cor. 5; 6; 8; 10; 11). Such events rarely have exact counterparts in twentieth-century England. Yet there are always applications that can legitimately be made from these passages to parallel or similar situations in the church today.

Relevance for today

Therefore a chapter like 1 Corinthians 14, which calls repeatedly for intelligibility and clarity, even bidding us to take into account the feelings and reactions of the uninitiated non-believer who may enter the assembly (vv.22-25), has much to say to us on the way we conduct our meetings and in particular our mid-week fellowships. As we look at verses 26-28, using this exposition as an illustration of how I am not 'blue pencilling' the chapter by my view that these gifts have ceased, we firstly see that *there was real sharing and participation* with different members taking part. Just because some house groups have gone hay-wire, there need not be an embargo on group discussion for the next century. It was a Brethren writer who described some churches as being 'like comets, with a brilliant head and a long nebulous tail'. [29] Such a picture may be flattering (perhaps in a wrong sense) to a minister but, if true, it would not really flatter any church. Our forefathers were not so wary in this matter. 'Mr Roger Williams, according to the custom, proposes a question, to which the pastor, Mr Smith, speaks briefly; then Mr Williams prophesies (or explains); and after, the Governor of Plymouth (who had studied the Hebrew language and antiquities) speaks to the question; after him, the elder (a man of learning); then two or three more of the congregation; then the elder (agreeably to Acts 13:14,15 etc.) desires Governor Winthrop and Mr Wilson to speak to it, which they do . . .' [30] Sometimes the Pilgrim Fathers must have felt they were sitting on the edge of a volcano, but they did not react by clamping down on the Sunday afternoon meeting for sharing. Obviously there was oversight and control. But equally plainly there was real participation by several men.

What then about the excision of all items in worship which leave the worshipper a mere spectator, and often a bemused one at that? John Wesley, in particular, saw the message of this chapter as applicable to certain types of singing in his day when he wrote, 'In the evening I preached at Pebworth Church, but I seemed out of my element. A long anthem was sung; but I suppose none beside the singers could understand one word of it. Is not that "praying in an unknown tongue"? I could no more bear it in any church of mine than

Latin prayers.'[31] (Incidentally, this is not to assume that a worshipper is a 'mere spectator' simply because he is listening to someone else speaking and praying.)

Secondly, the clear implication of verse 26 is that *there was a measure of preparation*. People were thinking beforehand what they were going to bring to the fellowship. A hymn was prepared. Is this not applicable today? Should there then be a mad scramble to find a tune? Ought the man at the front, who has forgotten to print a chorus on a sheet, glibly to say, 'Of course, you'll all know the chorus,' leaving half the number desperately trying to mouth something like the right words as they lip-read their neighbours? I think not. Should the people have three hands, as Hudson Pope used to say – a right hand and a left hand and a little behind hand? Should the missionary prayer board not be properly prepared? Ought not the room to be set out well beforehand, welcoming and warm? Should not the people be garnering from their own quiet times with God in preparation for the meeting?

Thirdly, we note the obvious truth, stressed much in the whole chapter, that *what was to be done must 'be done for the strengthening of the church'* (v.26). While we must not in a wrong sense prepare specifically for individuals, in the right sense we ought to bear in mind the needs of a particular group at a given time. Some things may be too difficult. Some may be inappropriate. Some may just display the speaker's ability and fly over the heads of the hearers.

> I shot an arrow in the air.
> It came to earth I know not where.

This happens so often and it is nothing but a tragedy when it does.

How often is evangelical preaching or speaking orthodox and yet abstract and vague, the preacher, in the vivid description of Quiller Couch, 'perpetually shuffling around in the fog and cotton-wool of abstract terms'! [32] Such preaching is gross contradiction of the call of this chapter. 'Again, if the trumpet does not sound a clear call, who will get ready for battle?' (v.8). One can hear notices in some churches where newcomers hear mention of mystic entities like Tear Fund and the B.E.C. and where even an invitation to a simple home

Bible study is couched in the language of an invitation to an Elizabethan get-together! Just because some are turning to drama, there is no need for us to turn to drabness. Just because some are turning to anarchy, we need not cling to archaisms. The whole emphasis of Paul is that of the need for freshness, intelligibility and contemporaneity in the right sense.

Fourthly, *the meeting must be governed and controlled by the Word of God*. It must not be vague and uncontrolled, or even wild and very unprofitable 'sharing', that predominates. This can be deduced from the centrality given to the word of instruction, the revelation, the other language and the interpretation, which was the way in which God gave his Word before the completion of the canon of Scripture. It will have been noted that the Pilgrim Fathers centred their discussion round the Word of God. We must seek to do likewise. The only authentic and infallible word we have is Scripture, and while there should be sharing, it must be governed by the Word.

Fifthly, *it must be orderly*. People should speak 'one at a time' (v.27). Wesley commented on the love feast at Burslem as follows: 'Such a one as I have not known for many years. While two or three spoke, the power of God so fell upon all that were present, some praying and others giving thanks, that their voices could scarce be heard; and two or three were speaking at one time, till I gently advised them to speak one at a time; and they did so, with amazing energy.' [33] Because the power of God comes, that is no excuse for disorder. Wesley again saw this in terms of the application of this passage.

Sixthly, *there must be accuracy*. We have seen that interpretation of another language means translation. The Word of God must never be treated in a vague, casual or generalizing way. This should affect how a passage is chosen. Has a portion been taken out of context so that it may contain a blessed, uplifting thought, with an essential accompanying condition being omitted? This is as bad as someone missing out a vital bit of the translation of another language when God gave such to the church. Is a speaker in any way manipulating Scripture? God's Word is not to be so used. In this context, I feel it is legitimate to ask, 'What about the use of a good, modern version of the Bible translated by evangelical men?' The translators of the Authorized Version realized the need for this. In fact they applied this very chapter to their own quest. This is how they put it in the Preface: 'But how shall men meditate in that which they cannot understand? How shall they understand that which is kept close in an unknown tongue? As it is written, Except I know the power of the voice, I shall be to him that speaketh a barbarian, and he that speaketh shall be a barbarian to me.' [34]

Seventhly and lastly, *there can be a value in a person being silent and communing with God in their inward being.* 'Blessed are they who have nothing to say and cannot be persuaded to say it,' is beatitude, which if taken seriously, would sometimes help a fellowship meeting! But perhaps even more to the point, and needing to be stressed today is the fact that there are real and precious spiritual experiences which should not be blurted out to all and sundry at the earliest opportunity. Much of modern-day sharing, even where genuine, is inappropriate. We need to pray over this.

I cannot close without throwing out a challenge to Pentecostal or charismatic groups at this point. How far do they themselves literally apply this chapter? Does the tongue-speaker remain silent when there is no interpretation? Do they never speak or even sing together? ('One at a time,' says Paul.) Are there regularly given two or three words of authentic prophecy at the meeting? Do the women stay silent? So very often not only are the above things not done at all in any scriptural way, but they in fact form a very small proportion of a meeting that is largely given up to other things – 'sharing', striking up a chorus, and increasingly today, dancing and miming. All this is but a further indication that the chapter cannot have a totally literal application today.

Readers may disagree with particular aspects of my application, but I have sought to show that evangelicals who do believe that the gifts have ceased do not run away from this chapter. In fact it is not a chapter from which we should flee with embarrassment. As believers in the entire Word of God, we have no place whatsoever for modernistic scissors or even blasphemous blue-pencil marks! We believe in the need for enthusiastic participation and sharing. Despite all its faults, the Corinthian church had this. We recall the simple comment of the negro, whose master took exception to the religious excitement of certain believers: 'Massa, is it not better that the water boil over than that it never come to the boil?' Order, yes. Proper scriptural interpretation, assuredly. Enthusiasm and sharing, why not?

4.
Tongues as practised today

The place of the mind

While we have dealt with some relevant issues in our discussion of 1 Corinthians 14, the crucial issue with regard to interpretation of the chapter has not yet been faced. It is not just a matter of how we apply certain verses in a contemporary situation, important though that is. The central issue of the chapter touches on a principle vital to our whole concept of God and his dealing with man. The question can be put as simply as this: does the true and living God ever deal with his people in ways that deliberately bypass their minds? While we sadly recognize that there can be a 'dead orthodoxy' and acknowledge that too often there is a tragic and pathetic pride in man's intellect, this should not therefore lead to an unbalanced disparagement of the mind or reason or intelligibility. Bernard Levin may have seen a notice outside the hall of an Indian guru, 'Minds and shoes left here.'[1] Could such a notice ever properly be displayed outside a true Christian church, or more relevantly, be put before the worshipper for even the briefest space of time in worship?

It is gloriously true that God's greatness 'no one can fathom' (Ps. 145:3). It is true that we constantly need the frame of mind in which Isaiah cried out, 'Who has understood the mind of the Lord, or instructed him as his counsellor?' (Isa. 40:13). With Job we must concede that even the greatest demonstrations of his power are but 'the outer fringe of his works' (Job 26:14). Particularly in the gracious matter of pardoning sinners, his thoughts and ways are far above ours (Isa. 55:6-9). Yet, when we have said that, we must not deny that it is 'his understanding' that 'has no limit' (Ps. 147:5). There is nothing mindless about God. It was by his understanding that the heavens were made (Ps. 136:5). If his thoughts towards each individual believer 'outnumber the grains of sand', what a mighty God he must be! (Ps. 139:18). Part of the endowment of his image upon man was the very gift of reason and even in man's sinfulness and stubborn rebellion God in grace continued to reason with him (Isa. 1:18).

From all these scriptures we may infer that, while there are countless aspects of God that are past understanding, this does not mean that God ever intends to bypass our understanding in dealing with us. There is one crucial text among many which puts the issue beyond any reasonable doubt. We have it on the authority of the Lord Jesus Christ himself that the most important commandment was 'Love the Lord your God with all your heart and with all your soul and with all your mind and with all your strength' (Mark 12:30). All the mind is to be constantly involved, just as the other faculties are. We have no warrant for dropping this word from the list for even the briefest moment. Pascal expressed it well when he wrote, 'Man is only a reed, the weakest in nature, but he is a thinking reed . . . Thus all our dignity consists in thought . . . [2]

Therefore we must see that the charismatic and Pentecostal misunderstanding of 1 Corinthians 14 is not concerned with just one issue. The whole question of our doctrine of God, of our understanding of his gracious dealings with sinful man and of the process of man's recovery is involved. The biblical position is that through the Fall man's mind has become tainted and perverted and, even from a purely intellectual angle, greatly weakened. This latter aspect is also instanced in the fact that man only utilizes a part of his brain power. 'So far down has the human mind sunk in our day in its average quality and capacity to use the brain that God gave us, that we are told by experts that even the greatest genius in the world never uses more than one tenth of one per cent of his brain capacity in his entire lifetime. Only one thousandth of the brain is used even by the most brilliant men of our world of our generation,' writes J.C. Whitcomb.[3] God intends to remedy this. In Christ the process of recovery for the believer begins on this earth. It is completed in heaven, when, as one old evangelical stalwart put it, 'God will not only wash our hearts, but our brains as well.'

Worshipping God with all the mind

Consequently, God wishes man to worship him with all his mind all the time. To say this is not to infer that there are no occasions when we find it difficult to frame the right words and no experiences which can never adequately be put into words (Rom. 8:26, 27; 2 Cor. 12:4). But this does not alter the principle that John Wesley so clearly enunciated when he told his preachers: 'You are in danger of enthusiasm every hour – if you lightly esteem reason, knowledge or human learning; every one of which is an excellent gift of God, and may serve the noblest purposes. I advise you, never to use the words, wisdom, reason, or knowledge by way of reproach. On the contrary, pray that you yourself may abound in them more and more. If you mean worldly wisdom, useless knowledge, false reasoning, say so; and throw away the chaff, but not the wheat.' [4]

The contrast with the charismatic movement is immediately stark and glaring and it surfaces most clearly with reference to tongue-speaking. Listen, for example, to the assertion of one of the founders of modern Pentecostalism who is speaking of this particular gift of 'other languages'. 'This phenomenon necessarily violates human reason. It means abandonment of this faculty for the time. And this is generally the last point to yield. The human mind is held in abeyance fully in this exercise.' [5]

Listen now to a leading modern proponent. He is asking why the gifts have been so neglected. He comments, 'Another big factor has been the tremendous emphasis in Western Christendom on the mind and human reason – leaving little or no room for more direct inspiration. If it is thought that the mind has a monopoly in the realm of edification, then there is obviously no room for the gift of tongues – in which the mind, according to Paul, is "unfruitful".'[6]

This type of approach is prevalent in the movement. The following are from a variety of sources: 'Speaking in tongues is a childlike act of faith. It involves no ability, but rather the setting aside of ability. 'Our minds are so used to regulating all that we do, that they rebel at this. Our minds need educating here to an appreciation of the fact that they must give up a part of their authority, for it is by offering ourselves to God and letting our minds be remade that we are able to discern the

will of God (See Rom. 12:1,2) . . . when we speak with a tongue
in a way that bypasses our mind.' 'You walk by the Spirit by
simply fixing your eyes on Jesus and stepping out *without
thought*.' 'The creative mind does not play a creative role in it.'
'The intellect, on the other hand, that does not understand the
language is humbled . . .' 'Whilst prayer with the
understanding remains a vital means of fellowship with God, it
is exceeded by a language of the Spirit unlimited in scope.'[7]
And in clear contradiction of all that has been said in the
previous chapter, 'Once we begin, we should expect the
language to begin to flow naturally. We will not understand
the words we are saying, nor should we expect to.'[8] The latter
quotation comes from a membership booklet of a house
church, which then cites 1 Corinthians 14:2; putting in heavy
print the phrase 'no one understands him'. Have none of their
members realized that if a person were to say, 'No one
understands me,' it does not mean that he does not understand
himself?

Manipulation by men

The group just quoted concede that only twice did the gift
come directly (Acts 2; 10). 'At other times, it is received by the
laying on of hands, as in Samaria (Acts 8),' they add, omitting
to point out that it was through the laying on of the *apostles'*
hands and proceeding to outline how readers can become
recipients as they build up in expectancy and then submit to
the laying on of hands: 'When the Spirit descends upon us, our
organs of speech are stimulated to form strange syllables or
words as we yield to his prompting.'[9]
    What is advocated here is common practice. No doubt the
element of 'intensity' varies from group to group. Someone
who has queried the whole experience has written, 'Not all
Pentecostals received their experience in an emotional
gathering. But a visit to a "waiting-meeting" is far from
reassuring. Certainly some Gospel after-meetings have a good
deal of emotion running through them, but even in those there
is not the dependence on the leader so dominant in the
gathering where people are longing for the "gift". It is not
unusual to see the leader walking along rows of candidates,

urging them to open their mouths and almost forcing them to speak in tongues. I have witnessed meetings of this nature myself, and it is the testimony of many others.'[10]

Instructions and guide-lines are often issued. An Assemblies of God handbook tells how to deal with a seeker after the 'gift of the Holy Spirit': 'Help the candidate see that the Gift is already given and that all that he has to do is receive it. Lead him to realize that anyone who is saved through baptism is prepared to receive a Baptism of the Spirit. Tell him that when hands are laid on him he is to receive the Holy Spirit: tell the candidate that he is to expect the Spirit to move on his vocal cords, but that he must co-operate with the experience as well: tell him to throw away all fear that this experience may be false: tell him to open his mouth wide and breathe as deeply as possible at the same time telling himself that he is receiving the Spirit now.'[11] And here is an Anglican charismatic giving guide-lines: 'Open your mouth and show that you believe the Lord has baptized you in the Spirit by *beginning to speak*. Don't speak English, or any other language you know, for God can't guide you to speak in tongues if you are speaking in a language known to you.'[12] The same writer says that on these occasions people may experience 'involuntary tremblings, stammering lips, or chattering teeth'.[13] He reassures them that it is all part of the package and may simply indicate that they have resisted him with their lips hitherto. But, as in all the other testimonies, no scriptural support is given for these practices.

Listen again to the writer of a booklet published by the Fountain Trust: 'In order to speak in tongues, you have to quit praying in English. After you have come to the Lord with your prayers and petitions in English, you simply lapse into silence and resolve to speak not a syllable of any language you have ever learned. Your thoughts are focused on Christ. And then you simply lift up your voice and speak out confidently, in the faith that the Lord will take the sound you give Him, and shape it into a language. You take no thought of what you are saying: as far as you are concerned, it is just a series of sounds. The first sounds will sound strange and unnatural to your ear, and they may be halting and inarticulate (have you ever heard a baby learning to talk?). You may even have the thought that you are just making it up. But as you continue to speak, and the lips and tongue begin to move more freely, the Spirit will begin to shape a beautiful language of prayer and praise.'[14] He adds that the devil will quickly be there to challenge the experience.

In answer to the following question, 'Some have said that they first began to speak in tongues by making noises with their mouths. Surely this means that tongues is a man-created thing?' the founder of the Fountain Trust replies, 'It is perfectly true that some have begun to manifest this gift in this manner, but it does not follow that the gift is man-created. Faith often involves us in activity. We have to make some practical response to the call of God. Going forward at an evangelistic meeting has never converted anyone yet! But it is sometimes a useful and practical response to a desire which has been given by the Holy Spirit. In a similar way, making sounds with the mouth is not "speaking in tongues", but it may signify an honest act of faith, which the Holy Spirit will honour by giving to that person the power to speak in another language. For this gift is always an act of partnership. Without the Holy Spirit we cannot manifest the gift, but without us, the Holy Spirit will not.'[15]

The man-centred nature of the above passages is blatant and the unscriptural nature of the whole approach hardly needs to be stressed. The gift of another language was a gift of the Spirit from heaven on the Day of Pentecost, in the household of Cornelius and to the group at Ephesus. There was no question of man co-operating, instigating – still less manipulating! Furthermore there was no putting aside human thoughts or starting to make sounds as a 'venture of faith'. In fact, a charismatic commentator writing on 1 Corinthians 12-14 really makes some 'give-away' remarks when he describes how another writer shows how this gift can be received. 'Experience seems to prove that the majority of those who reach out simply to God, do receive the gift of speaking in another language. Psychologically the only explanation that satisfies me is the fact that this is a potential capacity, dormant in most people, awakened in the Christian by the Holy Spirit and filled with meaning.'[16] The key phrase is 'a potential capacity, dormant in most people'. It is not from God. It is psychological – from within man.

In an article entitled 'Charismatic renewal and the instant

spirit of the age' a writer in *The Times* described how 'An American Jesuit . . . has even claimed that instant glossolalia can be induced by saying "La La La" over and over again.'[17] Wong Ming-Dao, the courageous Chinese Christian, has in fact described in his autobiography that it was by such a method that a Pentecostal induced him to seek and then claim this gift. In his case he was taught to repeat 'Hallelujah' without stopping. For a while he strenuously advocated this teaching, eventually concluding that 'It seemed to be the manufacture of tongues by man.'[18] A. Jackson Roddy was told to repeat, 'Praise Him, Praise Him, Praise Him,' or 'Glory, Glory, Glory'.[19] The important thing was to repeat the words without ceasing and without breathing. After all, were not the disciples 'continually in the temple, praising God' before Pentecost? The outcome was the recognition that the gift had been spurious.

Redefinition of the gift

As in the case of prophecy, we must be fully aware that in all these ways the charismatics are totally redefining the way the gift is received and rejecting scriptural teaching. The same must be said with reference to the nature of the gift. In no case have I found a testimony to the effect that the tongue-speaker understands his utterance as soon as it is uttered. The biblical evidence for this fact is never even considered since the gift is being defined in terms of individual experiences rather than Scripture. Therefore it is not surprising when certain spokesmen deny that interpretation is translation. They seem to think that it is almost a new revelation given to the interpreter, with no real relationship to the original tongues. Kildahl tells of someone he knew who was raised in Africa. He rose and said the Lord's prayer in an African dialect he had learned in his youth. It was interpreted as a message about the imminent second coming of Christ.[20] One who has had years of experience in the movement in England, Scotland, France and Holland writes, 'A regular tongues speaker in a church will, in a message in tongues, utter almost the same syllables week after week, only to have a different interpretation on each occasion.'[21]

The bypassing of the biblical teaching is vividly illustrated by the fact that nowhere do their spokesmen systematically expound the main chapter which treats of this gift. I have already indicated that they regularly use the question-and-answer method and change the order of the chapter, omitting to discuss the verses where the gift is specifically defined. Thus, when the reader's gaze has been turned from a detailed study of Scripture, they continue to redefine the gift in non-scriptural terms. Let us listen to them. 'He is edified, not indeed in his understanding (cf. v14), but by what has been called "the glow of soul associated with the exercise of the gift".' 'An almost spontaneous expression of otherwise unutterable emotion.' 'Essentially, therefore, tongues is a private, devotional language – a "love-language" if you like.' 'For me . . . the gift of tongues turned out to be the gift of praise. As I used the unknown language which God had given me I felt rising in me the love, the awe, the adoration pure and uncontingent, that I had not been able to achieve in thought-out prayer.' '"What's the use of speaking in tongues?" The only way I can answer that is to say, "What's the use of a blue-bird? What is the use of a sunset?" Just sheer, unmitigated uplift, just joy unspeakable and with it health and peace and rest and release from burdens and tensions.' 'When I started praying in tongues I felt, and people told me I looked, twenty years younger . . .' 'The idea of Tongues is therefore seen to be associated with Jesus upon the cross, when He hung there an uncomely "thing", a spectacle to God, men, devils and angels.' 'Tongues thus seem to fulfil a function not unanalogous with that of art and music for some.' 'You see, I have a little play language that I talk for my children when we're having fun together.'[22] The author who believes this last instance to be a genuine case of speaking in tongues also writes of the man who allegedly exercised the gift under his own ministry but then did not realize he had done it. (He had to be told that he had!) Since I have made clear the biblical position it is no part of my task either to reconcile the above views with each other or with Scripture!

Reference has been made in the section on prophecy to a

long-awaited book by a Reformed writer on the Holy Spirit. I have already expressed my disappointment with his treatment of prophecy, yet his treatment of tongues beggars description! I have forborne quoting him in support of my own views, though he constantly hints that edification does mean that the speaker of tongues understands, and does declare that the tongues of the New Testament are not to be equated with the tongues spoken today: 'Current charismatic phenomena do not fully correspond to those of 1 Corinthians 12-14.'[23] At several points he does seem to agree with the views of Hodge, saying at one point, 'Hodge's axiom that edification presupposes understanding is hard, biblically to get round; accepting it, however, would seem to entail the conclusion that glossolalia as practised today cannot edify, which is a most unfashionable view to hold.'[24]

Yet it would seem not insignificant that this quotation is taken from a footnote and, despite all the above asseverations, the same writer in so many places expresses approval of modern practices, even concluding that since 'many who pray in tongues pray much and for long periods of time; it is doubtful whether those who do not pray so much have any right to criticize what they are doing'.[25] (How does he know this?) What is saddest is the kind of justification he does in fact give for the practice: tongues are like learning to swim, 'confidence in entrusting oneself to the medium (the water in one case, babbling utterance in the other)'; 'comparable to the fantasy language of children, the scat singing of the late Louis Armstrong, yodelling in the Alps and warbling under a shower in the bath'; 'exalted fun before the Lord'; 'Wordless singing, loud perhaps, as we lie in the bath can help restore a sense of rational well-being to the frantic, and glossolalia might be the spiritual equivalent of that; it would be a Godsend if it were.'[26] Throw-away remarks like this last one leave me totally bemused at this whole light-hearted approach.

But not less bemusing were the reactions of some reviewers. One reviewer began by commending the author for being a man 'who will insist on following biblical principles ruthlessly, thoroughly, and without regard to the "names and sects and parties" into which evangelicalism persists in dividing itself'.[27] With regard to the treatment of the gifts this is just the thing the author signally and abysmally fails to do! (The first part of

his book on the Holy Spirit and sanctification is excellent.)
Another reviewer chose to contrast the book with two others
by Reformed writers. Whereas the other two writers 'will be
read for what the reformed position says', this book by
contrast 'will be read by both reformed and charismatic for a
fresh look at what the Bible says', the reviewer concluded.[28]

Not only have the reviewers been beguiled by the author's
reputation, they have insulted any genuine charismatic. At
least let me put it like this. I would expect the genuine
charismatic strongly to rebut my own position unless
convinced by Scripture and, if he were a conscientious
believer, I would be on the way to respecting him. But if he
spoke in tongues and cheerfully accepted the interpretations
given by the afore-mentioned writer ('exalted fun' etc.) I
would have little respect for him at all. He would, like the
writer of the book, have trivialized the whole issue. Another
reviewer, a professor from the Free Church College in
Scotland, got it just right. 'He (the author) obviously has a lot
of charismatic friends and he is frightened to offend them . . .
Sometimes the book just plays to the gallery . . . The
Charismatic Movement is a huge, dynamic and prestigious
phenomenon and it is easy for academic theologians (a
despised breed) to lose their nerve when confronted by it. It is
a sad day indeed when men of this stature are beginning to
judge it by its own criteria, arguing that an experience (or
doctrine?) is valid if you personally find it challenging and
uplifting.'[29] The reviewer goes on to affirm that we must keep
our heads and insist on more stringent biblical criteria.

Minimization of Pentecost

Some of those within the charismatic movement who
maximize modern experience end up by minimizing Pentecost.
Some deny the element of stupendous miracle when tongues
were first given, or at least refuse to acknowledge that the gift
of tongues to the Corinthians was of the same type.[30] Often
this is argued because the writers wish to state that the tongues
of 1 Corinthians 14 were merely ecstatic utterances, or even
the languages of angels, and cannot be traced to any known
modern languages. It must be admitted that not all

Pentecostals drive this wedge between the two sections of Scripture. The argument on whether any do speak in recognizable languages today ranges to and fro. There are those who claim to recognize a language but few, if any, claims will stand serious scrutiny.[31] Wong Ming-Dao gives his testimony thus: 'At first I had no doubts. But doubts arose because some people simply repeated one sound such as "Ba-ba-ba-ba" or "Da-da-da-da" or "Go-di, Go-di" for several minutes or even several tens of minutes, always repeating the same sounds. I ask, how can you call this "tongues"? Even when angels speak they cannot use just one or two sounds to express many meanings . . .'[32]

Gromacki sums up his findings like this: 'The conclusions of the linguists indicate that modern glossolalia is composed of unknown sounds with no distinguishing vocabulary and grammatical features, simulated foreign features, and the total absence of language characteristics.'[33] The verdict of Hoekema is similar, as he states, 'It is significant to note that at least two competent linguists, after analysing taped samples of glossolalia, both came to identical conclusions: what they heard were not actual languages but types of ecstatic speech, with peculiar consonantal structure and very limited vowel sounds, which bore no resemblance to any language spoken on earth.'[34]

In view of all that has been said earlier, unless it were by direct satanic impersonation, we would not expect that real languages should be recognized. We may thank God that men such as Wong Ming-Dao have recognized the deception and manipulation in which they have been involved. There are many who have renounced the supposed gift and acknowledged a sense of liberation and freedom in so doing. They have also in many cases testified to a deepened consciousness of the truth of God's Word and the doctrines of grace. One who renounced the gift as spurious said of the movement that had encouraged him to seek it that it 'has at its heart a false mysticism which is contrary to the Word of God'.[35]

This is further illustrated, and indeed confirmed by the many examples which can be given where (a) the seeker is urged to make the mind blank or take no thought; (b) he is urged to make meaningless sounds in order to induce the experience and (c) he is peremptorily instructed not to query in any way what has happened or to listen to the voice of Satan insinuating doubts. That such things do occur and occur frequently has been amply demonstrated. To be sure, there are older Pentecostals who strongly deplore all the ways of inducing tongues which I have been describing. One of them gives illustrations from literature of the same type as I have quoted and roundly condemns such techniques.[36] One must not query his sincerity, yet in honesty it should be pointed out that he belonged to the denomination, the Assemblies of God, which issued one of the manuals from which I have quoted! Perhaps the height of all this absurdity is revealed in a magazine interview with a well-known Roman Catholic lady. She reported how at a meeting she was led to speak in tongues. 'I spoke a few halting words, but I didn't know if I was making it up or not. The Colonel encouraged me to keep using those words and it would develop more fully.' Then, speaking of a later experience she says, 'One of the most precious moments of my life came recently when not only was I baptized in the Spirit, but consciously and explicitly accepted Jesus as my saviour, accepting what he did for me through His death and resurrection.'[37] If this latter experience was genuine we praise God for it, but where does it leave the earlier experience? Once again I feel that it is not necessary for me to seek to reconcile the unreconcilable, but the testimony illustrates the confused and false teaching and manipulative theology that have grown up in so many quarters on this subject.

5.
When do the gifts cease?

'When perfection comes'

'Love never fails. But where there are prophecies, they will cease; where there are tongues, they will be stilled; where there is knowledge, it will pass away. For we know in part and we prophesy in part, but when perfection comes, the imperfect disappears. When I was a child, I talked as a child, I reasoned like a child. When I became a man, I put childish ways behind me. Now we see but a poor reflection; then we shall see face to face. Now I know in part; then I shall know fully, even as I am fully known. And now these three remain: faith, hope and love. But the greatest of these is love' (1 Cor. 13:8-13).

Discussion of this passage has centred on the phrase 'when perfection comes'. Some have said that the phrase refers to the completion of the New Testament Scriptures and others have found this position absurd, affirming that the phrase can only mean 'heaven' or the 'second coming of Christ'. Let us take exponents of the latter position first. A well-respected modern writer finds the former view 'quite ridiculous', arguing that Paul is manifestly aiming 'to contrast our present condition with our future state of existence'.[1] He and several other writers all underline verse 12, which speaks of 'face-to-face' knowledge and our knowing as we are known, and which in their view can only apply to heavenly knowledge. In fact one says, 'If we desire to dispose of prophecy – then logically we must also dispose of "knowledge", which is likewise going to pass away (v.8).'[2]

Another writer, after asking whether there can be 'any reasonable doubt' that Paul is referring to the second coming, as he is in chapter 11:26, goes on to say that he had not found any great commentators of the past who take 'perfection' to

mean 'Scripture'.[3] A Dutch charismatic likewise feels that
such an interpretation is 'so evidently untenable and beside
the mark of sound exegesis that most commentators do not
even mention it'.[4] Yet in his querying of the interpretation he
majors more on the state of Christendom since New
Testament times than on God's gift of a perfect revelation.
(This is a common error in writers of this persuasion.) He also
feels it incredible that a 'spiritual giant' like Paul could include
himself in this lack of knowledge. A letter to a Christian paper
described the view that the perfection is Scripture as 'ludicrous
exegesis'.[5] Another best-selling author states the two views
and then rejects the view that 'perfection' means Scripture
without attempting any exegesis at all. In justifying his
adherence to the other view, he merely says, 'I have come to
believe . . .'[6] In some quarters that is enough! And here is the
comment of the leader of another group: 'It assumes that the
Bible is "that which is perfect", whereas we know from
internal evidence that the Bible is incomplete. There are at
least three letters of Paul's missing, beside some works by
prophets of the Old Testament. The Bible is not in that sense
"perfect" although it is perfect enough for God's purposes by it
among men in this age.'[7] We notice that many pejorative
epithets are used in all this. The position to be expounded here
is 'ridiculous', 'ludicrous', 'evidently untenable'. Nobody in
the past has even held it. Yet, later we shall recount in some
detail how that spiritual pygmy Jonathan Edwards
(presumably not to be compared with the giants of the
twentieth century!) expounded it in just the way we are going
to do, namely, in the sense that 'when perfection comes' means
'when Scripture is complete'.

A whole array of evidence

There are many strands in the argument that follows. The
interpretation that I espouse must be seen as one that has a
whole array of scriptures in its support and is one which does
justice both to the immediate context of the phrase within the
passage and also to the wider scriptural background, both
New Testament and Old. It also has the support of events in
history, as we shall see briefly in this chapter and much

more fully later in the book. I shall put down the arguments in
a series of propositions.

1. When the apostle Paul speaks of prophecy, tongues and
knowledge, he is not speaking of a casual 'word from the Lord'
(mixed and partly spurious), a mysterious spiritual pick-me-
up, which produces a warm glow inside and knowledge in
general. In each reference he is *speaking of supernatural God-given
revelation.* We have studied this extensively in the cases of the
prophecy and tongues. John Wesley defined the gift of
knowledge in this way: 'Perhaps an extraordinary ability to
understand and explain the Old Testament types and
prophecies.'[8] This is the most feasible interpretation. An
example of it would be James' interpretation and application
of the prophecy from the ninth chapter of Amos to the
admission of the Gentiles into the church at the Council of
Jerusalem (see Acts 15:12-17).

2. Paul was infallibly inspired in every word he chose. In
this letter he had no difficulty whatsoever in expressing in an
unambiguous way that something was going to continue until
Christ's return. Thus with regard to the Lord's Supper, he
wrote, 'For whenever you eat this bread and drink this cup,
you proclaim the Lord's death until he comes' (1 Cor. 11:26).
Therefore we can legitimately ask, 'Why did not Paul use the
same language in 1 Corinthians 13 if he wanted to express the
same concept? Is he not intending to express something of a
different nature in the later chapter?' When Paul refers to the
second coming he is more prone to speak of a person coming
rather that of an event.

3. Paul also has no difficulty in this letter in referring to the
end *(telos),* which clearly means the second coming of Christ.
Thus he says just two chapters later, 'Then the end will come,
when he hands over the kingdom to God the Father after he
has destroyed all dominion, authority and power' (1 Cor.
15:24). Why again did he deliberately avoid using this word in
1 Corinthians 15? Do we believe that every word of Scripture is
deliberately and purposefully chosen by supervision of the
Holy Spirit? Do we believe that every difference in shade of
meaning is important?

4. Paul was guided by God to use the word *'to teleion'* in
verse 10 for 'perfection'. It is a neuter word (a very strange
way of referring to Christ) and means 'the completed thing'. A

Greek lexicon will reveal that it is used eighteen times in the New Testament and never once refers to heaven. As John Macleod has written, 'Not once in the New Testament does *teleios* refer to the Parousia or the consummation of all things brought about by that event.'[9] It is often translated as 'mature' and this is the case in 1 Corinthians 2:6. The New English Bible rendering of the passage particularly brings out this nuance of the coming to maturity or completing of a process. It puts it like this: 'For our knowledge and our prophecy alike are partial, and the partial vanishes when wholeness comes.' Of course, no great objection can be brought against the rendering 'perfection' as long as this background is borne in mind.

5.   Therefore it is the full development and maturing of prophecy, other languages and knowledge that is in view. These gifts are the three gifts whereby God communicates supernatural, authoritative, infallible truth. At the time when 1 Corinthians was written he did this in a partial but not imperfect way through the gifts. What is the final completed form of God speaking supernaturally, authoritatively and infallibly? Is it not beyond any doubt the New Testament Scriptures? These are the prophecy to end all prophecies and are frequently termed such (Rom. 16:26; 2 Peter 1:19; Rev. 22:18). Prophecy was given by 'revelation' and it was by 'revelation' that Scripture was written (Rom. 16:25; Eph. 3:3,5). Above all the 'other language' or tongue involved uttering a 'mystery', and many scriptural passages emphasize that the writers of the New Testament had a commission to 'make plain to everyone the administration of this mystery' (Eph. 3:9. See Col. 1:24-27). Where else is the will of God to save multitudes from every 'nation, tribe, people and language' more fully set forth than in the completed New Testament? There, as it were, the 'mystery' is openly and completely displayed. Where else but in the complete New Testament is the key of knowledge, the mode of interpreting the Old Testament Scriptures so comprehensively set forth? Whole chapters, such as Romans 9, Hebrews 1 and whole books, such as Revelation, show us how to interpret passage after passage, whether they be veiled symbolism, messianic prediction or prophecies relating to the church. Moreover these are perfect guide-lines. All that we need is given.

6.   Paul was inspired by the Holy Spirit to use a very strong word for the cessation of these gifts. He spoke of them being destroyed *(katargeō)*. He used this word again in 1 Corinthians 15:24,26. The verb is used in verse 8 with reference to prophecy and knowledge and again in verse 10 with reference to all these gifts. Judisch, in his excellent linguistic study of this chapter, has said, after pointing out the strong meaning of the verb, that 'The cessation of the prophetic gifts was to be a complete obliteration beyond recall. Paul left no room for any thought of temporary lapse and revival. If the prophetic gifts ever ceased, they ceased for all time. But that they did cease at one point or another is clear from history. Therefore they have ceased for all time.'[10] Our historical section will show that at least for long periods, sometimes it would seem for centuries, the gifts have apparently disappeared.

Charismatics resort to two desperate expedients to counteract this argument. Some resort to the analogy of the early and latter rain and misapply the quotation from Joel, used in Acts 2, to argue that the gifts are due to appear before the second coming of Christ. We shall deal with this argument both in our historical sections and in the last chapter. One book is typical of many others when it states that the gifts faded during the same period that 'the church's spiritual vitality as a whole declined'.[11] Usually it is said that they disappeared because of the growing worldliness and disobedience of the church. Let us look at this more closely. Corinth was filled with people who were disregarding the Lord in preference for favourite preachers. There was a terrible case of incest, which the membership had treated light-heartedly. Some were going to law against fellow members. And there was actual drunkenness and greed at the Lord's Table, not to mention very dangerous views on the resurrection of Christ. Quite bluntly the apostle addressed them, 'Brothers, I could not address you as spiritual but as worldly – mere infants in Christ' (1 Cor. 3:1). The Christians, so far from being Spirit-filled and deserving the gifts in some way, were not even spiritual! The Corinthian situation, if the reasoning of many modern writers is correct, would have been a classic case for instant withdrawal of the gifts. Yet it did not happen then simply because the gifts were gifts. They were sovereignly bestowed for a particular purpose (see 1 Cor. 12:11; Heb. 2:3,4). The very existence of the letter to the Corinthians, even if there were nothing else in the New Testament, ought to be sufficient refutation of the twentieth-century myth that the more Spirit-filled we are, the more likely it is that the gifts will be granted. But every age loves its myths, and it is particularly difficult to scotch this one.

7.   If we stay for a moment with the word 'perfection', it can easily be seen that this is an appropriate, legitimate and indeed frequently used description of the Scriptures. Does not Peter call them the 'living and enduring word of God', which 'stands for ever', and is 'pure spiritual milk' and in comparison with which all else is fading, ephemeral and unsatisfying? (1 Peter 1:22-2:2.) Does not the apostle Paul declare, in his classic statement to young Timothy, that in the Word there is full and adequate provision to meet all eventualities? 'All Scripture is God-breathed and is useful for teaching, rebuking, correcting and training in righteousness, so that the man of God may be thoroughly equipped for every good work' (2 Tim. 3:16,17). If these are not seen as descriptions of completeness and perfection in the sphere of God-given revelation in Scripture, we are compelled to ask what stronger, clearer terms could be used?

8.   We are told with regard to verse 11 that the language can best be applied to our experience of heaven, as the apostle writes, 'When I became a man, I put childish ways behind me.' But is this so? Firstly, we point out that we are not to envisage a child talking nonsense (he 'talked', 'thought' and 'reasoned') but rather a child who sees accurately, but only glimpses part of a much greater whole. This is typical of the thinking of children. Thus to a child who is taking part in his first little school play and who comes home full of the part he is playing, his mother, trying in vain to elicit from him a description of the play as a whole, says, 'You only come home with half a tale.' She is being charitable. He only has 1/100th of the tale, if that! He sees his own little entry and one or two incidents relating to his own little part, but that is all. Adults take in the whole picture. A child grasps his bit. This is the analogy. The supernatural gifts present but a fragment of revelation, albeit a perfectly true fragment. The Scriptures tell the whole story. Every act, scene, line, entry, exit are all clearly shown.

Moreover the phrase is the language of active resolution –
something we do. This is not how the apostle describes entry
into heaven. Just two chapters later he depicts the great
transformation in his typical way. Listen to the type of
language that he uses: 'The body that is sown is perishable, it
is raised imperishable; it is sown in dishonour, it is raised in
glory; it is sown in weakness, it is raised in power; it is sown a
natural body, it is raised a spiritual body' (1 Cor. 15:42,43).
Every act is an act of God's power. It is not something we do.
The very thought of a Christian reaching heaven and deciding
not to speak in tongues any more is ridiculous. It is strange
that so few have seen this. No, the heavenly transformation is
brought about by the great actions of a great God, not by our
puny decisions. 'Listen, I tell you a mystery: We will not all
sleep, but we will all be changed – in a flash, in the twinkling of
an eye, at the last trumpet. For the trumpet will sound, the
dead will be raised imperishable, and we will be changed' (1
Cor. 15:51,52).

9.   Some find it inconceivable that the apostle Paul could
include himself in this description. One writes, 'This greatest
of all the apostles rebukes the Corinthians for being babies in
Christ (3:2). Could we believe that this man in Chapter 13:8ff
speaks of himself as childish in his understanding of spiritual
things in comparison with God's children of later times,
ourselves included?'[12] Now I have respect for the thought
behind this. Not only do I greatly reverence Paul, but I have a
typical Englishman's concept of heaven:

> They all shall be there,
> The great and the small,
> For I shall shake hands
> With the blessed St Paul.

But the writer quoted above not only claims too much for
Paul, but also makes claims that Paul would not want made
for himself. He seems to think of Paul as so endowed with
knowledge at the time of writing this passage as to be himself
capable of receiving no more, nor of accepting truth revealed
through other apostles. When he wrote 1 Corinthians did he
already know the truth which God showed in his second letter
to Corinth? Was all the truth of his later pastoral letters to

Timothy and Titus already bestowed upon him in one lump? Was he so far advanced as to learn nothing from the letters of Peter or the writings of John? It is a purely arbitrary concept that is introduced.

10. In verse 12 Paul uses the image of looking into a mirror. 'The apostle is comparing the state of the church before the New Testament Scriptures were added to the Old Testament Scriptures to a person looking into a mirror made of polished metal and which reflected only a blurred image.'[13] The person saw certain things in a real but fragmentary way. This was the position of the Christian when God revealed his truth 'in part' through prophecy, tongue-speaking and knowledge. What was needed was a clear image where every detail and facet, both large and small, would be revealed. This the mirror of the New Testament Scripture perfectly provided. Is it accidental that Paul uses the word *'espotron'* for mirror and that the only other time the word is used in the New Testament is in James 1:22-25? James says that the mirror is Scripture: 'the perfect law' which gives a clear reflection and provides a man with all the evidence he needs on which to take action. The word used for perfect is *'teleios'*.

11. Because I believe that Judisch has commented so perceptively on this whole passage, I quote him somewhat fully on this section: 'Those who want "the complete thing" of verse 10 to be the state of eternal glory argue that the first clause of verse 12 is referring to seeing Christ in a dim way throughout this life and that the second clause speaks of seeing Christ face to face in a literal sense in heaven. Such an interpretation is dubious, however, for two reasons. First, it takes the "dimly" *(ainigmati)* of the first clause figuratively, but the "face to face" *(prosópon pros prosópon)* of the second clause literally; a more consistent approach to the intended contrast seems preferable. If we thought that the object of the verb *blepomen* ("see") were Christ, we should note that the concept of seeing Christ face to face occurs elsewhere in the Corinthian letters in a figurative sense (2 Cor. 3:18; 4:6). Second, however, supplying the object "Christ" or "God" or the like is a rather arbitrary procedure. Paul is talking about seeing someone in a mirror, whether dimly or face to face. And the face that one sees in a mirror is not the Lord's, but one's own (cf. James 1:23,24).'[14] This is confirmed by the fact that a

primary function of the completed, perfect revelation in the
Scripture is to show us ourselves as we really are. It is given to
explore the inner recesses of the heart: 'The word of God is
living and active. Sharper than any double-edged sword, it
penetrates even to dividing soul and spirit, joints and marrow;
it judges the thoughts and attitudes of the heart. Nothing in all
creation is hidden from God's sight. Everything is uncovered
and laid bare before the eyes of him to whom we must give
account' (Heb. 4:12,13). It is by the Word that we know
ourselves fully as we are already fully known to God.

12.   Above all we are incessantly told that the phrase 'then
we shall see face to face' must mean heaven. But, if Scripture is
allowed to interpret Scripture, this can soon be seen to be a
false inference. This is a very important principle, since there
are many phrases, such as 'first-born' as applied to Jesus
Christ, or 'last days' as applied to the times of the Messiah,
which can at first sight be misleading. Pascal very aptly cites
Augustine on this point: 'Anyone who wishes to give the
meaning of Scripture without taking it from Scripture is the
enemy of Scripture.'[15] Particularly important for the interpretation of this phrase in our chapter is the Old Testament
background. Older versions of the Bible, such as the Authorized
Version and the nineteenth-century Revised Version, give as a
marginal reference Numbers 12:6-8. These references were
given long before the emergence of Pentecostalism and
therefore were not adopted in reaction to it. Moffat in his
commentary published in 1938 supports their directions as he
writes, 'The sole point of the apostle's illustration is to contrast
indirect and direct knowledge. He is thinking of the well-
known contrast in his Greek Bible between ordinary prophets,
who knew the Lord merely through visions and dreams
(ainigmata), and Moses who was promised direct intercourse
and a vision of the Lord "face to face, not in any *ainigma*"'.[16]

Moffat then cites Numbers 12:6-3 which we will now give in
full:

> 'When a prophet of the Lord is among you,
>   I reveal myself to him in visions,
>   I speak to him in dreams.
> But this is not true of my servant Moses;
>   he is faithful in all my house.
> With him I speak face to face, clearly and not in riddles;
>   he sees the form of the Lord.'

The background is that there had been an outburst of prophesying (Num. 11:24-27). But it had been partial, fleeting and somewhat obscure. Moses, as the writer of the first five books of the Bible, at that time received revelation that was fuller and clearer, as opposed to the other which was 'in part'. The important things to note are that a 'face to face' experience was very much one on this earth and that the contrast was between two types of revelation, both infallible but one far more complete and clear than the other.

Two other incidents in the account of Moses' career support this interpretation. We are told that when Moses went into the 'tent', the people standing outside saw the pillar of cloud come down and then 'the Lord would speak to Moses face to face, as a man speaks with his friend' (Exod. 33:9-11). The very same chapter makes it clear that Moses could not actually look upon God (vv.18-23), and Numbers 7:89 suppports the meaning that the 'face to face' encounter meant clear revelation: 'When Moses entered the Tent of Meeting to speak with the Lord, he heard the voice speaking to him from between the two cherubim above the atonement cover on the ark of the Testimony. And he spoke with him' (Num. 7:89). At the close of Moses' life the phrase 'face to face' is again used to describe, not the experience of heavenly bliss into which he had undoubtedly entered, but rather his position as the great prophet who had clear revelations from God (Deut. 34:10). Indeed this same book depicts the great Prophet who shall arise, even the Lord Jesus Christ, as the true successor to Moses because, says God, 'I will put my words in his mouth, and he will tell them everything I command him' (Deut. 18:18). It was a characteristic of the Lord Jesus Christ that he told his disciples everything (John 15:15; 14:2).

Of course, we have to admit that in these Old Testament passages it is the contrast between partial and fuller revelation that is in mind and not, as in the case of 1 Corinthians 13, the contrast between partial and final revelation. Nevertheless the contrast is there, especially when we underline the fact that at this point Moses himself was the only one who had written down the Word of God. Whether he utilized earlier records or not is immaterial. Through his ministry came the complete, written revelation in his day, and the phrase that characteristically depicts him in that role is that he saw the

Lord 'face to face'. His pivotal position at this juncture of revelation history is clearly conveyed by the writer of the letterto the Hebrews, when he wrote, 'Moses was faithful as a . servant in all God's house, testifying to what would be said in the future. But Christ is faithful as a son over God's house' (Heb. 3:5,6).

13.   Obviously no Christian comes to Scripture and immediately understands everything. Far from it. Yet some would say to those who believe that the perfection is Scripture, 'Oh, so you understand Ezekiel's prophecy fully? So you have a perfect grasp of the New Testament and know completely the mind of Christ?' Anyone with a modicum of humility will have great difficulty in replying to this. In the same way anyone who believes that Galatians 2:20 is not only Paul's experience but his own will find it hard when someone challenges with, 'Oh, so you believe that you are dead and that Christ lives in you, do you? Why then did you utter the egotistic word, throw that proud glance, take that hasty step?' Obviously there is full and adequate provision in Christ's atonement, and there is a real sense in which the Christian is already dead to sin despite weaknesses and falls. Similarly, there is a full and adequate revelation in God's Word and there is a sense in which the Christian is now in a position to see fully and completely despite ignorance and misunderstandings. At least Paul did not deem it futile or unscriptural to pray for the Laodiceans as follows: 'My purpose is that they may be encouraged in heart and united in love, so that they may have the full riches of complete understanding, in order that they may know the mystery of God, namely, Christ, in whom are hidden all the treasures of wisdom and knowledge' (Col. 2:2,3). Certainly it is God's stated aim that the giving of Scripture is that the man of God should be 'thoroughly equipped for every good work' (2 Tim. 3:17). One writer also makes this point: 'We may observe that the verb "to know" is compound; it does not refer to absolute knowledge such as that which we, hopefully, may possess in heaven. It refers rather to practical awareness of a situation.'[17]

14.   The concluding verse of the chapter thoroughly supports this interpretation. It reads, 'And now these three remain: faith, hope and love. But the greatest of these is love.' Firstly, we note that in contrast to things that fail, (and the

only things in the chapter which are going to fail are the extraordinary gifts) three things are going to remain. But verse 13 must mean 'remain in this life', since in heaven faith becomes sight and, as Paul says elsewhere, 'Hope that is seen is no hope at all. Who hopes for what he already has?' (Rom. 8:24; 2 Cor. 5:7.) Adequate reasons have been given by other writers for taking the 'now' in this verse in this temporal sense. Strangely enough, even a charismatic writer confirms this interpretation in his commentary, saying, 'Love is the greatest of the three, for love is not only for the "now" but for all eternity – even after faith has become sight and hope become fulfilment.'[18] Therefore the implication is that the gifts are going to cease before the end, while faith, hope and love last.

But, secondly, what is rarely underlined is that the growth of faith, hope and love in the believer is the great theme of the perfect revelation and that, if one looks through the Scriptures as a whole, this is seen as the central and essential message. As Paul tells the Galatians, 'But by faith we eagerly await through the Spirit the righteousness for which we hope. For in Christ Jesus neither circumcision nor uncircumcision has any value. The only thing that counts is faith expressing itself through love' (Gal. 5:5,6; See also Rom. 5:2-5; Col. 1:4-6; 1 Thess. 1:3; 5:8). Both the writer to the Hebrews and Peter link the heavenly trio. 'Through him (Christ) you believed in God, who raised him from the dead and glorified him, and so your faith and hope are in God. Now that you have purified yourselves by obeying the truth so that you have sincere love for your brothers, love one another deeply from the heart' (1 Peter 1:21,22; cf. Heb. 6:10-12).

15.   As previous chapters have shown, charismatics who say that the gifts remain do not give a proper scriptural meaning to these gifts. They disagree vastly among themselves even about these false meanings. Is prophecy expository preaching? Is it fallible? Is it dependent on the spiritual condition of the prophet? Is it just a prophetic bit in the middle of a sermon? Is there a regular predictive element? Should the prophet feel physical sensations? Vastly different answers are given to all these questions simply because they have refused to let Scripture determine what exactly the gift is and whether it continues today.

Similarly, with regard to the treatment of 'knowledge' in

this passage, one of the leaders lands himself in absurdity. He even fails to recognize the elementary point that in the passage 'knowledge' refers not to knowledge in general but to the supernatural and extraordinary gift. He writes, 'If we desire to dispose of prophecy – then logically we must also dispose of "knowledge", which is likewise going to pass away (v.8).'[19] Because he has failed to recognize that the passage deals specifically with revelatory gifts, (healing, miracles and administration would not have provided a parallel with the 'completed thing' at all) he infers that there will be a time when knowledge in general is abolished. But the Christian is not moving towards mist and mysticism! 'The path of the righteous is like the first gleam of dawn, shining ever brighter till the full light of day' (Prov. 4:18).

It would be tempting to say that the charismatic books are full of confused exegesis on this passage. But that would hardly be true. The normal stance is to spend just a paragraph or two saying that the other position is ridiculous and then to assert that perfection 'obviously means heaven', and to move on without engaging in any close study of the wording of the whole passage or even asking the basic question as to why, with over twenty gifts to choose from, Paul specifically put the three gifts which are revelatory in contrast to the perfection which God provides. The whole charismatic movement, as we shall see in the closing chapter, is largely a move away from any close and detailed study of the Word of God, to which the truly born-again Christian seeks to bow and submit at every point. Thus the word 'mystery', so crucial in the biblical definition of tongues, is bypassed, the true nature of prophecy as set out in Scripture is ignored and careful interpretation of the whole of 1 Corinthians 13:8-13 is evaded.

16.   If it is true that it is only during periods when Scripture is being written that revelation is given, then it is fitting that at the close of the period of Old Testament revelation before a four-hundred-year period of silence the character of the next great prophetic figure should be foretold (Mal. 4:5,6; cf. Luke 1:17; Matt. 11:13,14; 17:11-13). So at the close of the New Testament prophetic era the culmination of all prophecy was the book of Revelation, which closed with a curse on all who added to or took away from its message (Rev. 22:18,19). No further revelation was to be given.

What an old divine wrote would seem to be a satisfactory explanation of this fact: 'That rich supply of supernatural or miraculous gifts with which the apostolic churches were adorned, was a standing pledge and sign that the inward miracle of inspiration continued . . . But during the whole time of their continuance, these miraculous gifts, and especially the gift of tongues – that is, the gift of speaking in languages which had never been learned – were a conclusive proof and illustration of the miracle of inspiration.'[20] This simply means that when Scripture is not being given there will be no such gifts. The presence of such gifts would indicate that God's Word was still incomplete. A contemporary writer, drawing on B.B. Warfield for support, has also tied all this up with the question of redemption itself and cogently shown that 'Intimately entwined with these great redemptive acts is God's special revelation.' He has concluded that 'Once it is seen that revelation is part of the redemptive work of God it becomes clear why there can be no further revelation today.'[21] Further revelation implies an incomplete redemption.

More supporting evidence

Other New Testament passages support the view that the perfection is Scripture. We will examine five of them.

1.   We note first of all a passage in 2 Peter, taking care to observe that this letter is obviously late in date, for by the time of its composition most of Paul's correspondence is complete, available and fairly widely known (2 Peter 3:15,16), and Peter himself is near the end of his earthly course and expecting the death which his Lord had foretold (2 Peter 1:13,14). He recalls an earlier precious experience shared with his Lord on the mount of transfiguration when he actually heard a voice from heaven. Surely, most people would argue, such an experience ought to be sufficient to bring absolute certainty to anyone. Yet Peter argues quite differently, going on to declare in some amazing words that Scripture, 'the word of the prophets made more certain', and the light it brings as it conveys Christ to the believer's heart, is even more certain than a voice from heaven. 'We ourselves heard this voice that came from heaven when we were with him on the sacred mountain. And we have the

word of the prophets made more certain, and you will do well to pay attention to it, as to a light shining in a dark place, until the day dawns and the morning star rises in your hearts. Above all, you must understand that no prophecy of Scripture came about by the prophet's own interpretation. For prophecy never had its origin in the will of man, but men spoke from God as they were carried along by the Holy Spirit' (2 Peter 1:18-21). What a contrast to some modern views of prophecy this is! Matthew Henry linked this passage with the ceasing of tongues, when he wrote on 13 July 1712: 'The gift of tongues was one new product of the spirit of prophecy, and given for a particular reason, that, the Jewish pale being taken down, all nations might be brought into the church. These and other gifts of prophecy, being a sign, have long since ceased and been laid aside, and we have no encouragement to expect the revival of them; but, on the contrary, are directed to call the Scriptures the more sure word of prophecy, more sure than voices from heaven; and to them we are directed to take heed, to search them, and to hold them fast' (2 Peter 1:19).[22]

2.   Paul's letter to the Ephesians gives further support to this view. In the opening six verses of chapter 3 we find that apostles and prophets are divinely inspired. But the closing verses of the previous chapter tell us that their work is foundation work. The church is 'built on the foundation of the apostles and prophets, with Christ Jesus himself as the chief corner-stone' (Eph. 2:20). The work of teaching the basic truths of the gospel in an infallible way needs no more to be done again, and can no more be done again, than the fundamental atoning work of Christ on Calvary. Both need to be declared afresh and with the Spirit's power to each succeeding generation.

3.   Because the vocabulary of the pastoral letters is somewhat different from Paul's other correspondence, some critics have assumed on these and other grounds that Paul was not in fact the author. However, the change in vocabulary, for the most part, reflects the change in the life of the church by this time and in particular the near completion of the Scriptures. It is generally accepted that these letters come from the close of Paul's ministry, just prior to his martydom (see 2 Tim. 4:6). A whole group of words and phrases not generally used in his other writings indicate that Scripture, or

a body of truth, was now generally available to his readers. Thus he refers to 'sound doctrine', 'the truth', 'the deep truths of the faith', 'the truths of the faith and of the good teaching', 'sound instruction', 'the pattern of sound teaching', 'the good deposit', 'the word of truth', 'the trustworthy message' (1 Tim. 1:10; 2:4; 3:9; 4:6; 6:3; 2 Tim. 1:13,14; 2:15; Titus 1:9). Of especial importance is his charge to Timothy in 1 Timothy 4:13 where he says, 'Until I come, devote yourself to the public reading of Scripture, to preaching and to teaching.' 1 Timothy 5:18 shows that, as well as the Old Testament, Luke's Gospel was regarded as Scripture, as it is only there that we find our Lord's saying: 'The worker deserves his wages' (cf. Luke 10:7). We have examined the strong statement on the inspiration of Scripture at the close of 2 Timothy 3 and it is also relevant to note that when in 1 Timothy and Titus detailed qualifications for eldership are given these do not include the ability to prophesy or speak in tongues. This is a very significant omission and, if the Pentecostal emphasis be true, an amazing one.

4.   A passage which we will deal with in more detail as we look at the gift of apostleship is Hebrews 2:3,4. It reads: 'This salvation, which was first announced to us by the Lord, was confirmed to us by those who heard him. God also testified to it by signs, wonders and various miracles, and gifts of the Holy Spirit distributed according to his will.' Says Judisch, 'In fact the use of the aorist indicative form in verse 3 *(ebebaiōthē)* implies past and completed action. In other words, the apostles had already finished their eyewitness confirmation of the truthfulness of the Lord's claim to be the divine Saviour of the world (even though they had not yet completed their proclamation of it) when this letter was written . . . Likewise complete by that time were signs and wonders, miracles, and apportionings of the Holy Spirit with which God corroborated the apostolic testimony. For the present participle connecting verses 3 and 5 *(synepimartyrountos)* indicates that the action of the dependent clause is contemporaneous with that of the main verb; that is, the reference is to the events in the past.'[23]

5.   I forbear quoting again the verses at the close of the book of Revelation which seem clearly to affirm that prophecy is complete (Rev. 22:18,19) and merely append the comment of Matthew Henry, who wrote, 'This sanction is like a flaming

sword to guard the canon of the Scripture from profane hands.'[24]

While it must be admitted that few commentators of the past expounded 'perfection' in 1 Corinthians 13 to mean Scripture, there were some. For the most part, writers largely ignored giving detailed consideration to the passage in relation to the gifts, for to most of them it was hardly a live issue. Yet from examination of such passages as we have just considered most of them did indeed firmly believe that Scripture taught the cessation of the gifts. A justly renowned commentary compiled in the nineteenth century is that of Jamieson, Fausset and Brown. Their comment is as follows: 'A primary fulfilment of Paul's statement took place when the Church attained its maturity; then "tongues" entirely "ceased", and "prophesying" and "knowledge" so far as they were supernatural gifts of the Spirit, were superseded as no longer required when the ordinary preaching of the word, and the Scriptures of the New Testament collected together, had become established institutions.'[25] In our own century A.W. Pink wrote of the gifts that 'They were designed chiefly for the authenticating of Christianity and to confirm it in heathen countries. Their purpose, then, was only a temporary one, and as soon as the canon of Scripture was closed they were withdrawn. As 1 Corinthians 13 plainly intimates, "Whether there be prophecies (inspired messages from God) they shall fail (to be given any more); whether there be tongues, they shall cease; whether there be (supernatural) knowledge, it shall vanish away" (v.8).' [26] More recently Gromacki, Unger, Chantry and Judisch have all expounded the passage in this way. There are very positive conclusions to be drawn from all this which we shall consider in the final chapter.

it is, then it is remarkably strange that the church at Ephesus could be warmly commended by God in these terms: 'I know your deeds, your hard work and your perseverance. I know that you cannot tolerate wicked men, that you have tested those who claim to be apostles but are not, and have found them false' (Rev. 2:2). This New Testament community would seem to have had clear-cut guide-lines for testing claimants to apostleship and to have acted accordingly. It is inconceivable that God was commending inspired and lucky guesswork. Moreover the apostle Paul refers to 'false apostles . . . masquerading as apostles of Christ', and obviously expects his readers to be able to detect such men and reject them (2 Cor. 11:13).

It is sometimes argued today that the very fact that false apostles are to be detected and exposed means that true apostles must continue to exist. Does then the fact that antichrists have come mean that the true Christ is still walking this earth as in days of old? (1 John 2:18.) The argument has only to be stated in this way to be seen in all its absurdity. The Lord Jesus Christ gave clear warnings that both 'false Christs and false prophets' would proliferate and would work 'great signs and miracles' of tremendous subtlety (Matt. 24:24). The presence of a false Christ does not mean that the true Christ is other than in heaven, where he will remain until he embarks on that triumphant journey to complete his church, to judge the damned and to ring down the curtain on world history. There can be false apostles and false prophets on earth when all the true representatives of these lines have long been resting in their heavenly home.

If in both 1 Corinthians and Ephesians the apostles top the list of the gifts and are indisputably God's 'first' ('In the church God has appointed first of all apostles,' 1 Cor. 12:28), and if indeed the church itself is 'built on the foundation of the apostles and prophets, with Christ Jesus himself as the chief corner-stone' (Eph. 2:20), then we are entitled to expect clear guide-lines as to how to recognize an apostle. Indeed God himself has given us such directives. We can draw most of them from a basic passage in Acts 1:15-26 and Acts 2 where we have an account of the appointment of the successor to Judas and a description of the first activities of the apostles.

The authority

Firstly we note the great *authority* of the apostles. We see this in Peter's whole approach. 'In those days Peter stood up among the believers . . . and said . . . '(Acts 1:15,16). He was not dictatorial, lordly or overbearing, but the authority was instantly recognized. This was also evident as he stood up on the Day of Pentecost. It comes out unmistakably in phrases used in the apostolic letters. We take an example from Paul's first letter to Corinth: 'If anybody thinks he is a prophet or spiritually gifted, let him acknowledge that what I am writing to you is the Lord's command. If he ignores this, he himself will be ignored' (1 Cor.14:37,38). It is an incessant note. 'If anyone does not obey our instruction in this letter, take special note of him,' aptly shows the undoubted ring of apostolic authority (2 Thess. 3:14).

Yet the authority was used in a gracious way. The apostles did not throw their weight around, bark out stentorian commands or draw attention to themselves. In fact, at times Paul seemed almost reluctant or embarrassed to exercise his powers. In his second letter to the Corinthians this emerges in his final chapter as he says, 'This is why I write these things when I am absent, that when I come I may not have to be harsh in my use of authority – the authority the Lord gave me for building you up, not for tearing you down' (2 Cor. 13:10). Certainly in many matters the apostles did not coerce people into instant obedience. 'Now about our brother Apollos: I strongly urged him to go to you with the brothers. He was quite unwilling to go now, but he will go when he has the opportunity,' is an interesting example of this (1 Cor. 16:12). Apollos was not expected to be an instant 'yes man' whenever Paul spoke. But to suggest, as one speaker does in a sermon on tape, that there is 'no inherent authority in the office' seems incredible. (The same speaker manages to advocate a doctrine of apostles for today without grappling with any of the major biblical marks of apostleship.)[10] Other Christians readily recognized the uniqueness of apostolic authority. Clement, writing later to the Corinthians, simply says, 'The Apostles are from Christ.'[11] Ignatius, an early Christian leader, writing between AD 100 and 115, makes a clear distinction as he declares, 'I do not lay injunctions on you as did Peter and

Paul; they were apostles . . .'[12] These were men whose
ministry God had sealed in a special, unique and powerful
manner.

Infallibility in teaching

*Secondly,*we observe that the apostles were *infallible spokesmen
and interpreters of God's Word*. This is displayed particularly in
Peter's use of Psalm 69:25 and 109:8 in Acts 1:20. These
passages from the Psalms are declared to be specific references
to Judas. They have predictive quality, for, as Peter puts it in
verse 16, 'Brothers, the Scripture had to be fulfilled which the
Holy Spirit spoke long ago . . . concerning Judas, who served
as a guide for those who arrested Jesus.' In all this Peter is
dogmatic and unhesitating. As men the apostles could fall. As
men they could sometimes clash with each other. Yet when
they stood up as spokesmen for the Lord they were infallible.

God through their lips has consequently been pleased to
give to his church certain infallible sermons and specimens of
scriptural interpretation. Thus we learn from the sermons,
speeches of personal defence and prayers of Peter and John
contained within Acts 2-4 how Psalms 16; 110; 118 and 2 were
predictions of various aspects of the death, resurrection and
ascension of the Lord Jesus Christ. As in the instances of the
Psalms shown to be applicable to the actions of Judas, without
the unerring guidance of the apostles, these truths would not
have been apparent either to their contemporaries or to
ourselves.

A vivid example of this message of 'knowledge', this
inspired God-given ability to apply Old Testament Scripture
in a binding and conclusive way, is, of course, the summing-up
speech of James at the Jerusalem Council. After the accounts
of Paul and Barnabas about God working so powerfully
among the Gentiles through them, and after Peter's reminder
that God chose him to make known the good news of salvation
to Gentiles, James stood up and gave the clinching word. He
simply quoted Amos 9:11,12 as a prediction of the way in
which God intended to join Jew and Gentile together in one
church. Once again I must emphasize that this is not a
scripture which I would readily have used. Indeed some still

find it difficult to accept the finality of James's interpretation. Listen to this Brethren writer commenting on the scene: 'It would also appear from Acts 15 that James had not travelled much farther (than the Old Testament writers to whom the mystery of Christ was not revealed) and thus quotes Amos as covering prophetically the opening of the door of faith to the Gentiles.'[13] Other writers of similar dispensationalist persuasion likewise use the ninth chapter of Amos with total disregard to the authoritative New Testament interpretation. For example, it is evident that two modern writers wish to reapply the passage to the 'Jewish situation'. With them 'Radio Jerusalem' is more important than the apostolic decision at the Council of Jerusalem.[14] Such an approach stems from disobedience to the Word of God and in particular from failure to submit to apostolic rules of biblical interpretation.

If Augustine's assertion that 'In the Old Testament the New Testament was concealed' and that 'In the New Testament the Old Testament was revealed' is true, as we believe it is, then it was vital that, before the New Testament was completed, we should have proper guide-lines for interpretation. If we accept the position that 'the only successors to the apostles are the epistles' then it is essential to assert that Christians today are bound by their interpretations. Many today reject in a cavalier manner the apostolic guide-lines for interpretation. This is why we have so many vagaries and weird views in the realm of biblical prophecy with reference to the second coming. It is also why, with reference to 1 Corinthians 14, many charismatics and Pentecostalists can blithely assert many false things about 'speaking in other languages'. They can only do this by ignoring the apostolic interpretation of certain key words in the chapter in question, words such as 'mysteries', 'spirit' and 'revelation', or by using them in a sense other than that of the New Testament.

Eyewitnesses of resurrection

Thirdly, we note that a genuine apostle must be an *eyewitness of the resurrection*. This emerges clearly as Peter says, 'Therefore it is necessary to choose one of the men who have been with us the whole time the Lord Jesus went in and out among us, beginning from John's baptism to the time when Jesus was taken up from us. For one of these must become a witness with us of his resurrection' (Acts 1:22). This is, of course, a point reinforced by other scriptures. It is a vital and essential qualification.

To the Corinthians Paul says, 'Am I not an apostle? Have I not seen Jesus our Lord? Are you not the result of my work in the Lord?' (1 Cor. 9:1.) And later on in the same letter, after listing the various resurrection appearances of Christ to individuals and to larger and smaller groups, he affirms, 'Then he appeared to James, then to all the apostles, and last of all he appeared to me also, as to one abnormally born' (1 Cor. 15:7,8). It is indeed clear that the apostle Paul saw the risen Christ. He gives many testimonies to this effect (e.g. Acts 22:6-10, 17-21).

The passage in 1 Corinthians 15 is especially important. Firstly, these verses show that Paul, 'abnormally born' in the sense that Christ appeared to him and called him outside the normal forty days of his resurrection ministry, was the last apostle to be called. It would seem that there is a ring of finality in that 'last of all'. Since Paul no further apostles have been called and commissioned. Secondly, the reference to 'the apostles' is interesting, especially as earlier in this chapter he had referred to the more closely defined group as 'the Twelve' (1 Cor. 15:5). Although apostleship was wider than the original group it was always connected with seeing the risen Christ. It may be that one extra qualification of 'the Twelve' or the 'twelve apostles of the lamb' (Acts 6:2; Rev. 21:14) was that, in addition to the fact that they had seen the risen Christ, they had an intimate and thorough knowledge of the whole of his earthly ministry. It would also seem from Galatians that they had some role in authenticating the ministry of Paul (Gal. 2:9).

Nor must we forget that, not only were the apostles men who had seen the risen Christ, but they were also great heralds of the resurrection. Peter's Pentecost sermon in its latter part becomes a fervent resurrection sermon. Soon after this we learn that the priests and Sadducees 'were greatly distressed because the apostles were teaching the people and proclaiming in Jesus the resurrection of the dead' (Acts 4:2; cf. 3:15;

4:10,11; 5:31). On one occasion Spurgeon felt obliged to admit
to his hearers that in preaching regularly on predestination he
had unwittingly neglected the predominant emphasis of the
apostolic preaching in Acts which was the resurrection.[15]

A direct call of God

In the *fourth* place we find from Acts 1 that an apostle was a
man who was *directly called and commissioned by God*. This
emerges clearly in four ways.

Firstly Peter did not act on his own initiative. He did not
decide that it was time to replace Judas. He acted only because
God in his Word had predicted this. Therefore Peter cited
Psalm 109:8 as determining their course of action: 'May
another take his place of leadership' (v.20).

Secondly, the very language of the prayer offered underlines
the sovereign choice of God: 'Lord, you know everyone's heart.
Show us which of these two you have chosen . . .,' pleads
Peter (v.24).

Our third illustration is taken from the last verse of the
chapter, which simply reads, 'Then they drew lots, and the lot
fell to Matthias; so he was added to the eleven apostles' (v.26).
With us today a lottery emphasizes chance. But this was not a
game of apostolic bingo. In the Old Testament the lot drew
attention not to chance, but to the sovereign choice of God.
'The lot is cast into the lap, but its every decision is from the
Lord' (Prov. 16:33).

Fourthly we note an omission. There was no laying on of
hands by men. This is very significant. We are not told in
Scripture how to appoint apostles, whereas the instructions as
to how to recognize and appoint an elder or deacon stand in
clear contrast. 'Where no command, no rule, no authority, no
directions are given for the calling of any officer, there that
office must cease, as doth that of the apostles, who could not be
called but by Jesus Christ,' concludes John Owen.[16] The
apostle Paul summed it up succinctly, piling phrase on phrase
so that the issue would be put beyond any doubt, as he thus
addresses the Galatians, 'Paul, an apostle – sent not from men
nor by man, but by Jesus Christ and God the Father, who
raised him from the dead' (Gal. 1:1).

Signs and wonders

For our *fifth* and final point we again have to demolish a widely believed myth. How often people speak carelessly of the church in Acts as a wonder-working church! Yet it would be more accurate to speak of a church with *wonder-working apostles*. It is the apostles who are prominent in the initial outburst of speaking in other languages. It is their spokesman who explains this to the crowd and preaches a mighty gospel sermon. At the close of the Pentecost account, we are told that 'Everyone was filled with awe, and many wonders and miraculous signs were done by the apostles' (Acts 2:43).

Other scriptures confirm this: 'The apostles performed many miraculous signs and wonders among the people' (Acts 5:12). 'The whole assembly became silent as they listened to Barnabas and Paul telling about the miraculous signs and wonders God had done among the Gentiles through them' (Acts 15:12). 'Therefore I glory in Christ Jesus in my service to God. I will not venture to speak of anything except what Christ has accomplished through me in leading the Gentiles to obey God by what I have said and done – by the power of signs and miracles, through the power of the Spirit' (Rom. 15:17-19). 'The things that mark an apostle – signs, wonders and miracles – were done among you with great perseverance' (2 Cor. 12:12). 'How shall we escape if we ignore such a great salvation? This salvation, which was first announced by the Lord, was confirmed to us by those who heard him. God also testified to it by signs, wonders and various miracles, and gifts of the Holy Spirit distributed according to his will' (Heb. 2:3,4). There are three aspects to these signs. There were firstly healings, secondly miracles and thirdly the ability to confer gifts on others.

Healings
There were remarkable healings. At the command of Peter the cripple at the gate called Beautiful did not merely stagger to his feet. He was 'walking and jumping, and praising God' (Acts 3:8). Even Peter's shadow or handkerchiefs and aprons that had touched Paul had healing powers (Acts 5:15,16; 19:11,12). The latter passage specifically tells us that 'extraordinary' miracles were performed and the former

passage, together with the last chapter of Acts, tells us that 'all' the people on a given occasion or in a specific locality were cured. There were no stewards selecting the people with backache or migraine and refusing the chronically sick and the folk with withered limbs. There were no failures or relapses. There was no need of apostolic rest homes or out-patients' departments. When crutches were thrown away, they were discarded for good.

Even the dead were raised back to life (Acts 9:32-43; 20:7-12). It is vital to note in the earlier of these instances, the one involving the apostle Peter, that when the Christians at Joppa sent for him to perform the miracle, he did not roundly rebuke them for their own lack of faith or failure to utilize some God-given gift. He assumed that it was something only a genuine apostle could do. It is also intriguing to note that after Paul restored to life the man who fell through the window he did not then major on this but rather gave them an even longer discourse from the Word of God. One verse in Acts sums it up perfectly and ties in with the teaching of Hebrews 2:3,4 which we quoted earlier: 'So Paul and Barnabas spent considerable time there, speaking boldly for the Lord, who confirmed the message of his grace by enabling them to do miraculous signs and wonders' (Acts 14:3).

No one would have witnessed in their presence the pathetic spectacle described by an observer at one meeting where 'it was claimed that God makes available for Christians health for their bodies just as certainly as he makes available for them the forgiveness of their sins, and that if a Christian is not healed of some illness or infirmity, it is solely due to a deficiency of faith'. At this point the observer counted the high proportion of people on the platform wearing spectacles and then settled down to hear how healing could come via the Lord's Supper, a handkerchief or even via the telephone. He continues, 'All these claims relative to healing reached an amusing pathos when in the middle of the Albert Hall rally the chairman announced that a person in the congregation who had been taken ill was in the St John's ambulance room, and if there was a doctor in the house would he please go there quickly.'[17]

Miracles

As we consider this whole question of the miraculous, we must realize that there were in fact other aspects than that of healing. Therefore we turn secondly to 'miracles' in general. At times the apostles were recipients of visions which were definitely of a predictive nature. (Acts 10:19,20; 16:8-10; 22:17-21; 27:23-26.) By angelic intervention Peter was delivered from prison (Acts 12). On at least two occasions apostles were instrumental in announcing miracles of judgement. Thus Peter solemnly pronounced the death sentence on Ananias and Sapphira and Paul brought in the name of God a temporary blindness on Elymas, an opponent of the gospel (Acts 5:1-11; 13:8-11). It will be noted that in 1 Corinthians 12 there are both gifts of healing and 'miraculous powers'.

Power to confer gifts on others

The third aspect of this sign-ministry is that the apostles had the unique power of bestowing gifts on others. This is clearly taught in some passages and implied in others. Although we do not know what spiritual gift or gifts were bestowed upon the Samaritans by the ministry of Peter, yet we do read that 'Simon saw the Spirit was given at the laying on of the apostles' hands . . .' (Acts 8:18). Similarly we read later of Paul's confrontation with the twelve men at Ephesus: 'When Paul placed his hands on them, the Holy Spirit came on them, and they spoke in other languages and prophesied' (Acts 19:6).

Likewise other passages of Scripture imply this gift. 'This salvation, which was first announced by the Lord, was confirmed to us by those who heard him. God also testified to it by signs, wonders and various miracles, *and gifts of the Holy Spirit* distributed according to his will' (Heb. 2:3,4). The bestowal of gifts of the Holy Spirit was one of the signs accompanying and sealing the ministry of 'those who heard him', that is the apostles. Therefore it is interesting to note that the only two wonder-workers mentioned in Acts apart from the apostles were Stephen and Philip, both of whom had received apostolic laying on of hands (Acts 6:8; 8:4-8; 6:5,6). It is even more interesting to record that, although Philip could himself work many 'miraculous signs', he could not by laying on of hands convey gifts as the apostles themselves could.

Moreover there are only two occasions when the gift of other languages came directly from God, and they are singled out and linked together by Scripture itself. The first occasion was obviously that of Pentecost and the other was the incident in the household of Cornelius. The words of Peter explaining the latter incident are highly signifcant. He says, 'As I began to speak, the Holy Spirit came on them as he had come on us at the beginning' (Acts 11:15). Does it not seem strange that he should describe it in this way? After all, it happened some seven years after Pentecost. Why did he not say that the Holy Spirit came as he always came? Surely because normally the gift of other languages was bestowed through apostolic ministry, as we read in the episode at Ephesus. Therefore these other two incidents were exceptional. How then did so many Corinthians speak in other languages? The answer is in a letter to Corinth, namely, 2 Corinthians 12:12, where Paul writes, 'The things that mark an apostle – signs, wonders and miracles – were done among you with great perseverance.' Since we know that Paul had an eighteen-month ministry among them, it is natural to assume that he was instrumental in bringing gifts (Acts 18:1-11). If everyone could confer these gifts or work these miracles, they would no longer be signs of apostleship. It is as simple as that.

Apostles had supreme authority. Men no longer have this role. They were infallible spokesmen and interpreters of God's Word. There is a total absence of such men in today's church. Their great privilege of being eyewitnesses of the resurrection is one that is not bestowed on Christians any more. They were directly called by God, who no longer acts in this way. They performed extraordinary signs, wonders and miracles as a badge of their office, but men in the contemporary church are no longer recipients of this power. Through God's working they were able to convey gifts to others by the laying on of hands. Twentieth-century men are not able to do this. Moreover, since in all but two clearly defined instances speaking in other languages was a gift conveyed to people by the laying on of the apostolic hands, this would confirm our earlier conclusion that the gift of tongues is no longer bestowed today.

Watering down the language

Of course, there are many attacks on this position today. One charismatic, following Vincent Taylor, finds four types of apostle. There were firstly the Jerusalem ones, embracing the original twelve and James the brother of Christ. Secondly, there were those from Antioch, whose brief was to evangelize the Gentiles. These included Paul, Barnabas and Silas. Then, thirdly, there were those with purely localized responsibilities, as in 2 Corinthians 8:23. Finally there were 'apostolic ministries (e.g. Timothy and Titus carried out certain apostolic services without ever being referred to specifically in the New Testament as "apostles")'.[18] Another advocate of apostles today finds three groups and he divides them in this way: Firstly, there is Christ the Apostle of the apostles (Heb. 5:1). Secondly there were the original Twelve who were unique and who have no direct successors. Thirdly there are those who are still given by the ascended Christ to the church as evangelists and church planters and among whom the apostle Paul stands pre-eminent. These are pioneers or 'trail-blazers'.[19]

I have no intention of disputing the undoubted and glorious fact that Christ himself is supremely the 'sent one' and the Apostle of apostles. On the other hand I do not feel it incumbent upon me to chase after a will o' the wisp and discuss apostles who are never named as such in the New Testament. But some of these points do demand comment. I abide by the primary commitment that the apostle was an eyewitness of the resurrection above all else. I would point out that the mention of the five hundred eyewitnesses in 1 Corinthians 15:6 leaves God plenty of scope, but it is nevertheless a limiting fact – they had all set eyes on the risen Christ. As Andrew F. Walls has put it, 'Paul's own apostleship makes such a breach in any more restrictive theory that there is room for others of God's appointment to pass with him . . . But everything suggests that an apostle was a witness of the resurrection . . .'[20] Rengstorf likewise affirms that 'We do not know how many apostles there were in the early days, but they must have been fairly numerous.'[21]

Therefore I cannot hold with Hendriksen and others that there were only 'the twelve' and Paul.[22] This view leads to

problems over the position of James. That our Lord's brother
was an apostle seems fairly clearly established. Firstly, he was
an eyewitness of the resurrection (1 Cor. 15:7). Secondly, he
acted together with Peter and John to ratify the ministry of
Paul. 'James, Peter and John, those reputed to be pillars,' is
how Paul strikingly describes them (Gal. 2:9; see Gal. 1:19). It
is obvious that while James is not one of the Twelve, he does
share their authority. In the third place, we see him presiding
at the Council of Jerusalem and giving voice to the 'word of
knowledge' which determines the final verdict. When we think
of 'apostolic authority', it is hard to think of him as having less
than this role at this august assembly.

It would also seem clear that Barnabas was an apostle. This
can be seen from a variety of passages. Acts 14:4,14 not only
speaks of him as such but verse 3 links him with Paul in the
performance of apostolic miracles. Moreover Paul introduces
him naturally into an argument in 1 Corinthians 9:1-6 which is
solely concerned with apostolic claims, privileges and
sacrifices. Furthermore Barnabas is associated with Paul when
the latter's apostolic ministry to the Gentiles is approved by
the 'big three'! (Gal. 2:9.) Some imply that he could not
possibly qualify because he came from Cyprus (Acts 4:36). But
this merely indicates his place of origin. From early times he
was well known and widely respected in the church at
Jerusalem and equally to the point is the comment of F.F.
Bruce that 'Barnabas, although not one of the twelve, may
have been one of the hundred and twenty believers of chapter
1:15 and a witness of the resurrection of Christ.'[23]

The fact that writers can go to 2 Corinthians 8:23 or
Philippians 2:25 for support for a theory of 'secondary
apostles' almost seems evidence of despair! The word basically
means 'messenger' in these passages and is rightly so
translated in the New International Version. The ministry was
undoubtedly loving ministry and real service but, as the
context indicates, in neither case was it apostolic ministry in
the sense that we have established. Epaphroditus was offering
personal service and help to Paul, and Titus was seeking to
ensure that the money flowed in and the accounts were properly audited in a generous act of famine relief among the
brotherhood. This is not to be disparaged. But can it in any way
be equated with apostolic ministry? Writing on Romans 16:7,

where some have gleefully seen the possibility of a woman apostle; James Hurley simply points out that Junias could just as easily be a man's name, that the reference could be 'well-known among the apostles' rather than 'outstanding among the apostles' and that it would be sheer irresponsibility to establish any doctrine on so unclear a text.[24] There are no criteria within Scripture for recognizing secondary apostles. The creature does not exist. The guide-lines are clear and the apostles who stand at the top of the list in both 1 Corinthians 12 and Ephesians 4 are unique.

Modern claimants to apostleship

As we come to our own century and attempt a brief survey of modern claimants to apostleship we will range wider than the charismatics. It is necessary to remember, (and we will return to this in our final section) that there are groups today who are quite happy with the concept of contemporary apostleship and new revelations and who are most unhappy with close and detailed analysis of Scripture, and these are the groups with which many charismatics (not surprisingly) show real kinship and affinity.

We begin with the claims of Rome. Someone has summed up the Roman Catholic emphasis in a rhyme:

> His twelve apostles first He made His ministers of grace
> And they their hands on others laid to fill in turn their
>   place.
> So age by age, and year by year, His grace is handed on
> And still the holy church is here, although her Lord
>   be gone.[25]

This, of course, is no dated issue. Here is the pope in his opening speech at Westminster Cathedral: 'I am happy that I can concelebrate this eucharist with my brother bishops who, together with me, are the successors of the Apostles . . .'[26] At Coventry Airport he asserted, 'On that first Pentecost our Saviour gave the apostles the power to forgive sins when he poured into their hearts the gift of the Holy Spirit.'[27] And even in the telegram sent to Cardinal Hume to thank him for the successful arrangements we find: 'I cordially impart my apostolic blessing.'[28] There is no retreat from the old Roman Catholic claims and no ambiguity, fuzziness or reticence in these pronouncements.

Secondly, trailing behind are the little group of High Anglicans, who, although their own orders are still declared to be invalid by Rome, yet through spokesmen such as E.L. Mascal can argue that 'Only a man who has validly received the divine commission through the apostolic succession can validly perform the eucharist.'[29]

One is reminded at this point of the old story of the farmer being shown, with a party of English tourists, round St Peter's at Rome. Having been dazzled with constant wonders, they were to be confronted with yet another. Taking them to a place where some hens were to be seen, the guide solemnly announced, 'These hens are the direct descendants of the cock which crew at Peter's denial!' After a period of stunned and awed silence an old farmer with a broad country accent said, 'Excuse me, zur, but be they good layers?'

If the farmer's interest lay more in apostolic success than apostolic succession, he does not stand alone. John Wesley trenchantly said of those ordained by the bishop and sent to America that they 'knew no more of saving souls than of catching whales'.[30] In his view those who did not save souls were no true ministers of Christ. Luther, putting the stress more on the preaching of the Word, wrote, 'A bishop who neither preaches nor practises the cure of souls is nothing at all but an idol, in spite of the name and appearance of a bishop.'[31] Their criteria of a true ministry was none other than faithful preaching of the apostolic Word, sealed by conversions.

How significant that in their common declaration of unity the pope and Archbishop of Canterbury should state that their quest was founded on the 'gospels and ancient common traditions'![32] Not only is tradition blasphemously elevated to the level of biblical authority, but the Gospels are mentioned to the exclusion of the New Testament letters. It is in the letters (notably in Paul's letters to Timothy and Titus) that the character and qualifications of the ministry are so clearly delineated in terms of teaching, preaching and evangelizing. Is this why they are not mentioned? Would not the descriptions in the letters prove utterly opposed to the claims of Rome and

High Anglicanism for the ministry? It is supremely in portions
of the New Testament outside the Gospels, which Anglican
evangelicals often purport to find so 'confusing', that clear
guide-lines on ministry and apostleship are given.

Oddly enough, the same Archbishop of Canterbury tells of
how Dom Gregory Dix was once at the consecration of a
bishop. Let us hear the story in his own words: 'At the point in
the service where the bishops all gather round the candidate
and lay their hands on his head and he is lost in a kind of
scrum, the neighbour asked Dom Gregory rather agitatedly,
"What on earth is happening?"; to which he replied, "They
are conducting an operation to remove his backbone".'[33]
Many a true word is spoken in jest. But above all it must be
asserted that those who do not truly preach the saving gospel
of Jesus Christ in heartfelt submission to the Word are no true
ministers of Christ, however they have been ordained.

Charismatic claimants

Our third point of contemporary application must be to the
charismatic movement. We briefly mention a group who are
perhaps the only genuinely consistent charismatics, namely
the Mormons. Let us quote two of 'The Articles of Faith of the
Church of Jesus Christ of Latter-day Saints.'

'6. We believe in the same organization that existed in the
Primitive Church, viz., apostles, prophets, pastors, teachers,
evangelists, etc.

'7. We believe in the gift of tongues, prophecy, revelation,
visions, healing, interpretation of tongues, etc.'

It is not with our tongue in our cheek that we say that the
Mormons are the only really consistent believers in the gifts.
They do have apostles. They do have new revelations. They do
have additions to the Scripture. (Other people often do, but
frequently deny it.) If the gifts were bestowed today, we should
expect new revelations (1 Cor. 14:2,6,30).

Yet there are groups within Protestantism which
strenuously argue for the gift of apostleship today and which
certainly accept the view that apostles are figures with
considerable authority. *First Apostles, Last Apostles* was the title
of one recent booklet advocating this. One reviewer,
commenting on this booklet together with others emanating
from a house-group movement, said that 'This booklet

attempts to justify, on the most incredibly flimsy evidence, the necessity, desirability and existence of apostles today.' With reference to another of such booklets, *Not Under Law,* the same writer spoke of the arrogant tone and the 'attempt to browbeat those who are aware of their lack of spiritual experience'.[34] The same tone can be seen in the words of the apostle of the Church of the Living Word who thus addresses his congregation: 'You'll be taught by the Spirit what is involved in . . . apostleship or you'll be left in Babylon. There's no halfway point. The only alternative you have to spiritual submission and to divine order is Babylon.' On how to recognize an apostle he affirms: 'You don't teach people this. Jesus did not go around saying, "I'm the Messiah" . . . A person who has an ear to hear and an eye to see and a spiritual hunger to reach into God, when hearing an apostle will know he is an apostle.'[35]

Scripture has once more fallen entirely by the wayside. Recognition of the apostle is not to be by scriptural criteria but by some inner awareness. (We note the similarity of procedure to that advocated in the recognition of a prophet.) Scriptural criteria are also almost totally abandoned in the definition propounded by one house group in their guidelines for church membership. Although they refer to a list of Scriptures, they engage in no close analysis. Writing of apostles they say, 'Paul is the classic example. He describes himself as "an expert builder" (1 Cor. 3:10), a kind of spiritual architect. An apostle is a big man in spiritual terms. He can see the overall "shape" of a church situation and has authority and wisdom from God to redirect it, to spot areas of weakness and to appoint leaders. Because of the chaotic state of the professing Christian world, one of the regular functions of apostles and prophets today is to *rebuild* on a proper basis churches which have fallen into disarray.'[36] Like others the group argue that Paul was the first of an entirely new group of apostles which is still here today. It is very interesting, in the light of Paul's avowed 'ambition to preach the gospel where Christ was not known, so that I would not be building on someone else's foundation' (Rom. 15:20), that they emphasize 'rebuilding' (in the original the word is in bold print). Is this emphasized to justify a practice of deliberately taking from other churches rather than evangelizing in virgin fields? Their concept of one church in the city (with apostles, prophets etc.) entitles one to view with wariness their plea, made in the same publication, for overtures of fellowship towards other churches.[37]

Charismatic alarm

Many warnings are now being given by charismatics and Pentecostalists about these groups and their partners in America. Thus the founder of the Fountain Trust now views with alarm the concept of one American that 'There cannot be more than one church in any locality.'[38] A Pentecostal wrote an excellent series of articles on the teaching emanating from Fort Lauderdale, Florida. Warning on the danger of the shepherding emphasis, (a proper scriptural doctrine taken to extremes), he quoted a well-known leader as saying, 'We do not obey those in authority because they are right, we obey them because they are in authority.'[39] In his final article, aptly entitled 'Protestant Popery', he quotes the arguments of the same leader that 'The autonomous church is an unscriptural carry-over.'[40] Such groups are seen by critics as very much a 'denomination with apostles', desiring to swallow up the other charismatic groups.[41]

Although it could well be argued that these are the more extreme groups, yet there are many who realize that if you are really consistent and 'believe in all the gifts', then you must believe in the gift of apostleship as fervently as any other, if not more so. After all it is God's 'first of all'. So we have two authors referring to Carey as an apostle to India and Judson as an apostle to Burma. It goes without saying that neither of these men believed for one moment that they were such. The apostles in the New Testament clearly knew their role. But now we have apostles who not only did not know they were apostles but who did not believe that apostles still existed! We may call them posthumous apostles! In reality apostleship, far from being a gift conferred by the Holy Spirit, is one conferred by historians some centuries later when the men are no longer able to speak for themselves! Some have recently conferred the title on Dr Martyn Lloyd-Jones, although he himself wrote, 'By definition there never can be or has been a successor to the apostles.'[42]

One well-known convention speaker feels he must rationalize this position and so he writes, 'Apostle: a person who is sent from rather than being called to a particular church, and has the God-given ability to pioneer new territory with church-planting goals.'[43] This is a very neat definition. But what does he make of Acts 8:1: 'On that day a great persecution broke out against the church at Jerusalem, and all except the apostles were scattered throughout Judea and Samaria'? It was Philip, a deacon, who in the days after this outburst of persecution was the evangelist and church planter. John and Peter merely turned up to view the church already planted! Of course, to be fair, some of the apostles were great missionaries and church planters and particularly is this true of Paul. But it is by no means the basic meaning of the gift. This writer has ignored the five clear marks and invented one that is not clear to justify the gift today.

The writings of one well-known author on practical aspects of the Christian life must have been a great help to many young Christians. But not so his contribution to the debate on the gifts. On apostleship we learn that there is a 'secondary sense of pioneer church-planting missionaries'.[44] But then, after arguing that the gift is for today, he suddenly begins to dither as he warns, 'On the other hand, I think there is a great danger in a recent book which says, "Let us watch and pray for apostles to be raised up . . . Let us recognize and submit to them as they appear."'[45] Why is he so wary? The reasons are obvious. In fact one even more cautious Pentecostal pastor wrote to a Christian newspaper to assure them that the denomination to which he belonged had never sought to restore such a ministry.[46] Fair enough – but what has happened to the belief that all the gifts are for today? You cannot have your cake and eat it.

This leads us to comment on two of the major errors or defects in the charismatic and Pentecostal movements. One is that they fail to give the full-blooded scriptural meaning to each gift, but rather give a watered-down interpretation so that some modern practice, which in reality has no direct relationship to the authentic New Testament gift, can yet erroneously be described as such. Thus in many modern groups apostle becomes church planter or missionary. While I am in no wise aiming to denigrate the great calling of missionary, nor to underplay the missionary vision of the apostles, I do not feel that this simple equation in any way ties in with the New Testament evidence on what constitutes an apostle. When a man becomes a missionary, he still needs five more clear marks before we can legitimately call him an apostle!

Many so-called apostles today remind one of a man who claims to be an England test cricketer. 'Oh, you played with Botham, Allott, Downton and Gower?' 'No, but I wear white flannels.' 'Well, you will have played at the Oval or Lords or some other test ground?' 'No, but I wear white flannels.' 'You know what it is to get that summons to play for the England team?' 'No, but I wear white flannels.' 'You've been awarded that prized cap with the England emblem on it?' 'No, but I wear white flannels.' 'You've been paid the proper amount that Test cricketers receive in our day?' 'No, but I wear white flannels.' Well, he may look nice in his white flannels, but some of us would hesitate to describe him as an England test cricketer. People who claim apostleship do not even sound nice. They are usurping a role which God has given to a uniquely chosen body of men, and as our historical chapters will abundantly show, wherever this happens there are large dangers round the corner.

7.
Montanism to Luther

Many charismatic movements

As we look at the various 'charismatic movements' down the centuries, our course will not be even. There were periods when there were few claimants, or even none at all, to the extraordinary gifts. Not surprisingly, little appears to have been written on this matter at these times. On the other hand, there have been far more periods than is usually realized when the gifts were claimed by considerable numbers. We are not attempting to cover them all. We shall be selective. After a glance at the earlier centuries we shall particularly look at the Reformation period, the Puritan era, the eighteenth-century awakening, the nineteenth-century and, finally, we shall seek to assess the developments within our own century. We will have three principal aims in doing this. Firstly, we shall be interested to see whether there were those in the past who made similar claims to the charismatics today. Secondly, we shall then enquire about the tendencies and developments of such movements. Thirdly, we shall look at the theological stature and biblical comment of those who opposed such movements and sought to expose and oppose what they saw as their unscriptural errors.

The early years

Our position for the very early years, and in particular the fifty years after the passing of the apostles, is basically that of B.B. Warfield, who wrote in reply to those who claimed that charismatic gifts continued for several centuries, 'There is little or no evidence at all for miracle-working during the first fifty years of the post-Apostolic church; it is slight and unimportant for the next fifty years; it grows more abundant during the next century (the third); and it becomes abundant and precise only in the fourth century, to increase still further in the fifth and beyond.'[1] At the same time, it cannot be denied that there are occasional allusions to the gifts in these early years, but it can also be argued that very rarely is anything precise and definite said.

Significantly, among the fathers who immediately followed the apostles there is hardly any mention of the gifts, even in a generalizing way, and little or no evidence that the gifts were practised. For example, when writers seize on the well-known and often-quoted reference to travelling prophets in the *Didache,* surely the reference illustrates more the decline, or even the non-existence of the genuine prophetic gift than it proves the opposite. Listen to this glaring contrast with what the Bible says: 'You must neither test nor examine a prophet who speaks in the spirit: for "every sin shall be forgiven, but not this sin." But not everyone who speaks in the spirit is a prophet; he is only a prophet if he has the ways of the Lord. The false and the genuine prophet will be known therefore by their ways. Every prophet who orders a table in the spirit does not eat of it: if he does, he is a false prophet.'[2] There is a similar allusion in *The Shepherd of Hermas* where it is asked, 'How can a divine Spirit receive money and prophesy?'[3] Apparently there were some travelling charlatans who desired most of all that all expenses should be paid and that there should be a slap-up meal by courtesy of the local church. To such trivia had the testing of prophecy descended. Biblical moorings had already been lost. The references indicate people who, like many today, despite all their talk, could not tell an elephant from a mouse prophetically speaking! This was because the gift had ceased. (I ignore the miracles related by Papias because he is clearly describing events in apostolic times as he refers to Philip, his daughters and to the Justus of Acts 1).[4]

Justin and Irenaeus

The only two witnesses for the gifts during the next period are Justin and Irenaeus. The references in the former are tantalizingly brief. Although he certainly does write, 'For the prophetical gifts remain with us, even to the present time,' he provides no further details.[5] And when in another passage he claims that 'Now it is possible to see amongst us women and men who possess gifts of the Spirit of God,' yet all the preceding passage, as well as what follows, refers to events in New Testament times, such as the Spirit resting upon Christ and the citation of Joel 2:28-32.[6]

Irenaeus speaks of the restoration of sight, the curing of deafness and challenges others in these terms: 'And so far are they from being able to raise the dead, as the Lord raised them, and the apostles did by means of prayer, and as has been frequently done in the brotherhood on account of some necessity – the entire Church in that particular locality entreating the boon with much fasting and prayer, the spirit of the dead man has returned, and he has been bestowed in answer to the prayers of the saints . . .'[7] Since we feel that very few charismatics will wish to be saddled with the responsibility of raising the dead (it is not one of the signs which new apostles are keen to perform, even though it is biblical) we hasten to add to their relief that in a later reference in the same work it would seem likely from the tenses used that he is speaking of events that took place in apostolic times, as he declares, 'Yes, moreover, as I have said, the dead even have been raised up, and remained among us for many years.'[8]Moreover it must be remembered that, as Warfield reminds us, 'Irenaeus's youth was spent in the company of pupils of the Apostle; Justin may easily have known of, if not even witnessed, miracles wrought by Apostolically trained men.'[9]

Therefore, when Irenaeus says, 'Others have foreknowledge of things to come: they see visions, and utter prophetic expressions. Others still, heal the sick by laying their hands upon them, and they are made whole,' we wonder whether he is giving a summary of incidents in such books as Acts, since at no point does he give a clear contemporary illustration. The same query can be made about his most famous statement, also from the same work, where he writes, 'For this reason does the apostle declare, "We speak wisdom among them that are perfect," terming those persons "perfect" who have received the Spirit of God, and who through the Spirit of God do speak in all languages, as he used himself also to speak. In like manner we do also hear many brethren in the Church, who possess prophetic gifts, and who through the Spirit speak all kinds of languages, and bring to light for the general benefit the hidden things of men, and declare the mysteries of God, whom also the apostle terms "spiritual", they being spiritual because they partake of the Spirit, and not because their flesh has been stripped off and taken away, and because they have become purely spiritual.'[10] Even here he could be speaking about people in the Corinthian church. There are two grounds for saying this. The first is the obvious allusion to 1 Corinthians 2:6, and secondly as Hoekema comments, 'The word translated "terms" is *vocat* in the Latin, a present indicative form of the verb *vocare*, "to call or to name". These people, Irenaeus is saying, Paul calls "spiritual". If Irenaeus meant to say that certain people in his own day were the kind of people whom Paul would have called spiritual if he were now living, why was this not made more clear? Why did Irenaeus not use a perfect subjunctive instead of a present indicative?'[11] However, he does concede that Eusebius thought that Irenaeus was in fact alluding to events of his own day. In another passage Irenaeus exclaims, 'Wretched men indeed! who wish to be pseudo-prophets, forsooth, but who set aside the gift of prophecy from the church.'[12] So it may after all be possible that Irenaeus was the leading charismatic of his day. The evidence is not conclusive.

Prophetic fervour in Montanism

Fortunately for us, the leading charismatics of the end of the second century, namely Montanus and his followers, did not content themselves with generalizing references. They were specific. Montanus gave utterances as though the Lord were speaking directly through him. Two statements in particular caused scandal: 'Behold, man is like a lyre and I hover over him like a plectrum. Man sleeps, while I awake. Behold, it is the Lord who makes men's hearts ecstatic and gives new hearts to men,' and 'It is I, the Lord God Almighty, who am present in a man. I am neither an angel nor an emissary; I, the Lord God the Father, have come.'[13] Here was a man who was undoubtedly, in his own estimation, on a hot line to heaven. Not surprisingly, one so self-assured won followers. His two leading ones were ladies who, to the scandalizing of many, left their husbands to join him. One of them, Priscilla, included herself among those for whom 'continence results in harmony and they see visions and, bowing their heads, hear distinct voices, at once salutary and mysterious'.[14] The other leading prophetess was Maximilla.

A hostile witness described how Montanus 'raved, and began to chatter and talk nonsense'.[15] The witness was sure that Montanus and his crazed followers were false prophets. Indeed Montanus predicted that Zion or Jerusalem would come down from heaven to either the village of Pepuza or Tymion in Phrygia. Priscilla confirmed this. 'Christ,' she affirmed, 'came to me in the form of a woman clad in a shining robe; he set wisdom in me and revealed to me that this very place is sacred and that here Jerusalem will descend from heaven.'[16] Inevitably followers were soon having to explain away the non-fulfilment of all this. Meanwhile Maximilla, facing criticism, retorted in this vein: 'I am driven away like a wolf from the sheep. I am not a wolf; I am word and spirit and power.'[17] These are dangerous words and later a hostile witness again pointed out how she had falsely foretold various wars and revolutions. He wrote, 'Surely it is now obvious that this too is a lie? Today it is more than thirteen years since the woman's death, and there has been neither general nor local war in the world, but rather – even for Christians – continuous peace, by the mercy of God.'[18] One man who felt very sceptical about the claims of these prophetesses put the issue very bluntly: 'It is thus evident that these prophetesses, from the time they were filled with the spirit, were the very first to leave their husbands. How then could they lie so blatantly as to call Priscilla a virgin?"[19] The same writer more than once spoke with contempt of the way they eagerly grabbed the takings, asking whether this was a mark of the genuine prophet. From all sides there was hostility at the way the Montanists seemed to think that none but their group could be genuine Christians.

Attraction for Tertullian

Yet there must have been genuine Christian notes in the movement and many would stress that the Montanists were orthodox on the main doctrines. In fact, with their emphasis on discipline, on continence, on the seeking of martyrdom and on the claim that their gifted leadership could remit sin, they were just the group to attract an earnest, zealous, ascetic soul like Tertullian, who himself became a full-blown Montanist at the beginning of the third century. In fact, Tertullian became the apologist for the movement. His writings show that the characteristics criticized by opponents were present in the movement. Had not opponents alleged that 'The pseudo-prophet speaks in a state of unnatural ecstasy after which all restraint is thrown to the winds. He begins with voluntary ignorance and ends in involuntary psychosis . . .'?[20] Far from denying this 'mindless' element, Tertullian gloried in it. He stated the issue dogmatically and unambiguously. 'We defend the position, that a state of ecstasy, that is, alienation of mind, is suitable to the spiritual gift. For a man who is in the Spirit, especially when he beholds the glory of God, or when God speaks by him, necessarily loses his reasoning faculties for the time, being overwhelmed, that is, by the divine power.'[21]

Having embraced the Montanist position, Tertullian went the whole way. Referring to those who denied the bodily resurrection, he commented, 'That was an illuminating remark which the Paraclete made through the prophetess Prisca about those people, "They are things of the flesh and they hate the flesh."'[22] Echoing the claims of Montanus with regard to the powers of the gifted leadership, he said that he found 'the Paraclete saying, through the New Prophets, "The Church has power to remit a sin; but I will not do it, lest they commit other sin."'[23] Dangerously he also asserted that it was right that since 'the New Law abolished divorce . . . the New Prophecy abolished second marriage'.[24]

In his work against Marcion he taunted and challenged these heretics as follows: 'Let Marcion then exhibit, as gifts of his god, some prophets, such as have not spoken by human sense, but with the Spirit of God, such as have both predicted things to come, and have made manifest the secrets of the heart; let him produce a psalm, a vision, a prayer – only let it be by the Spirit, in an ecstasy, that is, in a rapture *(amentia)* whenever an interpretation of tongues has occurred to him . . .'[25] For his own part he was confident that he had joined the right group. Therefore, in his treatise on the soul, he informs us that 'We have now among us a sister whose lot it has been to be favoured with sundry gifts of revelation, which she experiences in the Spirit by ecstatic vision amid the sacred rites of the church: she converses with angels and sometimes even with the Lord; she both sees and hears mysterious communications; some men's hearts she understands, and to them in need she distributes remedies.' He adds that when she reported these 'communications' they were probed with scrupulous care. Then he describes one of the wonderful visions she had received. 'Amongst other things,' says she, 'there has been shown to me a soul in bodily shape, and a spirit has been in the habit of appearing to me; not, however, a void and empty illusion, but such as would offer itself even to be grasped by the hand, soft and transparent and of an ethical colour, and in form resembling that of a human being in every respect.'[26] He then quotes from 1 Corinthians 12 in defence of her vision and also brings in other supposedly learned authorities to prove that she was right. And many have exhorted us to accept the worth of the movement simply because of Tertullian's judgement!

To such banality, and dangerous banality at that, the prophetess was reduced! One wonders whether this would lead in the same dangerous direction as the forbidding of second marriage, where the prophecy definitely contradicted and indeed superseded the plain teaching of Scripture that 'in the Lord' this is permissible (see 1 Cor. 7:39; 1 Tim. 5:14). Throughout the movement the Scriptures were increasingly receding into the background. Despite disclaimers to the contrary this always proves to be the case. Moreover the blatant advocacy of a 'mindless' experience while under the influence of the Spirit was both unscriptural and fraught with peril. Many prophecies were not fulfilled. Empty claims were made. Women were wrongfully prominent. Marriages were endangered. False teachings were given (Christ seen as a woman, the claim to remit sin, the weird prophecy about the soul). Of them, Clement of Alexandria rightly said, 'But among their falsehoods they said some things also that were true, and in truth they prophesied in a state of ecstasy, as ministers of the Apostate.'[27]

Chrysostom and Augustine

Among the fathers who follow, two main emphases are discernible, both of which strongly militate against their acceptance of Montanism, or indeed any other charismatic movement, as genuine. One is the simple fact that they confirmed that the gifts had ceased and the other is that through careful biblical exegesis they established that the prophet or tongue-speaker was never in a state where there was the suspension of the mental faculties. We take the former issue first. Two brief quotations from Chrysostom and Augustine, both of whom lived in the fourth century, should suffice. The former commenting on 1 Corinthians 12:1,2 and alluding to the gifts, said, 'This whole place is very obscure: but the obscurity is produced by our ignorance of the facts referred to and by their cessation, being such as then used to occur but now no longer take place.'[28] Augustine asserts, 'For who expects in these days that those on whom hands are laid that they may receive the Holy Spirit should forthwith begin to speak with tongues?'[29] Since these two men were contemporaries, and since they lived in different areas and were both much-travelled men, with their finger on the pulse of things, the widespread absence of the gifts to which they testify is itself a problem for all those who maintain that the gifts have been there for all time. Were these and others of their period such spiritual pygmies that the gifts could not be bestowed in their day? Or had the gifts ceased as God intended?

Furthermore, both of these writers had thought through the issue. In one of his sermons on Acts Chrysostom observed that miracles and signs were to the infant church like the supports and defences supplied by the gardener to a young tree, which 'Christ took away for the future' when it was strong enough to stand. He added, 'Wherefore at the beginning the extraordinary gifts of the Spirit were conferred even upon the unworthy, for ancient times needed such support as a confirmation of the Christian faith, but now they are not given even to those who are worthy to receive them, because the power of the Christian faith is such as no longer to need this help.'[30] Equally compelling and full of insight is the argument of Augustine when he writes, 'In the earliest times, "the Holy Ghost fell upon them that believed: and they spake with tongues", which they had not learned, "as the Spirit gave them utterance." These were signs adapted to the time. For there behoved to be that betokening of the Holy Spirit in all tongues, to show that the Gospel of God was to run through all tongues over the whole earth. That thing was done for a betokening, and it passed away.'[31]

No alienation of the mind

Convinced that the mind was thoroughly involved in tongue-speaking, Chrysostom wrote, 'For one person knew what he spake in himself, but was unable to interpret it to another.'[32] Theodoret, of the early part of the fifth century, declared, 'As the prophet bringing to light the things previously infused into his understanding by the Holy Spirit profits his hearers by his prophecy, so I, he says, wish to speak by a language which the church understands, so that it may hear and be edified; and not by a vain-glorious exhibition of Greek and Hebrew *to edify myself, who understand what I am saying,* and not the church.'[33] One other quotation must suffice on the topic of tongue-speaking, and it is to Basil that we turn for a comment on the phrase 'unfruitful' in 1 Corinthians 14: 'For when the words of a prayer are unknown to those present, the understanding of the person praying is unfruitful, no one being benefited. But when those present understand the prayer, so that it is calculated to benefit the hearers, then the person who prays has fruit in the advantage gained by those who profit by it. And the case is the same with respect to every promulgation of the words of God.'[34]

Writer after writer says the same things about the prophets. They did not suffer alienation of the mind. It is the mark of the soothsayer to be 'under a violent impulse' (Chrysostom). Prophets did not 'lose their understanding', as did those possessed by unclean spirits (Origen).[35] They comment on the fact that, even in marvellous visions, Isaiah, Ezekiel and Daniel were self-conscious and reflecting. Basil, in his commentary on Isaiah, puts it like this: 'But there are some who say that they prophesy in a state of ecstasy, their human understanding being overshadowed and obscured by the Spirit. But this is irreconcilable with their boast of having the Divine Presence with them, that it should disable the mind of him who is divinely inspired; and that when he has become full of the divine counsels, he should then be estranged even from his own understanding, and that when he is making himself useful to others, he should himself fail of receiving profit from his own words. In every respect, indeed, what probability is there, that a man should become like one mad from the influence of the Spirit of wisdom, and should incur the suspension of his intellectual powers from the influence of the Spirit of knowledge?'[36] Augustine, Jerome and Gregory the Great all concurred.

The real issue is then put by two other writers. Epiphanius (A.D. 375), after agreeing with all the above argument and observing how certain contemporaries claimed the gift of prophecy but did not do it in this scriptural way, said, 'But, if again, they shall say, the first spiritual gifts are not like the last, whence can they show this? For the holy prophets and the holy apostles prophesied like one another.'[37] And Hilary the Deacon (A.D. 380) exposed the whole fatal business of accepting the concept of fallible prophecy: 'For the spirits of the world often speak what is good deceitfully, and, as it were, in imitation; and in the midst of it introduce by stealth what is evil, that so they may gain acceptance by those things which are good . . .' He significantly adds, 'For no error can be found in the Holy Spirit.'[38]

The medieval period

We traverse the medieval period with seven-league boots. Any reader of Bede's *History of the English Church and People* will know that in this island alone there were countless examples of the pseudo-miraculous, with all the deviation from scriptural truth that this entailed. Few seemed to oppose or detect these fabrications. It was otherwise in Bohemia a century before the emergence of Luther. John Hus lived at a time when rival claimants to the papacy were each supported by 'prophetic figures' and 'workers of miracles', whose visions and signs obviously cancelled each other out! One of the activities which first brought Hus into prominence was his thorough-going exposure of the practices of the fraudulent priests at a shrine called Wilsnack. He was a man whose supreme rule was Scripture and who never made common cause with the seers of his day, many of whom were probably as glad to see him burned as were the cardinals and bishops.[39]

Luther

Forthrightness of Luther
In Luther's day the priests of Wilsnack were still raking in the proceeds from a gullible public. Since Luther refers to 'St John Hus', contrasting Hus in his stand for the Word of God alone with the spurious saints of the papacy, whose alleged miracles supposedly supported papal doctrine, it is not surprising that in one of his earliest works, *An Appeal to the Ruling Class,* Luther advocated that Wilsnack, along with other shrines, should be pulled down.[40]Although it is notoriously difficult to sum up Luther's conclusions with exactness since his output was so vast, the main drift of his thought would seem clear enough. The following are three quotations from his sermons on the Gospel of John: 'The spirit of prophecy is still present in Christendom, but not so markedly as in the apostles. We, too, can predict and know such things, but only if we have learned this from the books of the apostles.' 'But now that the apostles have preached the Word and have given their writings, and nothing more than what they have written remains to be revealed, no new and special revelation or miracle is necessary.' And after referring to 'the writings of the apostles' about the Antichrist he says, 'And since we have this sure prophecy which is being fulfilled at present – a reliable token of the pure doctrine – miracles are no longer necessary to confirm this doctrine. For the accompanying signs were given principally, as St Mark says in the last chapter (16:20), to substantiate the new message of the apostles. But we have not introduced a new message; we have simply restored this same old, confirmed doctrine of the apostles.'[41]
Luther was indeed very clear that some things were peculiar

to the apostolic age. Thus in his exposition of Galatians 1:1 he comments, 'That they be properly called Apostles, which are sent immediately of God himself, without any other person as means.'[42] He therefore sees the casting of lots, in its biblical context, as reinforcing this. From the *Table Talk* we learn that someone wanted to know whether the 'killing with a word' of the lying Ananias was a precedent for us today. 'The doctor replied: "That was something extraordinary. Moreover, I believe that Peter did not do this of himself but by revelation, for God wished to establish the primitive Church by means of miracles."'[43] Such an act was confined to the apostolic age.

However Luther had a significant, direct and well-documented encounter with the prophetic movement of his day. In the vicinity of Wittenberg in the early days of the Reformation were the notorious Zwickau prophets, Nicholas Storch with his 'long beard and his sombrero', Thomas Drechsel, a cultured man, and Mark Stubner. This group made claims to visions and revelations. Also sniping from the wings was Thomas Müntzer, with his repeated emphasis on visions and dreams ('God comes in dreams to his beloved as he did to the patriarchs, prophets and apostles') and his attacks of Luther, whom he derisively termed 'Brother Porky-boy', 'Brother Soft-Life' and one of 'our scribes' who 'want to send the Holy Ghost to college'.[44] And hovering in the background was a discontented and resentful former colleague Karlstadt, showing certain inclinations towards the prophetic fraternity without ever whole-heartedly supporting them.

Need for Luther's wisdom
It would be easy, and it is customary in matters like this, to dismiss all those we have been discussing as fringe extremists and not at all like modern charismatics. Melanchthon did not find it so easy to decide about them when, in the absence of Luther, the Zwickau prophets first made their entry. He was bewildered. In a letter to the Elector of Saxony, he said, 'I see strong reasons for not despising the men; for it is clear to me there is in them something more than a mere human spirit; but whether the spirit be of God or not, none except Martin can easily judge.'[45] Once again we are bound to ask the obvious question: if a top-ranking theologian like Melanchthon could not sort this out, how can every young convert easily discern in

such matters? Furthermore, the fact that Melanchthon and others were partly drawn towards them, or at least reluctant to condemn them, shows that the group were not at first sight obvious cranks and impostors.

We may be thankful that in all this Luther was his normal ebullient and forthright self and that above all his spiritual discernment did not forsake him in any way. He wrote in reply to Melanchthon's panic signals: 'Now let me deal with the "prophets". Before I say anything else, I do not approve of your timidity, since you are stronger in spirit and learning than I. First of all, since they bear witness to themselves, one need not immediately accept them; according to John's counsel, the spirits are to be tested. If you cannot test them, then you have the advice of Gamaliel that you postpone judgement. Thus far I hear of nothing said or done by them that Satan could not also do or imitate. Yet find out whether they can prove [that they are called by God], for God has never sent anyone, not even the Son himself, unless he were called through men or attested by signs . . . I definitely do not want the "prophets" to be accepted if they state they were called by mere revelation, since God did not even wish to speak to Samuel except through the authority and knowledge of Eli.'[46]

Soon after this Luther had opportunity to have a conference with some of them. We learn that he there 'patiently heard the prophet relate his visions; and when the harangue was finished, recollecting that nonsense was incapable of confutation, he briefly admonished him to take care what he did. You have mentioned, said he, nothing that has the least support in Scripture; the whole seems rather an ebullition of imagination, or perhaps the fraudulent suggestion of an evil spirit.' Whereupon, in a typical reaction one of the group 'expressed the most lively resentment that Luther should dare to say such things of so divine a personage'.[47] Luther was confronted with the customary defence that those who opposed the prophets did so for want of spirituality. Thus Müntzer in a letter to Melanchthon could complain, 'The doctrine of Luther was *not sufficiently spiritual;* it was, indeed, altogether carnal. Divines should exert their utmost endeavours to acquire *a spirit of prophecy,* otherwise their knowledge of divinity would not be worth one halfpenny. *They should consider their God as at hand, and not far off.*'[48]

Luther's grasp of essentials

During this perplexing period Luther wrote several letters and documents on this theme. Here are some excerpts from his 'Letter to the Princes of Saxony concerning the Rebellious Spirit' (1524), where he obviously had Müntzer (of Allstedt) in mind: '"You yourself must hear the voice of God," they say, "and experience the work of God in you and feel how much your talents weigh. The Bible means nothing. It is Bible – Booble – Babel," etc.' 'If I had known that as many devils as there were tiles on the roof at Worms took aim at me, I would still have entered the city on horseback, and this, even though I had never heard a heavenly voice, or of God's talents and works, or of the Allstedt spirit.' 'They have a much higher and more precious office than the Apostles and Prophets and Christ himself.' 'For they are not Christians who want to go beyond the Word and to use violence, but are not ready to suffer much else, even if they boast of being full and overfull with ten holy spirits.'[49]

Here are some further examples from a second and third tract. In his 'Letter to the Christians at Strassburg in opposition to the Fanatic Spirit' (1524), after saying that Karlstadt concentrates more on Christ as an example than as Saviour, he wrote, 'But turn to Christ as to a gift of God or, as Paul says, the power of God, and God's wisdom, righteousness, redemption, and sanctification given to us. For such matters these prophets have little sympathy, taste or understanding. Instead they juggle with their "living voice from heaven", their "laying off the material", "sprinkling", "mortification", and similar high-sounding words, which themselves never understood. They make for confused, disturbed, anxious consciences, and want people to be amazed at their great skill, but meanwhile Christ is forgotten.'[50] He felt that they had got the Scriptures topsy-turvy and inverted the proper order and emphasis. He vividly described his former companion in his treatise 'Against the Heavenly Prophets' where he wrote, 'From which you now see that Dr Karlstadt and his spirits replace the highest with the lowest, the best with the least, the first with the last. Yet he would be considered the greatest spirit of all, he who has devoured the Holy Spirit feathers and all.'[51]

Nor was Luther overawed by the stories of great men who

must be heeded because they have been so mightily used and have performed such great miracles. Thus in his debate with Luther, Erasmus taunted his opponent for having only the support of Wyclif and Valla, while all the great scholars and miracle-workers of the past were on his side. This evoked a blunt rejoinder from Luther: 'Suppose I should press the question, which of all those of whom you boast can you prove for certain to be, or to have been a saint, or to have possessed the Spirit, or to have wrought miracles . . . "Many are accounted saints on earth whose souls are in hell," is a true proverb!'[52] Elsewhere Luther contrasted the weird tales of the medieval saints with a true biblical picture of saintliness. He wrote of 'the multitude of other books which continually babble about the saints and their doings, but seldom or never quote their words . . . In comparison with the Book of Psalms, the other books, those containing the legends of the saints and other exemplary matter, depict holy men all with their tongues tied whereas the Book of Psalms presents us with saints alive and in the round. It is like putting a dumb man side by side with one who can speak: the first is only half alive.'[53] Luther is constantly urging us to go back to the Word of God, where clear teaching accompanies actions. No number of weird and wonderful stories of healings and exorcisms today, many of which are cast far more in the medieval mould than many either realize or would care to admit, should shake our belief as to what Scripture says. Therefore, if Scripture does teach that tongue-speaking has ceased and that originally the tongue-speaker understood what he uttered, then however marvellous a story we read of someone or some group being helped out of some predicament by an interpreted tongue, Scripture must stand against all comers.

Views of Calvin

As we move on to Calvin we must pause to deal with the statement in two charismatic books that God is able to raise up new apostles today and the citation from Calvin to this effect.[54] Rather remarkably they both omit the phrases put in italics in this passage from the *Institutes*. After speaking of the unique place of the apostles, Calvin says, 'Although I deny not, that afterwards God occasionally raised up Apostles, *or at least Evangelists,* in their stead, as has been done in our time. For such were needed to bring back the Church from the revolt of Antichrist. *This office I nevertheless call extraordinary because it has no place in churches duly constituted.*'[55]

This passage is from a paragraph of loose and inconsistent arguments. His definition of apostles as those who 'were sent forth to bring back the world from its revolt to the true obedience of God' is true enough but woefully deficient.[56] And yet he follows this with the following comments on the second group in the list in Ephesians chapter 4: 'By *Prophets,* he means not all interpreters of the divine will, but those who excelled by special revelation; none such now exist, or they are less manifest.'[57] All this is far from satisfactory and clear, it must be admitted, yet elsewhere in the same *Institutes,* Calvin writes, with respect to the passage from James 5 used by the Roman Catholics as their basis for the sacrament of extreme unction, 'They make themselves ridiculous, therefore, by pretending that they are endued with the gift of healing. The Lord, doubtless, is present with his people in all ages, and cures their sicknesses as often as there is need, not less than formerly; and yet he does not exert those manifest powers, nor dispense miracles by the hands of apostles, because that gift was temporary, and owing, in some measure, to the ingratitude of men, immediately ceased.'[58] This ties in with what he writes in the Preface to the *Institutes.* There, answering the challenge of Roman Catholics of his day, he states, 'In demanding miracles from us, they act dishonestly; for we have not coined some new gospel, but retain the very one the truth of which is confirmed by all the miracles which Christ and the apostles ever wrought.'[59] He then cites Acts 14:3 and Hebrews 2:4 to prove his point. Apostolic miracles confirmed apostolic doctrine. They were peculiar to the age of inspiration.

Much of what Calvin writes in his commentary on 1 Corinthians 14 is also unsatisfactory and affords little help. But it is interesting that on verse 14 he does say, 'For it is incredible (at least we do not read of any instance) that there were any people who spoke by the influence of the Spirit, in a language they did not know themselves,' and then adds that 'Paul thinks it a great fault if the understanding takes no part in prayer.'[60]

Beza on this same verse, combating the view that the
tongue-speaker did not understand, observes that 'It would be
too absurd to believe that the Holy Spirit ever moved anyone
to do that, nor can such things be called prayers, but mere
mockeries of God and the church.' And on verse 11, he says
that it 'was a barbarism unheard of in all former ages, by
which . . . they become barbarians to themselves, who use a
language unknown to themselves'.[61]

Catholic views

By contrast it was a commonplace of Roman Catholic interpretation that the tongue-speaker did not initially understand and
by this argument they justified the use of Latin in the liturgy.
Thus, Estius, one of their expositors says on 1 Corinthians
14:4, 'But if he who speaks in a tongue which he does not
understand edifies himself, it is therefore not useless either to
pray to, or to praise, God, in words not understood', and on
verse 14 he comments, 'My mind, i.e. my intellect, not attain-
ing the signification and meaning of the words, is deprived of
its proper fruit, which is to understand, etc . . . That of which
the apostle speaks, happens to those who, ignorant of Latin,
recite prayers in the Latin tongue; for *such, as far as regards the
spirit and feeling of devotion, are carried out towards God,* if they pray
with sincerity; but inasmuch as they do not understand the
words, their mind is without fruit, i.e. the fruit of knowledge
. . . But such prayers are not on that account to be
condemned . . . as useless.'[62] Replying to Cajetan, another
Roman Catholic, who had made a similar plea, Whitby would
have none of it and affirmed that 'His piety in speaking of
them could be no more than that of a parrot . . . nor could any
pious affections be raised in him by words not understood.'[63]
The same writer also commented that the tongue-speaker
could only speak to himself if he did understand.

Anabaptist extremists

Among the fringe groups of the Baptists, untold harm, even
intolerable anguish, was caused by those who believed that the

gifts were being restored as a sign of the end of the world. Views of this kind led to the wildness, polygamy, executions and massacres of Münster. It must be realized that the trail which led to this particular fuse had been lit long before it reached Münster and blew the town sky high. For example, Melchior Hoffman had made various predictions and sent forth 'visions and revelations', as one contemporary put it.[64] The fact that some of his early visions were fulfilled increased his following and continued his conviction that he would lead a mighty host of preachers 'with powers, signs and miracles, and with all such strength of the Spirit that no one could resist them'.[65]

All this was further supported when, to quote the words of a contemporary, 'One of the prophetesses also prophesied – and that through a vision – that Melchior was Elijah. She saw a white swan swimming in a beautiful river or watercourse, which swan had sung beautifully and wonderfully. And that, she interpreted to apply to Melchior as the true Elijah. She had also a vision of many death heads on the walls around Strassburg. When she wondered whether Melchior's head was among them, and she tried to see, she became aware of Melchior's head, and as she gazed upon it the head laughed and looked at her in a friendly way. Thereafter she saw that all the other heads came alive, one after the other, and they all began to laugh. This and many such like visions and revelations they brought to light, but only for the brethren. What use and profit came from this I do not know.'[66]

The same author who records this also records some of the weird visions of Ursula Joosten. Hoffman spent time editing the prophetic visions and revelations of this lady and her husband Leinhard and, comments a contemporary, 'gave them as much authority as Isaiah or Jeremiah'.[67] It has been said that the vagaries of the Joostens were harmless and that Hoffman never advocated violence. But there is no doubt that they paved the way for others and engendered the climate at Münster, the scene of awful violence and polygamy and a city founded on visions and revelations. Indeed Hoffman had given his sanction to the notorious Jan Matthys of Münster in the days when he was on the surface a much milder man. Soon Hoffman was a forgotten figure as other leaders rose up claiming ever more remarkable visions and miracles. An old man had predicted Hoffman's imprisonment for half a year. Whereupon Hoffman courted imprisonment, had his will and was put in prison until his death ten years later! (Another prophecy to be rapidly forgotten by the group!) Those who gathered at Münster for the coming of the kingdom eventually sent out 'apostles' to win over others. Obbe Philips heard some and recounts that they said 'how John Matthys had come to them with such signs, miracles and agitation of the Spirit that words failed them to describe it enough to us, and they said we should not doubt but that they were no less sent forth with power and miracles than the apostles at Pentecost. Those words I have reflected on a hundred times.'[68] As well he might.

Menno Simons

In firm and constant opposition to these extremists stood Menno Simons, a former Roman Catholic priest and the emerging Baptist leader. In his writings he could claim that 'from the beginning until the present moment' he had opposed the Münsterites and dissociated himself completely from their errors.[69] Fundamental to the errors of these groups was the belief that a new age had begun and that the gifts were being restored as a sign of the end. Much was built on false interpretations of the book of Revelation. In direct opposition Menno thus announced his commission: 'Brethren, I tell you the truth and lie not. I am no Enoch, I am no Elias, I am not one who sees visions, I am no prophet who can teach and prophesy otherwise than what is written in the Word of God and understood in the Spirit . . . I have no visions nor angelic inspirations . . .'[70] Would to God that more had heeded the simple biblical testimony of this man! Even though he did not have the charisma and personality of many of the leaders of the other section, he did have a balanced view of God's truth.

Luther, Calvin, Beza and Menno stood in succession to early writers such as Chrysostom, Augustine, Basil, Theodoret and others in their opposition to the charismatics of their day. One could hardly label the opposition as 'theological small fry'. Nor could one say that God abandoned them for opposing what many felt was a movement of the Holy Spirit.

8.
The Puritan era

Times of confusion

Prophets and prophetesses abounded in what we normally call the Puritan era. In fact it may be becoming increasingly apparent that they have not been such a rarity as is frequently imagined, especially by those who believe that there have been no claimants till relatively recent times when the gifts have been 'restored'. Thus after referring to the false prophets in biblical times and the fact that they were acted on by a delusion, John Owen, the prince of Puritan expositors, says, 'And no otherwise hath it fallen out with some in our days, whom we have seen visibly acted by an extraordinary power. Unduly pretending unto supernatural agitations from God, they were really acted by the devil; a thing they neither desired nor looked after, but being surprised by it, were pleased with it for a while: as it was with sundry of the Quakers at their first appearance.'[1]

Hence we have the absurd spectacle of the Army Council of Parliament solemnly paying attention to the weird visions of Elizabeth Poole, whose predictions Colonel Rich spoke of reverently as 'that testimony which God hath manifested here by an unexpected providence'. When she warned that the king should not be executed, even the sober Ireton went and had serious conversations with her and heard from her that she had seen a vision.[2] Later Anna Trapnell, a strange northern prophetess, saw Cromwell as the 'little horn', and another public figure was one of a mighty throng down the ages to find himself identified as the 666 of the book of Revelation.[3] On another occasion a party of Levellers disrupted a service and harangued the people on the need to abolish not only the sabbath and tithes but even the Bible itself. Everard, a discharged soldier, proclaimed himself a prophet and claimed to have a vision in which he and his followers were commanded to arise and dig and plough the earth. Whitelocke supplied an interpretation of the vision. 'They threaten,' he alleged, 'to pull down park pales, and to lay all open.' John Owen, called to preach a sermon to refute such wildness alluded to men, 'heady, high-minded, *throwing up all bounds and fences*'.[4] A better man to restore dignity, decorum, law and order and broken fences one could scarcely imagine!

During the Puritan era there were various claimants to the office of apostleship. In opposition an earlier Puritan, Richard Sibbes wrote, *'There is a particular revelation of God's Spirit. This the prophets and apostles had, but now we have no such rule.'*[5] Thomas Watson saw the miraculous powers certifying their distinctive role as he wrote, 'Miracles were used by Moses, Elijah and Christ, and were continued, many years after, by the apostles, to confirm the verity of the Holy Scriptures.'[6] This, of course, is what we have seen taught in Hebrews 2:3,4. 'Many require miracles or new apostles, that maketh them turn seekers,' declares Thomas Manton.[7]

Alluding to the variety of claimants, Thomas Goodwin writes, 'I hear there are apostles abroad, at least those that say there are to be apostles still in the Church, and to the end of the world; and those that affirm it are not of the Romish party only, who make the popedom a perpetual apostleship in the Church, but of those who would be in all other things most contrary to the Pope.'[8] Not content with merely asserting this, Goodwin expounds the passage from the first chapter of the Acts of the Apostles very much as has been done earlier in this book. The upshot is that apostles are seen not merely to be unique in one respect but in many. John Owen agreed, describing their 'extraordinary *call*', 'extraordinary *power*', 'extraordinary *gifts*' and also 'extraordinary *employment* . . . requiring extraordinary labour, travail, zeal, and self-denial'.[9] These are qualities that are not often spoken of in connection with the office. It was not merely privilege!

Therefore the prince of Puritans lists the qualifications of the apostles as (1) *an immediate personal call from God himself,* (2) *a commission to all nations and all churches;* (3) *an authority in all churches;* and (4) *'a collation of extraordinary gifts,* as of infallibility in teaching, of working miracles, speaking with tongues, and the like'.[10] With reference to those who in his day claimed to be apostles, Owen simply alludes to the saying of the Latin author: 'It seems amazing that a soothsayer does not laugh when he sees a soothsayer.'[11] According to Flavel apostles, prophets, evangelists were offices both 'extraordinary and temporary'.[12] Bunyan was clear in his mind that apostles and prophets were with Christ the foundation of the church. He explains Ephesians 2:20 in this way: 'Christ is the foundation personally and meritoriously; but the apostles and prophets, by doctrine, ministerially.'[13] They had no equals and they have no successors. 'Further, the apostles were in that marvellous manner endued with the Holy Ghost, that they outstript all the prophets that ever went before them . . . They, as to their doctrine, were infallible, it was impossible they should err . . .'[14] Paul and Barnabas were both seen as apostles in association with the twelve.[15]

Investigations of Flavel

John Flavel, the celebrated Puritan preacher from Dartmouth, also met with men and women convinced that prophecy was being restored. He refers to the various prophetic outbursts at the time of Luther and mentions Thomas Müntzer by name. (Those who ignore history are destined to repeat it; Flavel was a wiser man than this.) In his case he was dealing with the Familists and their 'pretence unto the spirit of prophecy', together with 'their very pleasing predictions and prophecies'. He sadly affirmed, 'And how catching and bewitching these things are, gaining more respect among these vain spirits than the divine unquestionable prophecies of Scripture, this age hath full and sad experience.'[16] He then quoted the Puritans' great text whenever this subject arose, namely 2 Peter 1:19. The Scripture is sufficient. We need no more. 'The Scripture (saith Luther) is so full, that as for visions and revelations, *Nec curo, nec desidero,* I neither regard nor desire them. And when he himself had a vision of Christ, after a day of fasting and prayer, he cried out, *Avoid Satan, I know no image of Christ but the Scriptures.*'[17]

What a contrast with the climate of expectancy today and what a contrast to a book published in Flavel's own area, where in 1649 Ann Wells and Matthew Hall made free confession of deluding the people of Wheatfield in Suffolk 'with such pretended voices, visions, prophecies, and revelations, the like have scarcely been heard of in England, since the reformation. Multitudes of people were deluded by them'! Again we note the large numbers deceived, and the interesting fact that when the woman recanted, 'her partisans laboured four days to suppress and stifle it, but to no purpose'.[18] In the light of this, Flavel reminded those who glibly told people to accept prophecy but at the same time to test the spirits: 'Consider how difficult, yea, and impossible it is for a man to determine, that such a voice, vision, or revelation, is of God; and that Satan cannot feign or counterfeit it; seeing he hath left no certain marks by which we may distinguish one spirit from another . . . Sure we are, Satan can transform himself into an angel of light; and therefore abandoning all those unsafe and uncertain ways, whereby swarms of errors have been conveyed into the world, let us cleave inseparably to the sure word of prophecy, the rule and stand of our faith and duty.'[19]

The devil and prediction

Gurnall in *The Christian in Complete Armour* simply declared, 'When I see any miraculously gifted, as the prophets and apostles, then I shall think the immediate calling they pretend to is authentic.'[20] It is obvious that in his experience no prophetic figure had passed the test. However, he was convinced that there were those who qualified as false prophets and his analysis of how Satan was able to gain credence for them is a masterly one. 'And predictions surely may pass very well for secrets,' he begins.[21] The devil longs to compete with God, whose unique power it is to predict. He cites Isaiah 41:23. But what can we say of the devil who desires a reputation in this sphere? 'But alas! his predictions are no more true prophecies, than his miracles are true miracles.' 'For his predictions are either dark and dubious, cunningly packed and laid, that, like a picture in *plicis* – folds, they carried two faces under one hood; and in these folds, the subtle serpent wrapped himself, on purpose to save his credit, which way soever the event fell out.'[22] Gurnall gives three methods the devil uses. Firstly, he can spot natural causes and tendencies, as a doctor can predict by observing tell-tale signs that a man is dying. Secondly, he can weigh up political and moral causes, and make a shrewd guess. '*Third*. God may, and doth, sometimes *reveal future events to Satan*, as when God intends him to be his instrument to execute some of his purposes, he *may and doth, acquaint him with the same, some time before*. And you will not say the hangman is a prophet, that can tell such a man shall, on such a day, be beheaded or hanged, when he hath a warrant from the king that appoints him to do that office.'[23] Thus Satan, having been permitted by God to afflict Job, could have predicted this by some means. But prophecy from God is of a totally different order. 'Who but God could tell Abraham where his posterity should be, and what should particularly befall them, four hundred years after his death? For so long before was he acquainted with their deliverance out of Egypt, Genesis 15, which accordingly came to pass punctually on the very day foretold, Exodus 12:41. How admirable are the prophecies of Christ the Messiah, in which his person, birth, life, and death, even to the minute and circumstances of them, are as exactly and particularly set down, many ages before his coming upon the stage . . .'[24]

The teaching of John Owen

As is so often the case, the most thorough-going treatment of this question comes from the pen of John Owen, who turns to this theme in many of his works. His simple argument is that the prophets received new revelations and infallible inspiration from God. Speaking of the Spirit he says, 'The first way of his teaching is by immediate inspiration, communicating new sacred truths from God immediately unto the minds of men. So he taught the *prophets* and *apostles*, and all the penmen of the Scripture.'[25] Their utterances, as they themselves knew, were then infallible.[26] Listen to this categorical affirmation in response to a former writer who held a view of prophecy as a 'mixed phenomenon'. 'That men receiving any revelation from God had always an assurance that such it was, to me seems most certain: neither could I ever approve the note of Gregory on Ezekiel 1, – namely, "That prophets, being accustomed to prophesying, did often-times speak of their own spirit, supposing that it proceeded from the Spirit of prophecy." What is this but to question the truth of all prophetical revelations, and to shake the faith that is built upon it?' After citing various scriptures, he then states, 'But that any true prophets should not know a true revelation from a motion of their own hearts wants not much of blasphemy.'[27] Moreover all true prophets were endowed in a supernatural way, even though this might often be 'the power of discerning', rather than the performance of a miracle.[28]

Revelation is complete

Now the extraordinary gifts bestowed for the establishment of the gospel have ceased, in Owen's view: 'For nothing in such a way shall ever again take place, God having ultimately revealed his mind concerning his worship and our salvation, a curse being denounced to man or angel that shall pretend to revelation for the altering or changing one jot or tittle of the gospel.'[29] What then of claimants to revelation apart from that given to understand the mind of God in the Scripture itself? His answer once more is plain and decided. Speaking of revelations he says, 'They are of two sorts – objective and subjective. Those of the former sort, whether they contain doctrines contrary unto that of the Scripture, or additional thereunto, or seemingly confirmatory thereof, they are all universally to be rejected, the former being absolutely false, the latter useless. Neither have any of the operations of the Spirit pleaded for the least respect unto them; for he having finished the whole work of external revelation, and closed it in the Scripture, his whole internal spiritual work is suited and commensurate thereunto. By subjective revelations, nothing is intended but that work of spiritual illumination whereby we are enabled to discern and understand the mind of God in the Scripture; which the apostle prays for in the behalf of all believers (Eph. 1:16-19) . . .'[30]

All this leads to constant warnings from the brotherhood against those who seek guidance or assurance via such revelations, voices or vision. Brooks, after asking, 'How shall we know the whispering of the Holy Spirit from the hissing of the old serpent?' warns specifically against those who advocate listening for an 'outward voice'.[31] Elsewhere 2 Peter 1:19 is again his stand-by and, after alluding to the experience of Luther, he quotes Augustine's very relevant plea: 'Lord, let the holy Scriptures be my pure delights, in which I can neither deceive or ever be deceived.'[32] Then he recounts the counsel of one of old to a lady who had importuned him to pray that he might receive a 'revelation' assuring him that her sins had been pardoned. His answer is very apposite: 'That it was a hard and altogether useless matter which she required of him; it was difficult for him to obtain, as being unworthy to have the secret counsels of God to be imparted to him, and it was as unprofitable for her to know: and that, first, because such a revelation might make her too secure; and secondly, because it was impossible for him to demonstrate and make known unto her or any other the truth and infallibility of the revelation which he had received to be from God, so that, should she afterwards call into question the truth of it, as well she might, her troubles and doubtings concerning her salvation would have been as great as they were before.'[33] In this context he speaks of many hundreds in the nation being deluded in this kind of way.

We append a paragraph from many which could be culled from the writings of Flavel where he gives an identical emphasis: 'The teaching of God, and our hearing and learning of him, is not to be understood of any extraordinary visional appearances, or oraculous and immediate voice of God to men: God indeed hath so appeared unto some (Num. 12:8). Such voices have been heard from heaven, but now these extraordinary ways are ceased (Heb. 1:1,2) and we are no more to expect them; we may sooner meet with satanical delusions than divine illuminations in this way. I remember, the learned Gerson tells us that the devil once appeared to an holy man in prayer, personating Christ, and saying, "I am come in person to visit thee, for thou art worthy." But he with both hands shut his eyes, saying, *"Nolo hic Christum videre, satis est ipsum in gloria videre;"* i.e. "I will not see Christ here; it is enough for me to see him in glory." We are now to attend only to the voice of the Spirit in the Scriptures: this is a more sure word than any voice from heaven (2 Peter 1:19).'[34]

Gifts and the unconverted

This leads Puritan writers to say times without number that Balaam and many others had the gifts but were not saved.[35] Brooks puts it succinctly: 'The devil hath greater gifts than any man on earth, and yet he is a devil still.'[36] With reference to those times when predictions from false prophets come true, Flavel has a very discerning word about this perplexing problem. He writes, after alluding to the fact that those indulging in witchcraft may help to detect a murder or fraud, (shades of the police force consulting spiritists in our day!), 'Though it be not his (the devil's) interest merely to discover it, yet it is certainly his interest to precipitate wicked men, and hasten their ruin by the hand of Justice; and he will speak the truth, and seem to own a righteous cause, to bring about his great design of ruining the souls and bodies of men.'[37] Ultimately he wishes to lead people astray from the Word. There are many examples of him seeking to do this in the Puritan era. Thus John Bunyan describes how the Quakeress Ann Blackly, in the midst of a large group, bade him, 'To throw away the Scriptures! His prompt reply was 'No, for then the devil would be too hard for me.'[38] Bunyan vividly describes how the devil 'labours to render the doctrine of the Lord Jesus, and salvation by him alone, very odious and low: and also his ordinances, as hearing, reading, meditation, use of the Scriptures . . .', and also 'pretends to lead them up into some higher light, mysteries, and revelations of the Spirit, into which a very few have attained or can attain'.[39] John Owen likewise sees his tactics in these same areas: 'Not long since, his great design, as I manifested, was to cry up ordinances without the Spirit, casting all the reproach that he could upon him; – now, to cry up a spirit without and against ordinances, casting all reproach and contempt possible upon them. Then, he would have a *ministry* without the *Spirit:* – now, a *Spirit* without a *ministry*. Then, the *reading* of the word might suffice, without either preaching or praying by the Spirit; – now, the *Spirit* is enough, without reading or studying the word at all.'[40] In all this we see how the evil one loves to drive people to unbiblical extremes. He can, to further this end, use lying miracles, as Bunyan avers, though Owen contends that these are always, when closely scrutinized, false miracles, since

Satan cannot work a real one.[41] Flavel narrates in some detail how the devil can use apparitions and all kind of fascinating lying wonders to further his own ends.[42]

To the Word alone

'To the word alone!' is the clarion call of the Puritan brethren as a whole. 'God never intended to abolish his Word by giving his Spirit,' declares Flavel.[43] Therefore he warns of those following the Spirit without the Scriptures: 'So dangerous it is to separate what God hath conjoined, and father our own fancies upon the Holy Spirit.'[44] Scarcely has this concept ever been put more finely than by Brooks when he wrote, 'The word is that triumphant chariot of the Spirit, wherein he rides conquering and to conquer the souls of men.'[45] 'Here a lamb may wade, and an elephant may swim; here is milk for babes, and meat for strong men,' he also writes.[46] And Greenham reminds all those who would turn aside and study countless other themes: 'A young disciple asking an old rabbi whether he might not have time to learn the Greek tongue, he said, if he would do it neither by night nor by day he might, because by night and day he was to study the law: hereby he intimated that scholars' greatest study should be in the word of God. Paul therefore exhorts Timothy to give attendance to reading, to exhortation, to doctrine; he bids him "meditate upon these things, give himself wholly to them," (1 Tim. 4:15); his whole strength and time should be in them. Man's life is short; and if it were never so long, it should be spent in the knowledge of the Holy Scriptures.'[47]

There is a sense in which the Scriptures displace all the gifts. Many of the other gifts of the Spirit have not been discussed in this book. Yet I would agree with John Owen who said that all those gifts listed in 1 Corinthians were extraordinary.[48] Let us take one example to illustrate the argument of this paragraph, namely, the gift of discerning spirits. Says Owen, 'And upon the ceasing of extraordinary gifts really given from God, the gift also of discerning spirits ceased, and we are left unto the *word alone* for the trial of any that shall pretend unto them.'[49] Flavel in a work significantly entitled *The Touchstone of Sincerity or The Signs of Grace, and Symptoms of Hypocrisy* admits, 'I pretend not to any gift of

discerning spirits: such an extraordinary gift there once was in
the church, and very necessary for those times (wherein Satan
was so busy and the *canon* of Scripture not completed) which
the apostle calls the gift of *discerning spirits* . . .' He then
mentions Acts 5:1-11 as an example of this gift of infallible
discernment and says that we have it in this way no more. But
he adds, 'But the ordinary aids and assistances of the Spirit are
with us still; and the lively oracles are among us still; to them
we may freely go for the resolution of all doubts . . .'[50] Any
reader who feels that the Puritans are inferring that we are
deprived in our age has not understood them. In their
incessant appeal to 2 Peter 1:19 they are stating that God has
given us a surer word.[51] Therefore God gives us 'wisdom' and
'discernment' via study of the Word and even the passage on
tongues is not rendered irrelevant for them. Bunyan draws
from it the lesson that prayers must be understood and not
based on empty recitation of the Book of Common Prayer![52]
Owen says we can draw lessons from it by 'the way of analogy'.[53]

Puritan views on 1 Corinthians 13

It must be conceded that most Puritans applied 1 Corinthians
13 to heaven, despite the fact that they felt that Scripture
taught that the gifts had ceased. Thus Brooks movingly
expounds this passage in relation to our deeper knowledge in
heaven, feeling sure that our knowledge there will be complete.
Yet he does refer in the course of his exposition to 'the glass of
his word'.[54] Owen likewise sees the passage as referring to
heaven but lands himself in inconsistencies. He has to say that
our knowledge here is so fitful and incomplete. But then he
goes on, 'But here it must be observed, that the description
and representation of the Lord Christ and his glory in the
Gospel is not absolutely or in itself either dark or obscure; yea,
it is perspicuous, plain, and direct. Christ is therein evidently
set forth crucified, exalted, glorified. But the apostle doth not
here discourse concerning the way or means of the revelation
of it unto us, but of the means or instrument whereby we
comprehend that revelation. This is our faith, which, as it is in
us, being weak and imperfect, we comprehend the
representation that is made unto us of the glory of Christ as

men do the sense of a dark saying, a riddle, a parable; that is, imperfectly, and with difficulty.'[55] Owen here has moved away from exposition of the text. And this is also what Bunyan has to do when he discusses the passage in *The Saints' Knowledge of Christ's Love,* an exposition of Ephesians 3:18,19. In a very moving passage Bunyan, rightly in my view, says that even if all the knowledge of the redeemed were shared and all angelic awareness thrown in as well, we would never fully know the love of God and Christ. He candidly admits the difficulty: 'I know it says also *that we shall know even as we are known.* But yet this must not be understood, as *if* we should know God as fully as he knows us.'[56] Well said, John Bunyan! It needs saying. The passage is not referring at all to that kind of knowledge which, even in heaven, would not be possessed by humans. So let the reader get down to sorting out the real meaning and here again in a passage of imagination rather than strict exposition John Bunyan will prove the most helpful. We turn in fact to *Pilgrim's Progress,* where we read of Mercy seeing a looking glass in Interpreter's house and discovering what the glass was: 'Now the glass was one of a thousand. It would present a man, one way, with his own features exactly (James 1:23), and, turn it but another way, and it would show one the very face and similitude of the Prince of Pilgrims himself (1 Cor. 13:12). Yea, I have talked with them that can tell, and they have said, that they have seen the very crown of thorns upon his head, by looking in that glass; they have therein also seen the holes in his hands, in his feet, and his side (2 Cor. 3:18). Yea, such an excellency is there in that glass, that it will show him to one where they have a mind to see him; whether living or dead; whether in earth or heaven; whether in a state of humiliation, or in his exaltation; whether coming to suffer, or coming to reign.'[57] It must be noted that here Bunyan applies 1 Corinthians 13:12 to the Word of God! In another work, *The Water of Life,* he writes, with reference to God's throne: 'We must also labour for more clear Scripture knowledge of this throne; for the holy Word of God is the perspective glass by which we may, and the magnifying glass that will cause us to behold "with open face, the glory of the Lord" (2 Cor. 3:18).'[58] Gurnall too refers to the Word as a 'glass'.[59] Surely Richard Sibbes was not far from the mark when he exclaimed, 'The opening of the Scriptures is the opening of heaven.'[60]

Conversion as a great miracle

Not only are we not impoverished today with respect to God's revelation, but also we are not behind people of the New Testament in our experience of the miraculous. Flavel, like all the Puritans, knew that conversion was the greatest of all miracles. 'There are no wonders in nature like those in grace,' is rapidly followed by an exhortation to 'remember the work of grace is creation work'.[61] For Bunyan, to see a man turning to Christ is 'one of the highest wonders in the world'.[62] Gurnall puts it like this: 'When souls are converted, "the blind receive their sight." You were "darkness", but now "light in the Lord". "The lame walk" in that the affections – the soul's feet – are set at liberty, and receive strength to run the ways of God with delight. Lepers are cleansed, in that filthy lusts are cured, and foul souls are sanctified.'[63] Listen to Thomas Watson extolling conversion: 'The power of God is seen in the conversion of souls. The same power draws a sinner to God that drew Christ out of the grave to heaven (Eph. 1:20). Greater power is put forth in conversion than in creation. When God made the world, he met with no opposition; as he had nothing to help him, so he had nothing to hinder him; but when he converts a sinner, he meets with opposition. Satan opposes him, and the heart opposes him; a sinner is angry with converting grace. The world was the "work of God's fingers" (Ps. 8:3). Conversion is the "work of God's arm" (Luke 1:51). In the creation, God wrought but one miracle, he spake the word; but, in conversion, he works many miracles; the blind is made to see, the dead is raised, the deaf hears the voice of the Son of God.'[64] And how beautifully does Thomas Adams depict the whole process! 'Yea, even still God works miracles, though we take no notice of them. That our hearts should be converted by preaching, this is a miracle. That our faith should believe above reason, this is a miracle. That Satan doth not destroy us, this is a miracle. If he does not fetch water out of a rock, yet he fetcheth repentance out of sin, and makes the stony heart gush out tears; this is a greater miracle. If he does not turn water into wine, yet he turns our sorrow into joy; as great a miracle. If he does not feed five thousand bodies with a few loaves, yet he feeds five thousand souls with one sermon; as great a miracle.'[65]

Obviously marvellous happenings were not discounted. Bunyan refers to the uncanny experience of a great wind during the season of his conversion, something which 'in twenty years' time' he has not been able 'to make a judgement of'. 'I lay not the stress of my salvation thereupon, but upon the Lord Jesus, in the promise,' he adds.[66] There is scarcely a more ecstatic account in all extra-biblical literature than that of Flavel's heavenly meditations while travelling on horseback, so that with his nose running with blood, he arrived at his destination hardly knowing where he was. Yet he adds, 'He many years after called that day one of the days of heaven, and professed he understood more of the light of heaven by it, than by all the books he ever read, or discourses he ever had entertained about it.' 'This was indeed, an extraordinary fore-taste of heaven for degree, but it came in the ordinary way and method of faith and meditation.'[67] Flavel also refers to the prognostications of John Knox and certain strange deaths and Bunyan, especially in *The Life and Death of Mr Badman*, is not averse to telling a hair-raising story of judgement.[68] But always the stress is on the final judgement of Scripture on all things.

We leave the last two words to Owen and Flavel, who have perhaps provided us with the bulk of our quotations. Owen writes sadly on the state of real religion in his time: 'There is, indeed, a broad light fallen upon the men of this generation, and together therewith many spiritual gifts communicated, which, with some other considerations, have wonderfully enlarged the bounds of professors and profession; both they and it are exceedingly multiplied and increased. Hence there is a noise of religion and religious duties in every corner, preaching in abundance – and that not in an empty, light, trivial, and vain manner as formerly, but to a good proportion of a spiritual gift – so that if you will measure the number of believers by light, gifts, and profession, the church may have cause to say, "Who hath born me all these?" But now if you will take the measure of them by this great discriminating grace of Christians, perhaps you will find their number not so multiplied.'[69] Flavel pertinently remarks, 'Nothing is more common in the world, than for an old error to obtain afresh under the name of a new light. Satan hath the very art of turning stale errors after the mode of the present times, and making them current and passable as new discoveries, and rare novelties.'[70]

9.
The French prophets

The French prophets had an influence on a number of groups in various eras. We shall look at them as one looks at a stream which at times flows underground but surfaces and is clearly visible on at least six occasions. Firstly, we shall look at their origins in France around 1688. Secondly, we shall look at their re-emergence in France at the turn of the century in the year 1700. Thirdly, we shall trace the first rising of the stream in England in events between 1706 and 1710. Fourthly, we shall return to France for a very important debate on this whole matter in the 1720s. Fifthly, we shall observe the stream again bursting forth in England during the first years of the Methodist Revival from 1738 onwards. Our sixth and final glimpse will be when the stream reappeared and joined with other currents in New England in the 1740s. It will be particularly important to notice in the last three stages the reaction of prominent evangelical men to this movement and their assessment of it and of kindred groups.

Origins of the movement

The movement seems to have had its origin in Dauphine, among the Huguenots, or French Protestants, in the Mont Peyrat region in the year 1688. To a people harried by sorrows and persecutions a glass-blower brought back from his travels a treatise on the book of Revelation called *Accomplishment of the Prophecies of the Approaching Deliverance of the Church,* which was a work which interpreted the death of the two witnesses in Revelation 11 as having recently take place. It then foresaw their coming to life again as foreshadowing a deliverance of the church which would take place in 1689. Youths and children

were apprised of this teaching and amid sensations of heat and
frequent paroxysms they gave forth a stream of utterances.

One authority comments on this: 'It was reckoned one of
the miracles of the phenomenon that peasants unable to read,
and young children who spoke habitually in patois, should
pronounce long exhortations in good French; but this was
easily accounted for; their oracular eloquence was only a
reminiscence of what they had heard at the meetings.'[1]
Despite the imprisonment of these juvenile prophets the
movement continued to gain ground in Dauphine and the
Vivarais. Women were also prominent and when a travelling
advocate from Grenoble heard one of them preach and pray,
he said, 'I thought... I was listening to an angel. The sermon
was so pathetic yet animated.'[2] Soon afterwards this particular
preacher was imprisoned and consigned to an unknown fate.
Other women proved equally outspoken in face of danger.

Meanwhile at La Capelle, a little girl tending cows
professed to see an angelic vision. A child of her own size,
dressed in a white robe, emerged from a bush, declaring, 'My
sister, I am come down from the Lord Jesus to forbid thee to
go any more to Mass.'[3] Soon folk began abandoning the
Roman Catholic churches and parents alarmed at this trend
sought to shut up their children and even threatened to kill
them. A rich peasant and his wife were hanged for allowing
their two sons about twenty to prophesy. Then, just as
suddenly as it had arisen, the agitation subsided. For several
years little was heard of the prophets. Yet it was but a brief
pause, before the movement gathered greater force and
became even more prominent.

Re-emergence after decline

In 1700 the second phase began, when the embers were fanned
to a flame. Amid continuous and remorseless persecution
against Protestants, the prophets reappeared. Because of this
background one writer has understandably commented that
'This state of unnatural excitement was the result of
protracted and relentless persecution, mental and bodily
suffering, the reproaches of conscience, and the deprivation of
those religious exercises which the people so dearly loved.'[4]

Prophetic figures ranged from older men, like Daniel Raul leaving his plough, to young girls of five years of age. At the meetings prophets silenced each other. There were periods of fasting. Roman Catholic priests were alarmed at outcries against the mass and the labelling of their church as Babylon. Children were even sent to the galleys. In due course prophets laid claim to other gifts, such as healing the sick, exorcising demons, passing unharmed through fire and practising clairvoyance.

Excitement intensified as prophets, goaded by physical atrocities against Protestants, proclaimed that God was going to raise 40,000 prophets and urged that priests, seen in a vision as 'black oxen' gobbling up the produce of a garden, should be driven out. Typical of their mood were the words of one at the capture of a leading persecutor when he said, 'The Spirit wills that he should die.'[5] One of their number, Cavalier, often compared to an Ironside, described them thus: 'Neither quarrels, nor grudges, nor calumny, nor larceny had any place amongst us. All our possessions were in common; we were of one heart and one soul. Swearing, cursing, filthy conversation were wholly eschewed; and the overseers whom we had appointed to preserve order had the poor and the sick especially under their care.'[6] Considerable weight must be given to this testimony. They were not just a band of ragamuffins and rogues. There were high ideals in the movement. There was real care. Yet dangerously the prayer meeting and council of war were often identical.

However, as butchering and vengeance killings continued, one of their own highly respected preachers, himself suffering in prison and condemned to be broken alive, addressed a plea to them. He spoke bluntly of 'incendiaries and murderers' and of 'troops of madmen who boast of being inspired by the Holy Spirit', who were yet 'blinded by the demon of pride'.[7] Sadly few heeded him or the contradictions as amid a spiral of violence one prophet declared for a person's death and another against. Women prophetesses were often most bloodthirsty, many of them marching with the army. Inevitably after one terrible defeat faith in the prophets was shaken and we have the sad spectacle of a leader, Roland, having to draw lots to see which prophet was right after two had badly clashed after being consulted. Many of the prophets when captured died with an almost brutal courage. Attempts to gain sympathy from abroad were largely failures as they were regarded as rebels by most foreign governments.

The group reaches England

Some of the inhabitants of England had opportunity to assess their claims when, in 1706, a group came to England. Despite the fact that the Huguenot church in London repudiated them and that in 1707 three of their leaders were sentenced to the pillory, they soon gained a following even among the rich and well-to-do. Among their followers were Francis Moult, a chemist, Nicholas Fagio, a learned foreigner and Francis Misson, the author of *A New Voyage to Italy*. (The presence of scientific, foreign or literary names on a society's notepaper does not automatically mean biblical orthodoxy.) Sir Richard Bulkeley was also a fervent patron and we have a picture of him under the influence of the levelling prophet Abraham Whitrow, who 'preaches up the doctrine of levelling, or that the rich must part with all their estates, and become poor, if ever they designed to enter the Kingdom of Heaven'.[8] (It is also evident that titled patronage is in itself no guarantee of soundness!)

The best known of the converts actually opposed this levelling doctrine and since he himself was a prophet we can see that the oracles were not always in agreement. This was John Lacy, who wrote extensively in favour of the movement. A former member of the congregation of Dr Calamy at Westminster, he caused heated discussion when he claimed to be following the command of the Spirit to leave his wife and co-habit with a young prophetess. It is noteworthy that the Shakers later claimed to have been directly influenced by the movement, that another prophetic figure Richard Brothers read Lacy's works and, later still, Edward Irving had some of Lacy's writings reprinted.[9] That we are not dealing with someone who was immediately recognizable as unorthodox or extremist is shown by the comment made by John Wesley much later, on 15 August 1750, when he wrote in his journal, with reference to a book published by Lacy, 'By reflecting on an odd book which I read on this journey, *The General Delusion of Christians with regard to Prophecy,* I was fully convinced of what I had long suspected: (1) That the Montanists, in the second and third centuries, were real, scriptural Christians; and (2) That the grand reason why the miraculous gifts were so soon withdrawn, was not only that faith and holiness were well nigh lost, but that dry, formal, orthodox men began even then to ridicule whatever gifts they had not themselves, and to decry them all as either madness or imposture.'[10] This must be balanced, as we shall see, by other judgements of Wesley and it must be stressed that he was in the habit of making snap judgements as he journeyed and read on horseback (perhaps not the best place for reflective study), yet all these factors lead us to see that the French prophets out of the setting of the wars in France had some appeal for a variety of men.

Lacy described how there were agitations and trances and how boys and girls 'of the dregs of mankind, who could not so much as read, quote many texts of the Holy Scriptures'.[11] One of them, urged in England to renounce these gifts, replied, 'I am in no wise the framer of these bodily agitations I suffer in my ecstasies, I do not move my own self, but am moved by a power independent that overrules me; and for the words that proceed from my mouth, I protest with the same awful solemnity, they are formed without my intention, and glide forth of my lips without my direction, my mind no ways bearing any part in that marvellous operation by preceding forethought, or any attending will to deliver what I do at that instant.'[12] Thus he attributed it to another power and stressed the non-involvement of the mind in its conception and utterance.

Claims to supernatural insights

Elias Marion, the most noted of those who came to this country, spoke similarly of being 'taken over' and was able to reveal in detail the sins of another person so that the one thus exposed could affirm that he 'set them forth before all the company, as if he had seen or read them in my own heart'.[13] After quoting a previous incident involving a girl of fourteen or fifteen who was able to describe by revelation the result of a battle that was taking place some distance away, Lacy writes, 'Abundance of people of sobriety and reputation have assured me it was common with the inspired to discover the thoughts of others, and to reveal many things which they could not be acquainted with in a natural way. When this girl came to herself, I asked her if she could repeat what she had said; she answered, No.'[14] Yet it must be recalled that, despite the fact that they were convinced that it was by the Spirit's direction that they had taken arms against the king's troops, they were defeated quite decisively and their predictions about the speedy downfall of Babylon, or the Roman Catholic Church, were not fulfilled.

These preoccupations with battles and this undercurrent of violence seem to have spilled over on the English scene. One young printer drawn to the movement describes how his sister, 'a lusty young woman', flung another prophetess on the floor and violently trampled upon her, stamping furiously. 'This was adjudged to be a sign of the fall of the whore of Babylon,' he explains.[15] Here we have prophetic symbolism with a vengeance! The same witness also describes prophets dragging each other about at the home of Francis Moult. He adds these very significant words: 'For my part I had such a thorough belief of the divinity of the spirit presiding, that had John Potter ['a great prophet'], under operation, commanded me to kill my father, mother, or even the late Queen on the throne, I sincerely believe I should immediately have attempted.'[16] All the terrible dangers of suggestibility are summed up in this honest testimony.

All the prophecies of Mr Lacy which were in print were larger than all those of Scripture put together. Although he admitted it was difficult to prove their authenticity conclusively from Scripture yet he claimed it was God's voice though 'it admits no demonstration to sensual persons'.[17] Referring to the world's opposition he asked rhetorically why real believers should suffer unnecessarily if God had not spoken to them. 'Was there ever anyone acted by a spirit of delusion, that hath not advanced, uttered, anything contrary to the Scriptures or dissonant from them?'[18] Furthermore, was not his attack on the devil and his followers proof of this genuineness? Was it not true that 'the apostles so received the holy anointing that the same was to be diffused more than in their days'?[19] He claimed to speak in other languages such as Latin, Greek and French, obviously referring to the gift of tongues. Sir Richard Bulkeley claimed to have heard Mr

Dutton 'utter with great readiness and freedom complete discourses in Hebrew, for near a quarter of an hour together, and sometimes much longer'.[20] (B.B. Warfield ironically suggests that the attestors to all this often were as ignorant of the languages spoken as most boys are of Latin today.) There were also claims to healing, including one reported cure of blindness.

Specific predictions
However, ultimately the group in London made clear predictions. One of these was that dreadful judgements were going to fall on London within three weeks. When this did not happen, although the prophet had originally said they were normal weeks they suddenly became 'prophetic weeks', which were somewhat more elastic! (Even with the reprieve the prophecy proved a dud!) There was also an express prediction from several prophets that a Dr Emes, who died on 22 December 1707, was to be raised from the dead on 25 May 1708. Inevitably a paper had then to be written: 'Squire Lacy's reasons why Dr Emes was not raised.' Lacy said the miracle had been postponed because of the danger of the large crowd molesting the risen prophet. It is an old, old story. Daniel Defoe, observing all this in the April before the predicted date, wrote, 'I shall readily own with them, that if the God of life pleases to restore the soul to his abandoned carcase, according to their prediction, this thing is of Him; but I would caution my readers to hold them to the point, that, if it fails, they may own they were deluded.'[21] Is it not true that we need today more people who will 'hold them to the point'?

As the date was approached Defoe also noticed their wavering and vacillating and shrewdly observed that 'Foreseeing that a disappointment will at once bring their whole cause into contempt, they have laid a foundation for keeping the delusion on foot, and buoying up the credulity of their followers. Their champion, Sir Richard Bulkeley, has advanced a new hypothesis; which if they can reconcile to the nature of prophetic inspiration, is most politicly brought forward. It is this: that it is not essential to constitute a true prophet, that what he prophesies should come to pass. The Scripture tells us of prophesying lies; *They shall prophesy lies in my name.*'[22] With all these desperate expedients they sought to avert the derision and disbelief that undoubtedly awaited them. For his part Defoe thought they needed compassion rather than contempt and he expressed the hope that protection might be given to them by the civil authorities when an enraged mob found that the resurrection did not take place. (It was scheduled for a day which was a public holiday.)

After the failure in the performance of the miracle, Defoe exhorted the deluded people to return to their senses. 'I do confess,' he wrote, 'the prevalency of this delusion has been surprising, and nothing has been more strange to me in it, than to see men of sense and good character fall in with it; men that have been all their lives religiously disposed, masters of reason, well read in the Scriptures, and sound in the principles of the Christian religion. That these men should have been thus deluded, seems to signify something more than if it had been the common enthusiasm of men weak in judgement, wild in notion, and easy to be imposed upon.'[23] These words need pondering very much, especially by those who in our own day feel that a large group of sensible people cannot be imposed upon by such a delusion.

A vital debate in France

We return to France for the fourth episode in the story. It is largely the story of two men, Antoine Court and Benjamin Du Plan, both of whom had been called through the ministry of prophetesses. The former was deeply impressed by the word of a prophetess soon after his conversion, in which he was told: 'The sword which thou seest at my servant's side is my Word, which shall be in his mouth like a two-edged sword; the plentiful dew which thou has seen descend upon his head is the same Word which shall dwell abundantly with him.'[24] Almost instantly Court began preaching. He was applauded and encouraged by the small group, most of whom were women. Though he knew the suffering that lay ahead, he determined from then on to consecrate himself to the ministry of Christ's church.

Yet soon his feelings about the prophets and prophetesses underwent an abrupt and complete change. Concerned with the lack of discipline, he groaned at what he called their 'puerile utterances', feeling some were 'impostors' and some 'dupes'.[25] The fact of women preaching, the custom of speaking all at once and the whole aura of extravagancy led him to open opposition. He earned immediate antagonism as he recommended the silencing of the prophets. Yet so great was the drift away from Scripture and sound gospel teaching that in the year 1715 a manuscript had been circulated in Lower Languedoc, called *The Book of the Spirit*, in which it was asserted that 'God the Father had done His work, Christ had finished His, and it was now the turn of the Holy Spirit.'[26]

Court felt he must meet the 'inspired' head-on. Therefore when a prophetess had been speaking for a while in tongues and then began addressing each of her hearers in French, Court interrupted the customary applause which ensued and cried that this was not, from God. Many, angered by his protest, left. He then sought to convince others by vigorous door-to-door work. Some have felt that he acted with too heavy a hand and with too little discrimination. One writer, after arguing that people were often fed by the prophets who were preaching 'only repentance, pardon for sin, holiness, and charity', had claimed that 'The sober-minded among the prophets were always ready to submit their doctrines to the test of Holy Scripture.'[27]

This was certainly the view of Du Plan, who claimed to oppose deception and excess and who later addressed this plea to Court: 'I have always maintained both in public and private, that there have been amongst us, and still are, those who have received extraordinary gifts from the Holy Spirit. I could name some who possess the characters set down in your letter as essential to a true prophet.'[28] However, despite this seemingly moderate and balanced statement, Du Plan was in trouble with the church at home on various occasions for his contact with the prophets. After defending him on an earlier occasion, Court refused to do so again when, in 1744, his connection with the French prophets, now in London, formed one ground for his deposition. While it is good to know that later there were real reconciliations between these two courageous men, it is evident in view of what we shall say in a moment about the activities of the French prophets in London that Du Plan's judgement was hardly to be trusted.

In the letter of Court to which Du Plan alluded, Court had

gone right to the heart of the matter. The intensity of Court's feelings in 1721, when he spoke of the horror he felt that 'These people attribute their foolish imaginations and extravagancies to the Holy Spirit', ultimately led to this fine plea to Du Plan: 'The marks of a true prophet are holiness of life, a generous courage, knowledge of the future, power to discern men's secret thoughts. Above all, he must always speak the truth; if he swerve ever so little in this respect, he is a cheat, an impostor. Bring your prophets of the present day to this test, and you will discover only deceivers and liars.'[29] This was the issue then, is the issue today and will always be the nub of the matter.

Disruptive effect on Methodism

Despite the failure of the resurrection attempt, the French prophets were still very much in action in London in 1738. They seemed waiting in the wings to bring confusion and heartache to the leaders of the Methodist revival. It must be recalled that the Wesleys were converted in 1738 and by the following year, in company with Whitefield and others, they were on the road and in the field. Societies were being established. Converts were being built up. In January 1739 John Wesley was taken to a house where, in his words, 'there was one of those commonly called French prophets'.[30] He describes the 'convulsive motion' of her body and the signs, and recounts the prophecy, which was more or less a few Scripture sentences strung together. After she had spoken much ('all as in the person of God') on the fulfilment of prophecy and the spread of the gospel, 'she exhorted us not to be in haste in judging her spirit to be or not to be of God'.[31] Wesley then comments, 'Two or three of our company were much affected, and believed she spoke by the Spirit of God. But this was in no wise clear to me. The motion might be either hysterical or artificial. And the same words any person of a good understanding and well versed in the Scriptures might have spoken. But I let the matter alone; knowing this, that "if it be not of God, it will come to nought."'[32]

Six months later he was describing his experience with Mrs Cooper, another prophetess whose agitations were far less noticeable. She spoke for more than thirty minutes. One phrase she used to Wesley was 'Thou art yet in darkness. But yet a little while and I will rend the veil, and thou shalt see the King in his beauty' – strange and somewhat irrelevant words to a man who was converted and not in any particular mood of despondency.[33] Wesley concludes his comments with this: 'I felt no power while she spoke. Appearances are against her, but I judge nothing before the time.'[34] While it must be remembered that at this time both Wesley brothers were but babes in Christ, they certainly were not easily taken in by these pretensions, although others evidently were. Only a little later in the same month Wesley was having to call on Whitehead, whom he describes as 'hindered by some of those called French prophets'. That he immediately added, 'Woe unto the prophets, saith the Lord, who prophesy in my name, and I have not sent them,' clearly shows his feelings, especially as that very evening he strongly warned the society at Weaver's Hall about such matters.[35]The congregation there were strongly urged not to be unduly or dangerously impressed by any 'dreams, visions or revelations supposed to be made' to prophets and prophetesses but to test by the law and the testimony.[36]

Shrewdness of Charles Wesley

Charles Wesley had an encounter with the movement even before his brother. He tells us in his *Journal*,'I lodged at Mr Hollis's, who entertained me with his French prophets, equal in his account, if not superior, to the Old Testament ones.'[37] Notwithstanding his host's obvious admiration, when forced to share a bedroom with this man and hearing him speaking in tongues, ('gobbled like a turkey-cock' is Wesley's phrase) the evangelist began exorcising an evil spirit, so impressed was he by the genuineness of his partner! 'I did not sleep very sound with Satan so near me,' he adds.[38]

That Charles Wesley had a readier and more perceptive eye for rogues and charlatans in this matter, as in the case of the groaning, writhing 'converts', is quite evident, as is equally clear the group's own dislike of one who had seen through them. Thus on 7 June 1739, after writing that 'Many of our friends have been pestered by the French prophets, and such-like pretenders of inspiration,' and that his friend Bray had been deluded by them, Charles Wesley recounts his encounter with one of the prophetesses who first 'prayed most pompously' and concluded a discourse on the need for 'absolute perfection' with what Wesley termed 'a hellish laugh'.[39] Only a few days later he was having to investigate charges concerning her lewd manner of life and actual immorality, an investigation made all the more difficult in that she had acquired a significant following.

A meeting just a day or so later must be reported in full. Discussion was taking place about her great claims of intimacy with Christ, coupled with her evident and admitted immorality. At this point she entered. 'J. Bray was vehement in her defence; when she came in; flew upon us like a tigress; tried to outface me; insisted that she was immediately inspired. I prayed. She cried, "The devil was in me. I was a fool, a blockhead, a blind leader of the blind; put out the people's eyes" etc. She roared outrageously; said it was the lion in her. (True; but not the Lion of Judah.) She *would* come to the Society in spite of me; if not, they would all go down.'[40] Having seen Charles Wesley's humour in his sally about the tribe of Judah, we now glimpse his very real courage as he narrates the sequel: 'I asked, "Who is on God's side? Who for the old Prophets rather than the new? Let them follow me." They followed me into the preaching room.'[41] He rightly saw that it was a parting of the ways. Those who wanted the old prophets went one way. Those who wanted the new went another.

Over the next days, with his brother John's help and support, he sorted affairs out and saw those who had supported the prophetess much humbled. Obviously it was far from easy to challenge, as Charles Wesley later shows in his brief comment of another disciplinary matter. 'I am a poor creature on such occasions, being soon cast down, as in the case of Shaw and the Prophetess.'[42] Many years later Charles was still dogged by false and cruel prophecies. In February 1749 he writes, 'I was assisted to preach twice a day, the last fortnight; and pitied an unhappy friend for her confident assertion, that the Lord is departed from me. Let the rest of her words and actions be buried in eternal oblivion.'[43] One wonders whether it was the selfsame friend who, in all likelihood disappointed by his not marrying her, pursued him with a prophecy even to his very wedding day, for two months after this he states, 'At the church door I thought of the prophecy of a jealous friend "that if we were even at the church-door to be married, she was sure by revelation that we could get no further". We both smiled at the remembrance.'[44] It was good that he and his bride could smile.

Verdict of John Wesley
That Charles Wesley was clear on the question of the cessation of the gifts seems beyond dispute. While I cannot agree with the judgement of Warfield, who quotes with approval the view that Wesley 'was always far more afraid of being ungodly than of being credulous' and also the verdict that he claimed every apostolic gift except the gift of tongues, I have to admit that he was not as consistent as his brother.[45] I have already quoted his approval of Lacy's thesis that the gifts disappeared because of the worldliness of the church. Other words, quoted with relish by the Mormons, are these from one of his sermons on 1 Corinthians 12:31: 'It does not appear that these extraordinary gifts of the Holy Ghost were common in the Church for more than two or three centuries. We seldom hear of them after that fatal period when the Emperor Constantine called himself a Christian . . . From this time they almost totally ceased . . . The Christians had no more of the Spirit of Christ than the other heathens . . . This was the real cause why the extraordinary gifts of the Holy Ghost were no longer to be found in the Christian Church; because the Christians were turned heathen again and had only a dead form left.'[46]

These were careless statements. One wishes that Wesley had been as firm as his brother on some occasions and not just taken a Gamaliel stance (Acts 5:39). Yet it must be underlined again that when many of these events happened he was himself still a very young Christian even though mature in years. He clearly disbelieved the claims of the prophets he met and stood by his brother in his resolute purging of the society. Moreover in his published work he does voice other opinions on the continuation of the gifts and there were several later occasions in his ministry when he took a resolute stance against prophets. Thus, in December 1742, he dismissed John Brown's sudden outburst of prophetic frenzy and sent his follower home to cry out for deliverance from Satan.[47] The following year he writes, 'I talked pretty largely with George Newans, the supposed Shropshire prophet. I am inclined to think he believes himself, but I cannot believe God has sent him.'[48] This man, Wesley later described as 'full of himself, vain, heady, and opinionated'.[49] But perhaps the biggest test in this realm was when Thomas Maxfield, his first lay preacher, and George Bell, another faithful helper, both went off the rails. The former Wesley rebuked for encouraging 'visions and revelations'.[50] The latter crowned his fanaticism by a prophecy that the world would come to an end on 28 February 1763. Wesley disowned them in clear terms, finding Bell's 'thinking he had the miraculous discernment of spirits' ridiculous and writing to the editor of the *London Chronicle*, *Lloyds Evening Post* and, for good measure, the Countess of Huntingdon, dissociating himself from the prophecy.[51] He speaks of these men as 'those poor, wild men' and when many sat up terrified and expecting the end of the world, Wesley laconically observes in his Journal, 'I went to bed at my usual time, and was fast asleep about ten o'clock.'[52] Right at the end of his life, noting how prophets tend to abound in times of calamity, Wesley comments, 'They are seldom undeceived, even by the failure of their predictions, but still believe they will be fulfilled some time or other.'[53]

In his famous Oxford sermon of 1744, after refusing to decide whether there will be a restoration of the gifts at some point, he argues that even in the early church not all possessed these extraordinary gifts and goes on to say, 'Without busying ourselves then in curious needless inquiries, touching those *extraordinary* gifts of the Spirit, let us take a nearer view of these his *ordinary* fruits, which we are assured will remain throughout all ages . . .'[54] In another sermon dealing with the question of assurance of faith he refers caustically to 'madmen, French prophets and enthusiasts of every kind' and strongly dissociates himself from them.[55] And in his discourse specifically entitled 'The Nature of Enthusiasm' he showed that the endeavour of the prophets to raise Dr Emes had still not faded from the public memory as he writes, 'A second sort of enthusiasm is that of those who imagine they have such gifts from God as they have not. Thus some have imagined themselves to be endued with a power of working miracles, of healing the sick by a word or a touch, of restoring sight to the blind: yea, even of raising the dead, – a notorious instance of which is still fresh in our own history. Others have taken to prophecy, to foretell things to come, and that with the utmost certainty and exactness. But a little time usually convinces these enthusiasts. When plain facts run counter to their predictions, experience performs what reason could not, and sinks them down into their senses.'[56] In this sermon he warns against those who are frequently mistaken in relying on visions, impulses and dreams as they are 'misled by pride, and a warm imagination'.[57] Although God may occasionally guide in an extraordinary manner, to be expecting this constantly is to walk contrary to his will.

Very near the end of his life, in April 1786, hearing of extremism in some remote mountainous regions as folk prayed all together and even screamed, Wesley again compared them with the French prophets.[58] When we consider the above statements and especially his fine exegesis of 1 Corinthians 14, mentioned in an earlier chapter, we can perceive that Wesley's overall judgement was not as unbalanced on this matter as some would allege. Even though he believed that the gifts had been lost by the worldliness of the church, he did not express the view that they were going to be restored, expounded a view of tongue-speaking which would rule out all such today as non-biblical and rejected many contemporary claimants to prophecy as false. His final judgement on this contemporary charismatic phenomenon is surely to be found in a couple of sentences from his long letter to the editor of the *London Magazine* on 12 December 1760: 'Q 14. "Do you not commend the Quakers?" Yes, in some things. "And the French prophets?" No.'[59] This terse monosyllable expresses his final verdict.

Cennick and Whitefield

Naturally other revivalists could not escape this contagion. John Cennick, who accepted that one of their number answered in Latin or Greek, was disturbed in his soul and plunged into deep spiritual anguish when he discovered the wildness of their ways and noted that 'Some prophesied, and some uttered the worst of blashpemies against our Saviour'.[60] This was obviously not a rare incident for he adds, 'Things of this kind were frequent everywhere, and all manner of fancies

were preached by such means.'[61] Both Cennick and George
Whitefield felt with some justification that Wesley's requiring
of signs with regard to people being thrown down in
convulsions hindered rather than helped the situation. Hence
Whitefield addressed his co-evangelist in this way: 'I think it is
tempting God to require such signs. That there is something of
God in it I doubt not; but the devil, I believe, does interpose. I
think it will encourage the French prophets, take people from
the written word, and make them depend on visions,
convulsions, etc, more than on the promises and precepts of
the Gospel.'[62]

However, when a Commissary in New England wished to
draw opprobrium on the head of Whitefield he compared him
with 'all the *Oliverians, Ranters, Quakers, French prophets,* till he
came down to a family of the Dutarts' (a group of notorious
murderers), to use Whitefield's own words.[63] This was most
unfair. In 1740 a friend defending Whitefield from charges of
fanaticism wrote as follows: 'He renounced all pretensions to
extraordinary powers and signs of apostleship – gifts of
healing, speaking with tongues, the faith of miracles, things
peculiar to the age of inspiration and extinct with these.'[64]

This defence is substantiated by a long letter Whitefield
wrote in 1739, the year when the Wesley brothers were
struggling with the false teachings of the French prophets.
Here are a few excerpts: 'I hear there is a woman among you,
who pretends to the spirit of prophecy, and what is more
unaccountable, I hear that Brother . . . (whom I love in
the bowels of Jesus Christ) seems to approve of her. Need
therefore, great need have you, my brethren, at this time to
take the apostle's advice, and to try the spirits whether they be
of God. For the devil is beginning to mimic God's work, and
because terrors will not do, he is now transforming himself into
an angel of light in order more effectually to gain his point.
Brother . . . also, I cannot but think, at present is under a
spirit of delusion. He, as well as Brother . . . I believe imagines
there will be a power given to work miracles, and that now
Christ is coming to reign a thousand years upon the earth. But
alas! what need is there of miracles, such as healing sick
bodies, and restoring sight to blind eyes, when we see greater
miracles every day done by the power of God's word? Do not
the spiritually blind now see? Are not the spiritually dead now

raised, and the leprous souls now cleansed, and have not the poor the gospel preached unto them? And if we have the thing already, which such miracles were only intended to introduce, why should we tempt God in requiring further signs?'[65] God had begun a great work. Further than this Whitefield does not desire to know. 'It is sufficient for me to do the work of the day in its day . . .'[66] He feared lest, like Uzzah, some might be unwittingly laying hands on the sacred ark and running without a call and speaking without God's warrant. He continued: 'I would all the Lord's servants were prophets, but then I would not have people think themselves prophets of the Lord, when they are only enthusiasts . . . If Mr . . . is acted by a good spirit, why is he not patient of reproof? Why does he fly in a passion, when contradicted? Why does he pretend to be infallible, and that God always speaks in him?'[67] His concluding remarks bid his readers be wary of 'Satan's devices' and purge out the 'leaven'.

10.
The assessment of Jonathan Edwards

Wildfire in New England

There had been some wise assessments from the Wesleys and George Whitefield but a definitive, thorough-going demolition of the entire charismatic scheme awaited exposition from an even greater theological pen. There were a variety of factors which moved Jonathan Edwards to turn his attention to this theme. Firstly, he was himself aware that 'agitations of body were found in the *French prophets,'* accompanying their claims to inspiration.[1] The sixth phase of their movement was its appearance in New England. One of the leading opponents of the revival movement of which Edwards, Whitefield and others were participants and supporters was Chauncy. His first work attacking the movement was indeed called *The Wonderful Narrative: or, a Faithful Account of the French Prophets, their Agitations, Ecstasies, and Inspirations. To which are added, several other remarkable instances of Persons under the influence of the like Spirit in various Parts of the World, particularly in New England; with an Introduction, directing to the proper Use of such Extraordinary Appearances in the course of Providence.*[2] Chauncy's aim was to bring discredit on the revival by linking it in people's minds with the impostures and false claims of the French prophets. It must be borne in mind that much of Edwards' writings on these matters was in reply to Chauncy's accusations, though he rarely, if ever, alludes to Chauncy.

However, it was not merely among the French prophets that such beliefs were held. In the general atmosphere of revival in New England during the visits of Whitefield and on other occasions there were those who claimed such gifts. Thus one pastor reported that a few people spoke of 'trances, visions, extraordinary missions and immediate revelations', but he stressed that, contrary to common report, it was just a minority who did this. A brother minister in June 1743 also felt it necessary to issue this defence of the work of God among his people: 'We have not known visions, nor trances, nor revelations; but brotherly exhorting, with more modesty and affection than hath been represented.'[3] A third pastor, confronted by a lad who claimed to have had both a vision of hell, with its hideous roaring, and of Christ turning over the leaves of a book and telling him that his name was there, reports his response: 'I told him that these things were not to be depended upon, but that the apostle Peter has cautioned us, saying, that we have a more sure word of prophecy, to which we should do well to take heed.'[4]

Foremost among the fomenters of these practices was Davenport, himself a pastor with some talent, who had been encouraged and praised by no less a person than George Whitefield. Davenport was guilty of various irregularities. He often absented himself from his own congregation for periods without the consent of the local people. He intruded in the parishes of other men often stigmatizing their pastors as unconverted men and urging their people to ignore their ministrations. The following account hardly needs comment: 'He came very near attempting to work a miracle. A woman in an adjoining parish had been long insane, and for some time dumb. Davenport fasted and prayed for her recovery, and gave out that she would recover on a certain day that he named. On that day, she died. He claimed the event as an answer to his prayer, as she was relieved from her infirmity by being taken to heaven. This was in the summer of 1740; not far from the time when Whitefield saw him in New Jersey, and was so much pleased with his piety.'[5] The culmination of his folly was when, in an endeavour to cure a group of people of worldly things, a large bonfire was made, in obedience to messages which he claimed to have received through dreams. Wigs, cloaks, breeches, hoods, rings, jewels etc. were burned and for good measure he himself threw in his own plush breeches. A few days later a bonfire of books was made, including works by Flavel, Increase Mather and Beveridge, among others.

All this did not occur without remonstrations from his fellow pastors. Yet as soon as this happened another minister strongly protested that they should thus condemn a man being so signally used by God. Here is part of his protest: 'The honoured Association having been constrained to own him to be a truly pious man and a very useful minister, they go to butting and bounding him in the following manner. "He is a gentleman," they say, "much acted by sudden impulses, upon application of the Holy Scriptures to himself," etc. To which I reply: "What if he holds ten thousand impulses which others cannot so well see through; yet if it appears plain that the great God, who sends by whom he will send, improves him in saving many souls from hell, each of whom is worth more than the whole world, for God's sake let no one dare to do anything which hath a tendency to render his ministry contemptible, lest they kick against the pricks, and be found fighters against God."'[6]

It is an all too familiar story. Criticism is condemned as negative and unevangelical. Especially interesting is the closing plea of Davenport's defender. 'Nor have Mr Davenport's impressions done him any harm as yet: and to expect danger from that quarter, is fearing where no fear is; especially if we consider the uncommon sanctity of the man, and his trembling at the appearance of evil.'[7] All this took place before the wild extravagance of the bonfire, which was then followed by Davenport's own prostration through illness and by a lengthy and sincere apology and recantation from him called 'Mr Davenport's Retractions', in which he deeply regretted his own departure from sound scriptural reasoning and the following of impulses and his misguided zeal, 'which have been great blemishes to the work of God, very grievous to some of God's children'.[8] But for some it was too late to close the stable door, as the horse had already bolted. There were groups which had so been engulfed in this false fire that it was impossible to put it out. They merely felt that Davenport himself had become compromising and backsliding.

Although Davenport was a leading figure in this respect, there were others. Hugh Bryan, for example, had also been praised by Whitefield and was highly thought of by some. At length, imagining himself a prophet, he sent twenty closely written sheets of his journal, containing numerous predictions, to the Speaker of the House of Commons of the colonial legislature. After he had gained a following and displayed increasingly dangerous tendencies, he too recanted and admitted that he had fallen 'into a delusion of Satan'.[9]

That all this was part of a wider belief in the forthcoming restoration of the extraordinary gifts is evident from what Edwards himself writes. He describes how he gently led back to sanity a man whose delusion it was that the gifts should be restored![10] He also digs deeper and brings up a real theological objection against this theory: 'One reason why some have been ready to lay weight on such impulses, is an opinion they have had, that the glory of the approaching happy days of the church would partly consist in restoring those *extraordinary gifts* of the Spirit. This opinion, I believe, arises partly through want of duly considering and comparing the nature and value of those two kinds of influences of the Spirit, *viz.* those that are ordinary and gracious, and those that are extraordinary and miraculous. The former are by far the most excellent and glorious; as the apostle largely shows (1 Cor. 12:31 etc.).'[11]

Edwards urged to take up the issue

Obviously Edwards, with his finger on the pulse of things, knew what was going on. In the atmosphere of the revival this issue was not a small one. This is shown in a letter to Edwards from Mr Gillespie, written in November 1746, where he refers to Edwards' works *Thoughts on the Revival of Religion* and the *Treatise on the Religious Affections* and comments, 'I longed to see somewhat about impressions respecting facts and future events, whether by scripture texts or otherwise, made on the minds of good people, and supposed to be from the Lord; for I have had too good occasion to know the hurtful, yea, pernicious tendency of this principle, as commonly managed, upon many persons in manifold instances and various respects.'[12] Once again we underline that Gillespie was talking of a common occurrence. Although there were many relevant comments on this theme interspersed in writings of Edwards, Gillespie believed that it merited a full-scale treatment on its own. He goes on to plead, 'And as (if I do not mistake) Providence has already put that in your hand as a part of your generation-work, so it will give me, as well as others, vast satisfaction to find more said on the subject by you . . .'[13]

Two years later Gillespie returned to this matter, acknowledging that Edwards might already have said enough in treatises already published. He concludes by putting his finger on the real point at issue: 'I should have also mentioned, that it seems evident, the doctrine of immediate revelations must be simply denied as unscriptural, and thus well-founded in *no* case; or it must be allowed in its full compass and latitude, let the consequences of it be what they will, for if the thing is allowed *possible*, reasonings about its effects will not conclude nor avail; I can see no middle way between the two things.'[14]

Of course, Gillespie had indeed chosen the right man to whom to make his appeal. The enthusiasm of Dr Martyn Lloyd-Jones for Jonathan Edwards is almost unbounded. 'If I had the power I would make these two volumes compulsory reading for all ministers! Edwards seems to satisfy all round; he really was an amazing man,' is his well-known comment on the flyleaf of the recent Banner of Truth reprint of the works of Edwards.[15] Elsewhere, with regard to Edwards' deep spirituality and meticulous honesty as a commentator and writer, Dr Lloyd-Jones declared that 'He is one of the most honest expositors I have ever read. He never evades a problem; he faces them all.'[16]

This is no exaggerated commendation. And indeed if Gillespie did eventually possess the bulk of Edwards' writing he would have had a very thorough-going and detailed discussion of this whole question on the basis of Scripture alone. This was indeed, as his correspondent put it, part of his 'generation work'. Things in the revival were strikingly new to many, and Edwards, realizing that contemporaries were going to assess events by 'history' instead of Scripture, reminded them, 'It has all along been God's manner to open new scenes.'[17] Elsewhere he tells us that 'No deviation from what has hitherto been usual, let it be never so great, is an argument that a work is not from the Spirit of God, if it be no deviation from his prescribed rule.'[18] Moreover, everything must be ruthlessly scrutinized in the revival, with the wheat being sifted from the chaff, and people resolutely resolving not to rely on personalities alone or treat them with the blind and unthinking allegiance so many had unwisely given to Davenport. 'We go too far, when we look upon the success that God gives to some person, in making them the instruments of doing much good, as a testimony of God's approbation of those persons and all the courses they take.'[19] Would that more Reformed brethren would heed this counsel today after the departure of a great stalwart of the evangelical faith!

'Age of miracles' in first century

It is the emphasis of Edwards that the extraordinary gifts were revelatory gifts and that they were given because the New Testament era was specifically one of inspiration or miracle. According to him, it was rightly called *'the age of miracles'* and, after being thus established, Christianity was continued by more normal means. The gifts had a specific purpose: 'And by means of these extraordinary gifts of the Holy Ghost, the apostles and others were enabled to write the New Testament, to be an infallible and perpetual rule of faith and manners to the church.'[20] Prophets therefore spoke by 'immediate inspiration'.[21] He says this with reference to 1 Corinthians 14 and thus sees the gift as one of infallible utterance. It is also the case with apostleship. 'Those who are spiritual among us have no infallible apostles to admonish them,' is his firm conviction.[22] When he reluctantly ventures into print against his illustrious grandfather, he can indeed quote his relative in support of his own stance, which is that 'All protestants agree that there is no infallibility at Rome; and I know nobody else pretends to any, since the apostle's day.'[23]

In the proper sense Edwards draws attention to the role of the mind. Behind spurious faith is frequently found a lack of true understanding. 'Now there are many affections which do not arise from any light in the understanding; which is a sure evidence that these affections are not spiritual, let them be ever so high,' declares Edwards, in words which would rule out practically all, if not all, modern instances of tongue- speaking as spurious.[24] In the light of this it is not surprising to find that he believed that the tongue-speaker understood his utterance. 'Men receive nothing, when they understand nothing; and are not at all edified, unless some knowledge be conveyed; agreeable to the apostle's arguing, 1 Corinthians 14:2-6.' In that passage he goes on to say, 'God deals with a man as with a rational creature; and when faith is in exercise, it is not about

something he knows not what.'[25] He shows the balance of his
viewpoint in the following two utterances: 'Holy affections are
not heat without light; but evermore arise from some
information of the understanding, some spiritual instruction
that the mind receives, some light or actual knowledge.'[26]
Consequently John the Baptist is his ideal of the true gospel
minister since with him 'Divine light is attended with heat;
and so, on the other hand, a truly divine and holy heat and
ardour is ever accompanied with light.'[27]

Views on 1 Corinthians 13

Undoubtedly a key passage for Edwards, in his understanding
of the cessation of these extraordinary gifts, was 1 Corinthians
13. Here is his exposition as it is found in *Charity and its Fruits:*
'The extraordinary gifts of the Spirit, such as the gifts of
tongues, of miracles, of prophecy, etc., are called
extraordinary, because they are such as are not given in the
ordinary course of God's providence. They are not bestowed in
the way of God's ordinary providential dealings with his
children, but only on extraordinary occasions, as they were
bestowed on the prophets and apostles to enable them to
reveal the mind and will of God before the canon of Scripture
was complete, and so on the primitive Church, in order to the
founding and establishing of it in the world.'[28] Thus in his
view the above gifts were revelatory. They were bestowed as
an 'interim measure' by God before Scripture was completed.
Since, in his view, the 'perfection' of 1 Corinthians 13:10 was
the completion of Scripture, he can conclude, 'But since the
canon of the Scripture has been completed, and the Christian
Church fully founded and established, these extraordinary
gifts have ceased.'

Also in *Marks of a Work of the Spirit of God* he explains the
passage in the same way, referring to 'these gifts of inspiration
as childish things, in comparison of the influence of the Spirit
in divine love'.[29] On this occasion he also draws an argument
from the final verse of the chapter, where we read that faith,
hope and love are to abide. Two of these obviously abide only
in this life, since in heaven faith becomes sight and 'Who hopes
for what he already has?' 'Here is a manifest *antithesis,* between

remaining, and that *failing*, *ceasing* and *vanishing away*, spoken of
in the eighth verse.'[30] The conclusion is that the gifts cease in
this life when we have 'a complete standing rule established',
namely Scripture in its completeness.[31]

In his *Notes on the Bible* he discusses this passage again.
While he acknowledges that the passage has some reference to
heaven it must, he argues, also apply to the time when 'the
canon of Scripture was completed', when 'the gifts of prophecy
and tongues, etc. ceased at the end of the church's age of
childhood'.[32] Therefore, Edwards consistently beckons his
reader to accept fully Scripture's perfection. What of the
world's future? 'Nothing else sets before us how he will govern
it to the end, by an orderly prophecy of future events.'[33] What
is the significance of the book of Revelation and its concluding
chapter? 'Christ having given this last revelation to his church
to be added to the book of Scripture, with which the canon was
to be shut up (concluded) and sealed, by the instrumentality of
the apostle John, who lived the longest of the apostles, and
wrote this book, wherein such great future judgements are
revealed as coming on the wicked, and such an affecting
declaration of the future glory of the saints, to enforce the rest
of God's word and grace; and then intimates, that no more
revelations are to be expected . . .the next revelation that is to
be expected . . . is to be his immediate appearance in
judgement . . .'[34] Because 'the Revelation is a *prophecy*' and
because of the finality of its themes, it is the prophecy to end
all prophecies and nothing more can be said until God says it
in the person of his Son.[35]

Therefore Scripture is to be studied fervently and applied.
The increase in the extent of the canon from Old Testament
times lays on us a great obligation to dig yet deeper.[36] In a
passage of rare vision Edwards sees beyond the preponderance
of theological works by Anglo-Saxon divines to glimpse such
works by 'negroes and Indian' divines and, because he expects
a growth in the corporate knowledge of the church and 'a
wonderful unravelling of the difficulties in the doctrines of
religion, and clearing up of seeming inconsistencies', he cannot
believe that the end is yet nigh.[37] 'It is an argument with me,
that the world is not yet very near its end, that the church has
made no greater progress in understanding the mysteries of
the Scriptures.'[38]

In the passages in which Edwards asserts that the extraordinary gifts have ceased he strongly contends that we are not thereby impoverished. Saul, Balaam and Judas all had gifts, but not the gift. It is the possession of the gift of grace that matters. As a typical example of his mode of argument, he points out that Balaam had various immediate revelations from God, even one of the coming Messiah, the Star rising out of Jacob. 'But Balaam had no spiritual discovery of Christ; that day-star never spiritually rose in his heart, he being but a natural man.'[39] Who but Edwards could see that a man could even discern infallibly and accurately the godly estate of another man without himself even being converted? Edwards alludes to the case of Laban and Jacob.[40]Even if we were to receive from God direct instructions about where we should go, it would be no more than a common gift which even unsaved people can receive.[41]

False views of spirituality

In the light of contemporary events there are numerous references in his writings to those who feel gifted to predict the future or foresee future events. Many who were deceived about these things must also be deceived about their own supposed spirituality, feeling that they were advanced Christians because they were preoccupied with such things. Speaking of contemporaries who, he felt, were deceived by 'false discoveries and elevations' even to their own damnation, Edwards comments, 'The chief ground of the confidence of many of them are impulses and supposed revelations (sometimes with texts of Scripture and sometimes without) like what many of late have had concerning future events.'[42] In his view the experience of Brainerd was much more clearly based on Scripture and he tellingly quotes Brainerd's summary of some of the aspects of false assurance: 'A mixture of *self-love, imagination,* and spiritual *pride,* or perhaps the influence of Satan transformed into the angel of light . . . They have on a sudden *imagined they saw Christ,* in some posture or other, perhaps on the cross, bleeding and dying for their sins; or it may be, smiling on them . . . Some having had a passage, or perhaps many passages, of *Scripture* brought to their minds *with power* (as they express it) . . . some speak of seeing a great *light* which filled all the place where they were . . .'[43]

This factor of pride is one which Edwards analyses with great power. It has been said that Satan has consummated skill in managing the temptation of theological and spiritual pride because he 'was trained in the best divinity school in the universe'.[44] If even the apostle Paul, with all his great revelations, had to be exceedingly watchful in this regard, how much more do we need to be careful in the giving of testimony with 'the great tendency it has to spiritual pride'.[45] Two quotations from Edwards on this theme are exceptionally perceptive: 'A true saint, when in the enjoyment of true discoveries of the sweet glory of God and Christ, has his mind too much captivated and engaged by what he views without himself, to stand at that time to view himself, and his own attainments,' he shrewdly observes.[46] And in discussion of revival he declares, 'And here, I humbly conceive, some eminent servants of Jesus Christ that we read of in ecclesiastical history, have been led into a mistake; and, through want of distinguishing such things as these from immediate revelations, have thought that God has favoured them, in some instances, with the same kind of divine influences that the apostles and prophets had of old.'[47]

Failure of prophecies

As we pause to note that eminent servants of God can, according to Edwards, fall into this snare, we notice also the frequency with which people of his day thought they had the gift of prophecy: 'Some of the true friends of the work of God's Spirit have erred in giving too much heed to impulses and strong impressions on their minds, as though they were immediate significations from heaven to them, of something that should come to pass, or something that it was the mind and will of God that they should do, which was not signified or revealed anywhere in the Bible without these impulses. These impressions, if they are truly from the Spirit of God, are of quite different nature from his gracious influences on the hearts of the saint; they are of the nature of the extraordinary *gifts* of the Spirit, and are properly inspiration, such as the prophets and apostles and others had of old; which the apostle distinguishes from the *grace* of the Spirit (1 Cor.13).'[48]

Of course, it is well nigh impossible to reason with a man who is directly inspired from heaven or who feels that his friend is. But does the fact that many prophecies fail cause such people to stop and think more deeply? Not at all. 'I have seen so many instances of the failing of such impressions, that would almost furnish a history,' reports Edwards, adding that those who are convinced that prophecy is to be restored will not be convinced otherwise. From this he infers that 'It seems to be a testimony of God, that he has no design of reviving revelations in his church, and a rebuke from him to the groundless expectations of it.'[49] He also writes, 'I have seen them fail in very many instances, and know by experience that impressions being made with great power, and upon the minds of true, yea eminent saints – even in the midst of extraordinary exercises of grace, and sweet communion with God, and attended with texts of Scripture strongly impressed on the mind – are no sure sign of their being revelations from heaven. I have known such impressions fail, in some instances, attended with all these circumstances. They who leave the sure word of prophecy – which God has given us as a light shining in a dark place – to follow such impressions and impulses, leave the guidance of the polar star, to follow a *Jack with a lantern*. No wonder therefore that sometimes they are led into woeful extravagancies.'[50]

This allusion to 2 Peter 2:16-21 is in line with the constant use that the Puritans made of this passage. Edwards was satisfied with what God has given. 'And why cannot we be contented with the divine oracles, that holy, pure word of God, which we have in such abundance and clearness, now since the canon of Scripture is completed? Why should we desire to have anything added to them by impulses from above? Why should we not rest with that standing rule that God has given to his church, which, the apostle teaches us, is surer than a voice from heaven? And why should we desire to make the Scripture speak more to us than it does?'[51]

Conversion the greatest work

Above all conversion itself is the truly great work and the

stupendous miracle. It is in fact always a dramatic work, truly miraculous in its effects.[52] 'I am bold to say, that the work of God in the conversion of one soul, considered together with the source, foundation, and purchase of it, and also the benefit, end, and eternal issue of it, is a more glorious work of God than the creation of the whole material universe. It is the most glorious of God's works, as it above all others manifests the glory of God; it is spoken of in Scripture, as that which shows *the exceeding greatness of God's power, and the glory and riches of divine grace,* and wherein Christ has the most glorious triumph over his enemies, and wherein God is mightily exalted.'[53] In fact the main point of Christ's own miracles is that they were images of the great work he came to perform on men's hearts.[54] Yet without the truly great work of raising the dead sinner, no amount of outward displays ('There has rarely been a more degenerate time than that of Elijah and Elisha, who wrought so many miracles') and not even the sight of Christ himself ('Nay, all the world shall see him in his glory . . . yet this is far short of having the saving knowledge of him') can suffice for the saving of a soul.[55]

Infiltration of the devil

Moreover God has given his infallible Word and it is not an insignificant or harmless thing when people mistakenly claim to be inspired by God. 'One erroneous principle, than which scarce any has proved more mischievous to the present glorious work of God, is a notion that it is God's manner in these days, to guide his saints, at least some that are more eminent, by inspiration or immediate revelation. They suppose he makes known to them what shall come to pass hereafter, or what it is his will that they should do, by impressions made upon their minds, either with or without texts of Scripture; whereby something is made known to them, that is not taught in Scripture. By such a notion the devil has a great door opened for him; and if once this opinion should come to be fully yielded to, and established in the church of God, Satan would have opportunity thereby to set up himself as the guide and oracle of God's people, and to have *his* word regarded as their infallible rule, and so to lead them where he would, and to introduce what he pleased, and soon to bring the Bible into neglect and contempt. Late experience, in some instances, has shown that the tendency of this notion is to cause persons to esteem the Bible as in a great measure useless.'[56]

Thus the devil, by infiltrating the ranks of Christians, is able to inject into them a large dose of the 'pride and malice' that makes up his own character.[57] Whole groups of those who have the gifts are led into 'counterfeit love' and a kind of satanic *bonhomie*. They look down on others, who do not possess what they have, in what Edwards depicts as 'only the working of a natural self-love, and no true benevolence, any more than the union and friendship which may be among a company of pirates, that are at war with the rest of the world.'[58] Such circles, 'boasting of high degrees of spirituality and perfection, censuring and condemning others as carnal', he likens to those who sprang up in opposition to the Reformers: 'men that pretend themselves to be more enlightened than the reformers were ... hence they called those that did adhere to the Scripture, and would try revelations by it, Literists and Vowelists, as men acquainted with the words and vowels of the Scripture, having nothing of the Spirit of God.'[59]

Such abundant references show us that Edwards was not writing about something of little moment during the revival. He refers to the whole issue as the one which more than any other threatened to undermine the work. His treatment and rejection of claims to the gifts was thorough-going and decisive. He believed that Scripture taught that the gifts were revelatory, giving infallible utterances, whether in prophecy or tongues, and were an 'interim measure' until the perfect gift from God in the form of the completed Scripture was given. Confronted by a wide range of contemporary claimants to the gifts, he rejected them one and all as spurious.

It would be very easy to say that Davenport was a wild man and an extremist. It would certainly be legitimate to say that some of the prophetesses the Wesleys met were dubious characters. In the early origins of the movement there was an undercurrent of fanaticism and wildness. Yet at all stages there were many more seemingly balanced and non-violent people who were thoroughly taken in. We recall the defence of

Du Plan of the more sober of the prophets and his conviction that the gifts should continue, purged of excesses. Yet we have surveyed the movement for some decades after this and seen how in fact error and excess are built in because the very theology is faulty.

Educated people could be taken in. Defoe expressed his amazement at this. (Some people are convinced that the charismatic claims are true because some scientist, titled person or T.V. personality has written an article in a magazine.) Whole groups could be deluded and badly led astray. Churches could be split. And how could simple young believers easily assess and test all this when even John Wesley, admittedly himself a young believer at the time, dared not express a final verdict on the prophetess? Always there is the lurking fear that we might be resisting the Holy Spirit. Although Whitefield and Charles Wesley were ultimately firm, as Antoine Court had been earlier in the century, we may be particularly grateful to God for the thorough-going exposition and exposure of the movement by Jonathan Edwards. This is not merely to extol him as a great man but as one who painstakingly showed from Scripture how false countless charismatic notions are – that the tongue speaker does not understand what he says; that in the wake of countless false prophecies groups can still sail merrily on and never ask whether God is dishonoured; that an era of great miracles would automatically draw people to Christ; that the Scripture leads us to expect a restoration of the gifts in the last times; that a gifted person is one who has advanced in spirituality (he may not even be converted!). All these things badly needed saying then. They desperately need saying now.

11.
The nineteenth and early twentieth centuries

Edward Irving and his followers

The story of Edward Irving in the nineteenth century has been so well retold by Arnold Dallimore that little remains but to draw out the salient features. A perusal of his biography, together with the book of William Goode, shows that in charismatic matters, in contrast to his defective Christology, Irving stands squarely with the Pentecostals of the past and those of the present. The verdict of Strachan is indeed apposite: 'The beliefs and experiences of the various branches of the contemporary Pentecostal Churches are so similar to those of Irving and his followers that one might suspect they had been handed down by word of mouth, or discovered like some Deuteronomy of the Spirit. The fact that there was no collusion between the two movements . . . only emphasizes the power and validity of the comparison.'[1]

There were many unfulfilled, even foolish and banal prophecies (a man called Baxter admitted to forty-six of these himself), and the 'man of sin' was declared to be the young Napoleon and the Bible Society the 'curse' going through the earth.[2] Yet despite these glaring errors few wanted to investigate matters more closely. When Baxter ultimately renounced the gifts and went to confess his numerous failures to Irving, pointing out at the same time how other prophets had clashed and contradicted each other or said things that were manifestly untrue, Irving refused to investigate, taking refuge in the assertion 'that the same person might at one moment speak by the Spirit of God, and the next moment by an evil spirit'.[3] In many instances the 'tongues' were clearly induced by man and many of the first claimants (including not a few women) later recanted and even admitted deception. Yet Baxter, while speaking in tongues or prophesying, spoke regularly of the feeling of 'divine constraint' upon him. In a letter to his brother, while under the delusion, he wrote, 'I cannot for a moment doubt the reality of the manifestations; and the Spirit secretly bears witness with my own spirit that he has spoken in me, and leads me to the expectation that he may yet again constrain my utterances.'[4] The group as a whole were sure that a miracle of healing would be performed on a certain person, yet eventually Baxter had to write, 'The person on whom the miracle was to be performed is dead, never having been in the least degree restored.'[5]

Amazing gifts of discernment

Yet it must not be forgotten that in all this many people did possess amazing discernment in revealing things apparently known only to a listener. Baxter himself was able, like many today, to expose the thoughts of others, and he and his wife experienced at times what seemed to be amazing signs. They took these as proving that they were in the right way. Here is one testimony from Baxter: 'To several questions which were asked, answers were given by me in the power. One in particular was so answered, with such reference to the circumstances of the case of which in myself I was wholly ignorant, as to convince the person who asked it that the spirit speaking in me knew those circumstances, and alluded to them in the answer.'[6] Baxter goes on to say that he could relate innumerable instances of people reading the thoughts of someone even in the next room and testifies that many were convinced of the rightness of the movement by facts like this.

When Baxter, a man appearing so evidently gifted, was convinced of his call to apostleship, it was a matter of course that Irving should easily be persuaded to acquiesce. Yet the 'apostles' appointed by the Irvingite church certainly did not see themselves as church 'messenger boys' for very long, or as 'church planters' at all. Realizing that apostleship does imply real authority, they began to exercise it in an evil and dictatorial way, simply because they had with false motives usurped what God alone can authentically bestow.[7] Furthermore what had prepared the way for the whole delusion was an over-emphasis on the prophetic portions of

Scripture and a belief in the imminence of the second coming. Irving, despite his earlier disbelief, was finally convinced that the gifts would be restored 'anterior to the time of his second advent', to use his own words.[8]

Central to everything was the customary view that in great experiences such as tongues and prophecy God delights to bypass the understanding. Baxter, on his renunciation of the gifts, found that people in the movement shrank away from him and would not even discuss the Scriptures in question or hear arguments from the other side. He testified, 'There are some general characteristics in the work which, apart from doctrines or instances of failure of predictions, cast suspicion upon it. One is the extreme secrecy enjoined by the Spirit, and the manifest shrinking from public examination . . . Another is, the manifest denouncement and debasement of the understanding'.[9] Irving actually said that 'The mind, the understanding, and the feeling, or, as it is commonly called the heart, is only a serving creature', which one day we shall relinquish.[10] It is interesting that David Brown (of Jamieson, Fausset and Brown fame), who was assistant to Irving at one time and who examined and rejected the claims of the movement, was rebuked by Irving in this vein: 'Your intellect, Sir, has destroyed you.' Brown retorted, 'Yes, Sir, I confess it; my intellect has done the deed . . . I am responsible for the use of my intellect and I have used it.'[11] Brown meant, of course, that his intellect was submitted to Scripture and that within Scripture the intellect is never to be thrown aside, but rather renewed.

Now that more is known about Irving, many are claiming that he does not stand in true charismatic succession and it is customary to say that people today would have been far too discerning to have been taken in by the false prophecies that are now recognized to be such. 'I am certain that today's charismatic leaders would be shocked by Irving's reactions when "the gifts" appeared,' argued one correspondent to a Christian newspaper, also adding that many prophecies should have been sifted and seen as not from the Lord.[12] It is easy to have the advantage of hindsight and also the findings of Dallimore's book! But let the reader go back to the early chapters and look at the many *modern* quotations on the mind being in abeyance and compare these with the Irvingite emphasis. There is no difference! Let him do the same with regard to the view that prophecy is a 'mixed phenomenon'. Again it is obvious that there is no real difference!

It is very interesting to note a verdict on Irving expressed by a leading charismatic just a few years before Dallimore's book was published. Reviewing Strachan's earlier book on *The Pentecostal Theology of Edward Irving,* he never breathed a criticism of either Strachan's presentation or of Irving himself, even though he mentioned the factor of Irving's defective Christology and his deposition for heresy. The reviewer wrote, 'Irving believed that when men ascribed the manifestation of the Holy Spirit to an evil agency, they were in danger of blasphemy against the Holy Spirit and he saw a crisis rising in the church when "she must either decide for the Holy Ghost or against him, for her own salvation or her own perdition for ever and ever". This adds to the drama of Irving's trial, defence and deposition of which some scenes are described in graphic terms. The deposition of Irving is a sad and tragic story, but as Gordon Strachan points out, "Like a Knox in exile . . . although he is still without honour in his own country and among his own people, he would immediately leap from obscurity to theological prominence, should the Church of Scotland begin to take seriously the challenge of Pentecostal doctrine and experience."'[13] The reviewer saw Irving as an example and challenge to us today.

The view of Spurgeon

What said the voice of orthodoxy in face of all this? In the Metropolitan Tabernacle C.H. Spurgeon spoke with no uncertain voice. Commenting on Irving's sermon, where he exhorted missionaries to go forth without scrip or purse, he plainly declared, 'Edward never volunteered to go himself. If he had done so at the end of the sermon, we might have endorsed his philosophy. But he stayed at home and did not go.'[14] Spurgeon repeatedly asserted that miracles as performed by the apostles were finished. These were the great bells to summon people to the feast of the gospel at the outset. Apostles, who were supremely witnesses of the resurrection, were no more. He ridiculed the idea that miracles had been restored. Yet the greater works were being done: 'It is true we can work no miracles, yet we can do works which mark God's children . . . We can work spiritual miracles. Today, can we not stand at the grave of the dead sinner, and say, "Lazarus, come forth"? And has not God often made the dead to rise at our word, by the power of His Spirit?'[15] On hearing that such miracles were being supposedly restored he cryptically observed, 'A bottomless pit of fanaticism is yawning.'[16] To contemporary claimants to apostleship he threw out this challenge: 'The apostles were empowered to do many things, but who are you? Do you claim to be their successors? Then work miracles similar to theirs: take up serpents and drink deadly things without being harmed thereby; prove to us that you have seen the Lord, or even that cloven tongues of fire have sat upon each of you.'[17]

Would-be prophets were by no means absent from the scene. And Spurgeon, like Luther, believed in calling a spade a spade. Unlike certain delicate modern gentry, he did not foolishly fear to grieve the Holy Spirit because he plainly branded error as error. 'Certain would-be prophets tell us, that many wonders will occur in 1866 and 1867, though I notice a propensity to postpone the whole business to 1877. Is this postponement intended that there may be ten years longer in which to sell their books?' he mischievously asked.[18] 'Every now and then there comes up a heresy; some woman turns prophetess and raves; or some lunatic gets the idea that God has inspired him, and there are always fools ready to follow any impostor,' he declared. But what was the remedy in such a situation? Spurgeon tells us: 'Next, be sure to attend a teaching ministry. Do not be always running after sweets. Do not be running after prophesying and novelties. Try to see the whole range of Scripture.'[19] After mentioning the pseudo-prophetic fabrications in the *Koran* and the *Book of Mormon*, Spurgeon declared, 'It would be an insult to the judgement of the least in the Kingdom of heaven to suppose that he could mistake the language of these forgeries for the language of the Holy Ghost. I have had several pretended revelations submitted to me by their pretended authors: for we have more of the prophetic clan about than most people know of; but not one of them has ever left on my mind the slightest suspicion of his having the inspiration of John, or Paul. There is no mistaking the inspired Books if you have any spiritual discernment.'[20]

Therefore when he preached on the gift of prophecy and tongues and healing in the early church, he shrewdly expected that some within his congregation might crave such in his day. Yet he reassured them that times had not deteriorated! 'We cannot suppose that the Holy Ghost brought forth the best wine at first, and that his operations gradually deteriorated. It is a rule of the kingdom to keep the best wine till last, and therefore I conclude that you and I are not left to partake of the dregs . . .'[21] Then in his normal way he spoke of conversion as the great work. And how could anyone say that God abandoned Spurgeon for grieving his Holy Spirit? Indeed great instances of God working in his congregation seemed to abound.

Twentieth-century Pentecostalism

When we think of twentieth-century Pentecostalism we think of the movement which sprang from events which took place in Azusa Street in 1906, when W.J. Seymour preached a Pentecostal message and Agnes Ozman was the first of a growing number to seek the 'baptism' and then speak with tongues. One modern writer enthusiastically describes this significant event and likens it to another Pentecost. 'But when the same thing happens two thousand years later it causes a theological earthquake and the Church tries to get it out of its system,' he complains.[22] Some would reply that there are good and sound reasons for this reluctance to identify, or even link the two events.

In what follows, as well as utilizing testimonies from early Pentecostal leaders, I have drawn heavily on a book by a man who had contact with the emerging Pentecostalism from 1909 onwards. That he does not embrace my own position is evidenced by the following quotations: 'Speaking with tongues is certainly Pentecostal, nor do I question that the Spirit of God can grant this power today. I reject the theory that this and other gifts were not intended to be permanent in this age . . . Having no objection to the exercise of supernatural gifts, I did not look at the matter with prejudice or initial disfavour.'[23] 'That true God-given visions are possible I do not in the least question or I must reject Acts 2:17, "your young men shall see visions".'[24] In one of his other books he gives instances of prophecies that he does accept.[25] Yet, drawing extensively on personal experiences in different parts of the world, and utilizing many articles from magazines written in the early days of the movement by its own advocates (especially *Confidence* magazine) as well as later books by strong proponents, he paints a picture which is very disturbing indeed, especially since most of the evidence is from Pentecostals themselves. 'I will judge you by your own words . . .' might well be a fitting introduction to what follows (see Luke 19:22).

Frank Bartleman is described as the one who 'has given us the only available first-hand account of the important and standard Los Angeles beginnings of the Pentecostal movement.'[26] In what should be now a very familiar story he narrates these events in the following terms: 'Nothing hinders faith and the operation of the Spirit so much as the self-assertiveness of the human spirit, the wisdom, strength and self-sufficiency of the human mind. This must be crucified, and here is where the fight comes in . . . I never sought "tongues". My natural mind resisted the idea. This phenomena *(sic)* necessarily violates human reason. It means abandonment of this faculty for the time. And this is generally the last point to yield. The human mind is held in abeyance fully in this exercise.'[27] Once again we see the disparagement of reason even in the redeemed believer and the plea that the mind be abandoned. (Admittedly, pride does need to be cast down, but this is not the same as the abandonment advocated here.) An archdeacon, speaking of 'the baptism' at that time, said, 'If I might add a word of caution from experience, *it would be to use the greatest care to keep one's head out of the way*. It is not by way of one's head so much as by way of one's heart that the Holy Ghost loves to enter.'[28]

Therefore it is interesting to learn that T.B. Barratt, who was caught up in these events and who is generally regarded as the father of European Pentecostalism, was told in a letter that for some who sought sometimes a 'wonderful shaking' came over them.[29] Not surprisingly, as he approached the time of his 'baptism' (and for him there was a period of seeking), he had just a little while before the event 'some special manifestation in my jaws and tongue'.[30] When it happened he declared that someone saw 'a crown of fire over my head and a cloven tongue as of fire in front of the crown', and soon he was lying on the floor with his eyes shut, speaking in a whole variety of languages (he claimed seven or eight) until 'there was an aching in my vocal chords'.[31]

The highly charged atmosphere and the undoubtedly remarkable events must not blind us to the simple fact that all kinds of aberrations occurred that were totally absent from Pentecost, simply because it was in no way a repetition of the Pentecost event. For example, even though there were only fifteen in a room, T.B. Barratt was led to bellow forth words at top volume ('I know from the strength of my voice that 10,000 might easily have heard all I said'). Moreover with regard to his claim that he was divinely inspired because 'The words would rush forth like a cataract,' and that 'It seemed as if an iron hand laid over my jaws. Both jaws and tongue were worked by this unseen power,' it has been suggested that this sounds more akin to demon possession than the Spirit's work.[32] Amazingly T.B. Barratt is selected by a modern writer as an example of the balanced section of the early days of the movement!

Chaotic meetings
Perhaps, however, we can even find this description of Barratt credible when we listen to some accounts of early meetings selected by another official historian as commendable and worthy of imitation. We hear that there was 'walking about a hall and playing a piano with one's eyes shut: public weeping, shouting, dancing, leaping, lying in a heap on the rostrum before the congregation: falling backward across steps, constant speaking in tongues often simultaneously, tongues which usually no one understood and which mostly were not interpreted'.[33] We have an account by the English leader, Alexander A. Boddy, of a camp meeting which he attended in Georgia: '"Everyone pray; everyone talk with God," is the command shouted out by a leader, and some are singing the brightest quick-time tunes; others are with stentorian voices letting themselves go in ecstatic, ear-splitting prayers.' Boddy, fetched to help some people seeking the baptism, tells us that 'I can scarcely make myself heard in the religious din and

ecstatic turmoil as a leader marches up and down the platform, clapping his hands and shouting at the top of a tremendous voice, "Glory be to God. Hallelujah!"[34] Boddy, a man praised by the former leader of Fountain Trust, adds, 'I must confess I rather like such a scene just now and again, but it should come spontaneously and not be worked up.'[35] Obviously a man whose own meetings in Sunderland had been described as 'pandemonium in prayer' felt in his element.[36]

That there was much 'manipulation' is evident. It was there from the beginning even though some may have failed to discern this. Frank Bartleman gives this odd picture of the scene at an early meeting: 'Brother Seymour was recognized as the nominal leader in charge . . . Brother Seymour generally sat behind two empty shoe boxes, one on top of the other. He usually kept his head inside of the top one during the meetings, in prayer.'[37] But soon Bartleman was sadly lamenting the fall from the pristine simplicity of Seymour praying with his head in the shoe box: '. . . The truth must be told. "Azusa" began to fail the Lord also, early in her history. God showed me one day they were going to organize . . . As the movement began to apostatize platforms were built higher, coat tails were worn longer, choirs were organized and string bands came into existence to "jazz" the people. The kings came back once more to their thrones, restored to sovereignty. We were no longer "brethren". Then the divisions multiplied etc. While brother Seymour kept his head inside the old empty box at "Azusa" all was well. They later built for him a throne also.'[38] Now we know what is the remedy for preserving spiritual Eden – keeping the preacher with his head in a shoebox!

From fervent supporters come many descriptions of the type of meetings that must have been held regularly. Next in importance to the doctrine of the preacher with his head in a box must come the doctrine of lying on the floor! Here is Bartleman again: 'At the New Testament Church a young lady of refinement was prostrate on the floor for hours, while at times the most heavenly singing would issue from her lips. All over the house men and women were weeping. A preacher was flat on his face on the floor, crying out "Pentecost has fully come".'[39] At other gatherings many, including the preachers, were lying on the floor, purportedly 'slain of the Lord'. One preacher 'had his feet tangled up in a chair'[40] (a bit of variation to normal prostration!). From the Indian scene, which the movement had reached in 1909, we have a picture of ladies going round and decorously arranging the skirts of other ladies who were rolling and kicking on the floor 'or covering them with shawls'.[41] When Cecil Polhill, one of the Cambridge Seven, was temporarily caught up in all this and threw his home open, his sister-in-law wrote of people 'rolling and kicking, bellowing, rattling, cackling, singing, shouting in tongues, with words and without words'.[42] Meetings at the home of the Booth-Gibborns drew complaints from neighbours because of the noise but the family were undeterred for 'quilts, blankets were fastened over windows and doors, and the "heavenly music" went on unabated'.[43] Earlier the father of this family had been somewhat embarrassed by his young son walking through London singing in an unknown tongue. As two policemen bore down on them, the father's courage evaporated and he rapidly hailed a taxi. No wonder Bartleman was exhausted at the age of about thirty-four. He wrote '. . . so that my nerves were completely exhausted. I could hardly contemplate the writing of an ordinary postcard without mental agony at this time . . . I can sympathize with Evan Roberts' nervous breakdown after the revival in Wales.'[44]

In some instances there was moral as well as nervous collapse. One instance will suffice. Another widely respected leader in these early days was Aimee Semple McPherson. We have her testimony from the year 1908, together with many accounts of others receiving salvation, the baptism or healing through her ministry, since she was a widely regarded evangelist. Of her own experience she writes, 'All at once my hands and arms began to tremble gently at first, then more and more, until my whole body was atremble with the power of the Holy Spirit. I did not consider this at all strange, as I knew how . . . batteries hummed and shook and trembled under the power of electricity, and there was the Third Person of the Trinity coming into my body in all his fulness . . .'[45] We learn from the testimonies of her hearers that she particularly emphasized entire sanctification.

In view of this one account of her meetings is, to say the least, rather odd. 'Services would begin with Aimee, clad in white gown and long robe, walking down a circular ramp with a spotlight trained on her, to the music of recorded choirs. On one occasion she varied the procedure by roaring down the ramp on a motor-cycle, screeching to a halt, and shouting, "Stop! You're headed straight for hell!" In her way, Aimee was applying the maxim of stripper Rose Lee, "You've gotta have a gimmick".[46] Perhaps her sudden mysterious disappearing act was really not so mysterious especially as we know that she was the kind of person who had received a 'revelation' that her marriage was not of the Lord and she should enter another union.[47]

Spurious visions

Bad though all this undoubtedly is, we must nevertheless deal with an aspect that is even worse, though it is rarely recognized to be so. I refer to the spurious visions and false prophecies that proliferated at this time. We will look at the visions first, though obviously there is overlap. Some were, to use the words of my main source, just 'a jumble of metaphors'. Thus a magazine published a 'tongue' in 1917: 'The Lord hath exalted His people . . . from grace to grace, spirit to spirit, until the whole church is one solid block in the Lord, without spot or wrinkle, or any such thing. To this end as a choice vessel, keep thine house in order, filled with oil, waiting for the consummation.'[48] It simply does not make sense. Other weird visions were published. In one birds were speaking from a nest through pipes into a cistern, with vapours rising from the cistern to the throne in heaven.[49] No explanation is offered of this vision either!

Another vision reported in the same magazine tells how one person was lying on the ground shaking when 'Gradually I was caused by the Lord Jesus to turn on to my back.' At this the Lord himself appeared and showed her 'part of heaven. First, I went up to heaven and knocked at the Golden Gates, – they were opened wide and I entered in. The Lord Jesus placed on my head a golden crown. While in the presence of my Saviour I saw my two young sisters and my brother, who had gone to glory a few years before. One of them said to me, "Oh, B, isn't it beautiful?" and they took hold of my hands and began to dance for joy.'[50] This was followed by a vivid re-enacting of the sufferings of Christ on the cross. The whole incident is riddled with unscriptural concepts.

Let the reader work this out for himself or herself.

That false teachings and not merely muddled impressions were conveyed through such visions must be stressed. 'A sister saw a dove descend to a tree in full bloom but without leaves; but the bird flew away. Another part of the tree was without bloom but in full leaf. Again the dove would not alight. Next came a tree which fell dead, where also the dove would not settle. Finally there was a tree loaded with fruit, where the dove settled. "The fruit was the product of life in the tree, and the life of Christ must develop and mature and bring forth fruit. Then the Holy Spirit can take them up in the power of God and unite them with Christ".' Someone has commented thus: 'The lesson aimed at is good, even the need for the fruit of righteousness to abound in the believer, but the doctrine is wrong. We do not become united with Christ because we bear fruit, but we bear fruit as the result of union with Christ (John 15, vine and branch).'[51]

Some visions were communal and quite fantastic. 'It is related that in 1914 Stephen Jeffreys was preaching at the Island Place Mission Room, Llanelly, South Wales, when there came suddenly a supernatural picture upon the wall above the platform. At first it was the head of a Lamb; then it gradually changed and became the Face of the Man of Sorrows. There it remained in the sight of the congregation and of everyone who came in to see it. It was there for six hours, and many saw it.'[52] The same publication *Confidence* also narrates how in 1918 the said Stephen Jeffreys at Thornton Heath saw heaven opened and witnessed afresh the stoning of Stephen.

Many false prophecies
When such claims are made, many feel that a preacher or movement is signally authenticated and owned of God. But what of the prophecies that were made? Here surely is a very clear test. We turn first of all to the English scene. We read, 'In the very first days of the Movement in Sunderland another clergyman was an enthusiastic supporter. He was the Rev. J.M. Pollock, brother to Mrs. A.A. Boddy. He told me the following facts and confirmed them in writing. The smallest son of a neighbour was sick. Mrs Boddy received in "tongues" intimation that the child would recover and be well. She

requested her brother to take this comforting news to the father. On the way the "power" fell on Mr Pollock and by "tongues" and interpretation he received confirmation of the message: but on reaching the house he learned that the boy was already dead.' (We note that they both received the same 'tongue'.) The writer continues, 'He pressed upon his sister that it was evidently a deceiving spirit that was operating; but she, upon recovering from the first shock, said that she had received the explanation. They had misunderstood the message, the true import of which was that the boy was to be well *in the other world,* not in this world.'[53] Readers will recall that this kind of incident is not without precedent in previous eras.

In the hope that many readers are finding these excerpts very helpful in their assessment I have included another lengthy extract from my main source book. I have already mentioned the rapid spread of the movement to India. 'In India its principal advocate was Max Wood Moorhead, editor of the periodical mentioned, *Cloud of Witnesses to Pentecost in India.* The third number was dated October 12th, 1907.

'The movement promptly ventured on an audacious prophecy. There lies before me a copy of the handbill that first announced this. It reads:

> "A message from God
>   given September 23rd, 1907
> (The) Spirit saith –
>   Judgement is coming
> (In) ten months –
>   Colombo earthquake first
>   Ceylon sunk (in) sea.

This reached Mr Moorhead in Ceylon, who repeated the whole handbill, of which the above was the beginning, in the issue of his magazine mentioned. He stated that the message was given through a Swedish missionary, and that her fellow ladyworkers had received confirmation of it. He gave a lengthy account of how by tongues and interpretations the prophecy was confirmed to him on four occasions. The destruction was fixed for October 16 and 17. Many fled from the city.'[54] It is not surprising that those who were caught up in the movement

did just this. It is a relief to know that at least one man in India
near to that time, Lord Radstock, disapproved. If only more
had been like him!

The same author summarizes for us another area where
false predictions were rife and makes pointed and apt
comments: 'One further matter deserves special mention
because it provides a test in some other vital questions. From
the very first, and throughout all the early years, there was
persistent assertion that the second advent of Christ was just
at hand. From 1911 to 1917 there was given on the first page of
Confidence a brief summary of doctrines believed, which
included "the soon-coming of the Lord". This imminency was
emphasized in addresses, reports, and letters, so that few
pages of that magazine are without such a statement.' He tells
how through tongues and prophecies this message was
reinforced and continues, 'Fifty years have passed and He is
not here. It follows that the visions, tongues, and prophecies
which contained these unfounded statements were either not
inspired at all, but were merely the utterances of the natural
mind, or else they were inspired by lying spirits. Many of the
utterances were quite precise, as that the Lord will come "this
year", or within two years, or that this may be the last Winter
before He comes . . . This false prediction was so constant, so
emphatic, so universal as to constitute a major feature of the
whole Movement from its start, which forces serious doubt as
to the energy animating it.'[55]

Not the hand of God

This must be our verdict. These tongues, visions and
prophecies were not from God. That some real Christians were
caught up in it I do not wish to deny. That there were
countless remarkable incidents, as well as some grotesquely
engineered ones, I would not gainsay. The singing must have
been unearthly. 'The notes produced were often beyond the
compass of the human voice. Persons not musical would join
harmoniously in the grand music.'[56] But was it truly heavenly?
Many claims for healing were made, but were they truly
apostolic, especially when they seem 'super-apostolic'?
'*Confidence* gives many reports about him and by him [Smith
Wrigglesworth], and, if only half the cases be accepted, he
came not a whit behind the very chiefest Apostles as a

healer.'[57] But from this background of bombast, exaggeration and deceit can even half the accounts be accepted? The historian of the movement analyses the various claims of Bartleman for personal healing and shows how unreliable the testimony is.

Once more the constant emphasis was on stifling the mind. It is interesting to note the reaction of T.B. Barratt to the prophecy about Ceylon. In a letter published by Boddy in England in 1908, Barratt wrote, 'Of course mistakes have been made here in India as elsewhere. The Apostles even made mistakes after "Pentecost". But the Lord is taking us on and teaching us in His wonderful school daily. The prophecy concerning Colombo was a mistake. Mr Moorhead also very emphatically acknowledged it. But our adversaries are constantly trying to find fault and make a tremendous noise at every mistake thus made, as if *the whole Revival were to blame for it*. They ought to mind their own "P's and Q's".'[58] The writer sounded irritated. But should not people examine and test? Moreover, according to one commentator, it was not true that Mr Moorhead readily acknowledged the mistake. It had to be forced out of him. It certainly is not true that the apostles made mistakes of this kind. And one wonders whether the prominence given to this false prophecy was partly due to the fact that it was written down and could not be glossed over for want of proof! (Many others were soon forgotten!) In fact the prophecy was very harmful, for many would be led to question the truth of Christianity itself because of its failure.

Again and again the writer whose work I have heavily drawn on stresses the unwillingness of many within the movement to investigate properly. With regard to the uniformity of experience in the baptism of the Spirit, hardly any were willing to query. This was actively discouraged.[59] He points out that amid the sheer rowdiness of many meetings it was well-nigh impossible to think clearly, even if the increasingly exhausted leaders wanted their people to do so.[60] After William Booth-Clibborn had wandered through London singing in tongues and had been whisked into a taxi we learn of the father's reaction: 'Yet when the matter of imminent school examinations came up the next morning after the night described, he declared that the lad had been too hopelessly blessed to be any good as a student, and that this was not a time for school, for "once we have tasted of this wine we are incurable as drunkards! We always want more."'[61] When one man wrote a manuscript on the tongues issue and offered it to a lady caught up in the movement, she refused to look at it, saying, 'The Lord will not let me read *a thing like that!'*[62] Most important of all, it is reported that when a speaker from Los Angeles came to India and was asked to justify those occurrences from the Bible he could not do it.[63] Neither can I. But I am equally convinced that in many of the events, whether they be the noisy exhausting meetings or the many false prophecies, there was a considerable satanic element.

The sad thing is that in few contemporary books will the reader find the above facts. Instead the early leaders will invariably be portrayed as balanced, fervent Christians, exuberantly enjoying life on a supernatural dimension denied to many other Christians who were strangers to the 'baptism' and the 'gifts'. I do not wish to impugn the evangelistic zeal and basic orthodoxy of some leaders, but it is very important that this other side should be known. I have not engaged in needless muckraking. The facts I have presented ought to be known since they involve matters which lie right at the heart of the validity of charismatic claims. Truth never fears exposure to the light.

Anyone who has followed the biblical arguments at the beginning of the book and the detailed historical section cannot fail to recognize that distinctive patterns have repeatedly emerged. The sad thing, as these closing pages of the chapter will seek to demonstrate, is that the true picture has rarely been portrayed accurately or, worse still, seems in some cases to have been actively concealed. On the historical evidence the words of William Goode can scarcely be bettered when he stated that 'The principal points to which the writer wishes to call attention . . . are these two: viz. first, the dissimilarity between the characteristics of the supposed gifts of the present day, and those of the scriptural prophets; and, secondly, the remarkable similarity between them and those of the various false pretenders to such endowments in the past ages of the Christian Church.'[64]

Yet charismatics have so often failed to portray the past accurately. We have seen this in the case of Irving. Many other instances could be given. One leader has written a book surveying the various Pentecostal claimants down the centuries. While he admits excesses in the Montanists, he refers to Tertullian as 'one of the most brilliant Christian scholars of any age' using his stature and charismatic convictions to support his own claims.[65] Yet we have surveyed the dangerous unbiblical views of Tertullian and the puerile prophecies that he sanctioned. This writer also expresses the view that 'Perhaps the greatest book ever written on the subject of the Holy Spirit came from the pen of a Puritan – John Owen.'[66] There is, however, no mention of the fact that John Owen, we have already seen, firmly believed that the extraordinary gifts had ceased. And while quoting Jonathan Edwards' defence of the Revival from the attacks of critics, 'who were displaying that human weakness of "either approving or condemning all in a lump"' he himself displays gross historical weakness by never once telling the reader that Jonathan Edwards wrote prolifically and powerfully against his own position![67]

In some charismatic books and pamphlets a quotation attributed to Augustine appears. In it he supposedly writes, 'We still do what the apostles did when they laid hands on the Samaritans and called down the Holy Spirit on them by the laying on of hands. It is expected that converts should speak with new tongues.'[68] In no case is documentation given for this quotation. While it is permissible to quote from a secondary source from time to time, and I have done this particularly with regard to the book by William Goode (after checking many of his quotations and finding them invariably accurate) in this particular case the use of Augustine's name to bolster up a position would seem particularly reprehensible. This is because his contrary viewpoint is so well known from many quotations which can be verified.

Similarly, we have seen from various quotations from Luther that he not only dissociated himself from the charismatics of his day, but strenuously wrote against them and combated their influence. Yet a modern charismatic has written of Luther as follows: 'Martin Luther commenting on Mark 16:17,18, said, "The signs here spoken of (including that of speaking in tongues), are to be used *according to need*. When the need arises, and the Gospel is hard pressed, then we must definitely do these signs, before we allow the Gospel to be maligned and knocked down."' The writer does not give any reference and I have not been able to trace this quotation. He then adds, 'I believe we are in such a time as Luther alluded to. And I believe that the Scripture gives us every reason to believe that in such a time the Lord will give added power – yes, added gifts – to His Church to meet the challenge.'[69] In similar vein another leader of the movement has written, 'Sauer in his *History of the Christian Church* tells that Martin Luther was endowed with all the gifts of the Spirit. Certainly he experienced the supernatural in a remarkable way. We see for instance his faith in divine healing in a letter written in 1545 to a friend asking advice about a sick person: "When you depart lay your hands upon the man again and say, 'These signs shall follow them that believe; they shall lay hands on the sick and they shall recover.'"'[70] In context this latter passage envisages a period of sustained prayer rather than immediate healing. It hardly supports any charismatic programme. Moreover earlier quotations from Luther show that he viewed the signs of Mark 16 as peculiar to the apostolic age. Hence the use of his name in this way is simply dishonest.

Alleged prophecies in Scotland

Writers often quote experiences of John Knox, Alexander Peden and other worthies in Scotland. This is a period that we have not examined. It would seem plain that Knox did voice a strong conviction about the fact that he would preach again in Scotland and about the manner of various people's deaths. Yet when credited by his followers with prophetic gifts, Knox himself replied, 'My assurances are not marvels of Merlin, nor yet the dark sentences of profane prophecies. But *first,* the plain truth of God's Word, *second,* the invincible justice of the everlasting God, and *third,* the ordinary course of His punishments and plagues from the beginning, are my assurances and grounds.'[71] One would have thought this was a clear enough disclaimer and certainly one of his best biographers, who discusses this point in some detail, while firmly rebutting the view that he had special 'revelations', does believe that because of his close walk with God he saw more deeply into events and their consequences.[72]

In discussion in 1983 a leader of our day was quoted as saying with regard to Alexander Peden that 'It seems to me beyond any dispute that that man had the power of foreknowledge and did prophesy things that subsequently came to pass. The records are authentic and they can be read in the two great volumes of Select Biographies edited for the Woodrow Society.'[73] I have not been able to obtain this book, but Robert Woodrow's *A history of the Sufferings of the Church of Scotland from the Restoration to the Revolution*, Vol. IV, says of Peden that 'When removed from his people by force, I am told, he was very positive that no curate should ever be fixed in that parish, which, they say held true.'[74] In itself, for a man well aware of the feelings of his people in such a situation, this was not a particularly remarkable prediction! Nor, in view of the mood of the day, is the prophecy that his corpse would be disinterred after burial and then hung on a gallows surprising in its narration and its fulfilment.

Yet Woodrow goes on to describe at some length how Peden has been much abused since his death by having false or non-existent prophecies foisted upon him. One that he mentions is that King William was to have warred with Spain – an event that never happened. Woodrow's verdict is balanced and fair. 'That the secret of the Lord was with this fearer of him, I do not doubt; and the attested hint I have given of his foretelling the disturbing of his dead body, before he died, may fully satisfy to this; and I am apt to think this prediction, with some others I have pretty well vouched, together with the additions that are generally made by too many to such accounts, when they are in conversation, indistinctly told and handed about, may have given a handle to some designing persons, for their own ends, to shape and frame prophecies under Mr Peden's name.'[75] When one is confronted with the description of Peden's awareness of the death of a friend at the hand of Claverhouse's troops and the mourning of his widow, even if we assume that all the details that have come down to us are accurate, we are surely confronted more with the aspect of the blessed communion of saints than with some charismatic gift.[76] There are many such incidents and premonitions described in the *Days of the Fathers in Ross-shire* where the author, like the biographer of Knox, explains it rather in terms of Psalm 25:14, where we read that 'The Lord confides in those who fear him' and never sees these incidents in terms of a recurrence of the charismata.[77]

There are many worrying features in the arguments of many Methodist charismatics with regard to John Wesley and early Methodism. We saw that although, admittedly, John Wesley himself held weak views on the reason for the actual cessation of the gifts, both the Wesleys and Whitefield consistently opposed the tongue-speakers and prophets of their day. None of them gave the slightest indication that they believed the gifts would be restored. In fact John Wesley opposed such manifestations to the close of his ministry and expounded a view of tongue-speaking which would mean that all instances today are spurious. That this was his ultimate position would seem irrefutable and the evidence for it is not difficult to find.

Yet, blatantly ignoring the fact that these early Methodists faced courageously and biblically the charismatic claimants of their own day, a booklet entitled *The Charismatic Movement in Methodism*, citing the view of one of their modern leaders, states, 'It could well be that because the first Methodists did not expect to receive the charismata, and indeed did not particularly want them, that they created a mental or spiritual block to their reception.'[78] Yet it was a biblical block that they erected! They examined and rejected the claims to gifts on scriptural grounds. It is very sad that in this publication and in another article entitled *John Wesley's Charismatic Ministry* none of the evidence adduced in this book is even so much as mentioned.[79] Therefore when another modern writer, who is not himself a Methodist, blithely writes that 'The early Methodists are a few examples of those in earlier days who spoke in tongues,' we must continue to put large queries against the honesty of much of the scholarship of the movement.[80] Since this same writer also says that 'probably Martin Luther' spoke in tongues as well, it seems appropriate to append an important scripture and leave the reader to ponder the challenge perhaps more seriously than he or she has ever done before:

> Lord, who may dwell in your sanctuary?
>   Who may live on your holy hill?
> He whose walk is blameless
>   and who does what is righteous,

> who speaks the truth from his heart
>   and has no slander on his tongue,
> who does his neighbour no wrong
>   and casts no slur on his fellow man
>   (Ps. 15:1-3).

It may be that some of the assertions of these men are simply mistakes. It may be that I have made mistakes in what I have written and need to ask God's forgiveness. But I can honestly say before God that I have sought to investigate the matter properly, remembering that it is a terrible sin to slander a man of the past and to wrong a neighbour, even though that neighbour lived many centuries ago. We certainly do this when we ascribe to them views which they not only did not hold, but also clearly opposed.

12.
A contemporary delusion

A call for a sympathetic understanding of Pentecostalism

Today we are being urged on all sides to look sympathetically at the emerging Pentecostalism in our midst which is now very firmly established in many historical denominations as well as in the older Pentecostal churches. In the 1960s and 1970s one magazine played a significant role in this regard. At the beginning of 1964 readers were told of the rapid spread of the movement and given the choice between 'Pentecost or Holocaust'. They were told of High-Church and academic converts to the movement and the commendation of a well-known Reformed Anglican was cited. He was thrilled at the prospect of nominal churchgoers being converted. 'Your editor met individuals and groups whose lives had been affected by it. He attended their prayers and worshipped with them, and visited the homes of some. He heard some praying in an unknown tongue. It was all restrained and calm, and immediately someone else would interpret what had been said.'[1] The writer felt that, with the healings and testimonies to victory, it was very like the situation in Acts.

Another writer, confronted with the phenomena in our day and convinced of a vast change in Roman Catholicism, wrote of the weakness of quoting 1 Corinthians 13:8 for the cessation of the gifts and said, 'Anyone who mixes, as I do, in wide enough circles to meet with dozens of Christians from all kinds of denominational backgrounds, into whose lives there has obviously come, through receiving this gift of tongues, a new dimension of warmth, love of Christ, love of people, zeal to witness, knows that it is absurd and indeed blasphemous to call this satanic.'[2]

In an article calling for 'a Charismatic Truce', the author

said that, in the face of today's claims while 'we can deny the
validity of their experience – to most of us this would be
intellectually and scientifically dishonest; we can admit they
are gifted, but claim the donor is not the Holy Spirit but the
Devil – this would be a highly dangerous claim to make; or we
can accept that, whether we approve of his activity or not, we
are watching the Holy Spirit distribute his gifts, both
miraculous and ordinary.'[3] He opted for the last attitude. Not
surprisingly the article was welcomed by the secretary of
Fountain Trust and others, although one non-charismatic did
perversely, but one would feel accurately, point out that
'While calling "truce" he surreptitiously shifts his boundary
line several yards into my territory.'[4]

The 'periodicity view'

One Reformed writer in particular has had a vast influence
within the ranks of non-conformist evangelicals. While I
gladly acknowledge my deep indebtedness to this man, on this
subject I have had to part company with him on many matters
– on the commendation of the treatment of tongues in a book
by a well-known Bible teacher, on the assertion that prophecy
is given merely 'in certain strange and extreme circumstances'
and, not least, in the latter part of the following assertion:
'Furthermore, I would suggest that in the Bible itself there is
surely discernible a kind of periodicity in the appearance of
these supernatural happenings. For instance, there is clearly a
periodicity in the Old Testament. These things happened at
special given times, and for clear and obvious reasons. The
same is seen in a measure in the New Testament; and we are
told that the Spirit is the Lord of these matters and dispenses
His gifts according to His own will. This is something
therefore that can happen at any time when it is the will of
God that it should happen. Who are we to determine when
this should be?'[5] Before any readers rush to claim this
conclusion as supporting their views on the subject, it would
seem that they ought honestly to ask whether they really
believe in such a view of the gifts as he here expounds, or
whether they do not rather believe with many others that the
gifts are always available.

Undoubtedly there has been a shift of emphasis in the main articles in one Christian newspaper. This has been especially evident in a column which ran for about three years. On many issues the writer of this column has written in a biblical, stimulating and provocative way but on this issue I would only apply the last of the three adjectives. In the early days of his column he sounded a warning shot when he urged that churches, to show themselves as New Testament churches, 'should not panic if this is sometimes demonstrated in the exercise of such distinctive supernatural gifts as Paul recognized and approved (1 Cor. 12-14) by some members of the body'.[6] It was he who said that prophets in New Testament times were fallible and errant. It was he who warned us against building too much on apostleship, but gave us no guidelines with which to build anything. It was he who charged that those who deny the reality of the gifts today come perilously near to blue-pencilling two whole chapters of the New Testament. It was he who declared, 'I have never spoken in tongues nor have I ever wished to do so (I am however rebuked in this piece of nervousness by the apostle Paul who wrote: "I want you *all* to speak in tongues"!)'[7] Yes, the apostle Paul did say this but we might at least be permitted to hear what tongues were and whether they have ceased!

It will be noted that the writer who emphasized 'periodicity' left the door open for a restoration of the gifts. This has always been a Pentecostal position. One of their historians of the Los Angeles revival puts it in what for them is familiar imagery: 'But here we are with the restoration of the very experience of "Pentecost", with the "latter rain", a restoration of the power . . .'[8] Another of their spokesmen argues that their movement is really the latter rain, i.e. the prelude to the end. 'The latter-rain out-pouring of the Holy Spirit is God's final great movement of power to provide a strong witness to the church and the world before the coming of the Lord Jesus Christ.'[9] Thus in a book by a former member of the Brethren and published by Fountain Trust the author can say, 'Joel's prophecy to which Peter referred on the day of Pentecost has yet to be fulfilled in the days immediately preceding "the great and terrible day of the Lord" (Joel 2:31), and its fulfilment will be accompanied by "wonders in the heaven above and signs in the earth beneath". The Pentecostal outpouring was indeed a foretaste of that fulfilment, and seeing that tongues was a special feature on that occasion we should have thought that this fact alone would serve as strong presumptive evidence of its appearance together with prophesying, dreams and visions, as one of the signs which will accompany the fulfilment in the end time.' He then goes on, 'Indeed may not the world-wide reappearance of charismatic and other supernatural gifts in recent years serve as a solemn warning that we are now approaching the end of this age?'[10] In tune with this one group in America refer to themselves as part of 'God's end-time army'.[11]

While we are ever being urged not to lump charismatics together and to recognize that Reformed charismatics are of a much more stolid, stable frame of mind, it has not proved easy to do this in our study, especially when we read statements such as the following: 'I do not feel that any of us need, in principle, at any rate, to question God's sovereign *right* to restore such things to the church if he wills, especially if that church is in the last hours of the "last days" and on the verge of apocalyptic events both sublime and terrible.'[12] Or again, 'God can work miracles today as He has done in past ages. Perhaps we should expect Him to do so as the days are darkening, and the forces of evil seem to be emerging in an unusually aggressive and potent manner.'[13] Oddly enough, this last quotation forms the final pages of a pamphlet in which the author spends much time in warning about satanic gifts and signs. Despite many helpful things that are said, it is a pamphlet that seems to lack real biblical firmness. These Reformed writers would in fact seem to concur with the judgement of a modern evangelist, who has likewise written, 'Certainly we cannot blind ourselves to the fact that many of the sign gifts which vindicate the authenticity of the gospel are reappearing at this moment.'[14]

Who really limits the Holy Spirit?

The immediate reply to this is that there is no indication in Scripture that the gifts will be restored. If my exegesis in the earlier chapters has been correct, God has declared that when the gifts cease, they cease for all time. This in itself is sufficient reason for rejecting the plausible argument that we might be restricting God's sovereignty if we reject the restoration of the gifts. Judisch, answering those who argue that this view limits the Holy Spirit, has well written, 'The charismatic movement of course warns us not to limit the Holy Spirit in this way. The truth of the matter, however, is that we must recognize and respect the limits that the Holy Spirit has set upon Himself. Indeed we limit the Spirit if we insist that He conduct Himself in the same way in every age – if we argue, that, because He bestowed miraculous powers on men in biblical times, He must bestow miraculous powers on us today as well.'[15] And, of course, the majority of charismatics do not really accept this 'periodicity' view. They believe that the gifts have always been available, but have been refused or forfeited through the worldliness or unbelief of the church. This leads them perilously near to the view of Irving, to the effect that 'For fifteen hundred years and more the church has been shutting her door against the glory of Christ,' and that previous ages of the church had been totally deficient of the earnestness and piety that in his day qualified some to receive the gifts.[16]

It must also be pointed out that the quotation from Joel used by Peter in his Pentecost sermon is not a text projected into the future. Referring to the events of his own time, he prefaces the quotation by these words: 'No, this is what was spoken by the prophet Joel' (Acts 2:16). However difficult we might find it initially to apply all the words from the quotation to events around Pentecost, this can be done. Charismatics often treat this text as dispensationalists treat the quotation by James of Amos 9 at the Council of Jerusalem. They refuse the apostolic guidelines, which would apply the words to first-century events, and make them refer to events immediately prior to the return of Christ. It goes without saying that there is much scriptural teaching about false signs and miracles prior to the return of Christ and to this we must turn in a moment.

But another simple historical fact remains to be faced. Why did all the other groups get it wrong in this respect? Let us look back over the historical chapters. The Montanists believed that the end was near. The Anabaptist groups linked the restoration of the gifts with a belief that the return of Christ was nigh. So did the French prophets. So did the Irvingites.

So did the early Pentecostals. So they do today. Are we at last in the period when they have got it right? Can we just sweep away the past periods with an airy wave of the hand and some remark about grim and grisly stories of the horrors of the past not being able to sap our confidence today? Listen to the French prophet Lacy: we need 'an extraordinary dispensation to prepare for so extraordinary a revolution'.[17] Is this not strangely familiar? With those who argue that all this is conducive to holiness, William Goode disagrees, pointing out that if the prophecy proves false then the whole fabric might be queried. Christ's argument for watchfulness came from the very uncertainty of the time (see Mark 13:33-35).

A second danger is that the missionary nerve of the church will be cut. People will either become absorbed in the signs of the end, to the exclusion of the missionary mandate, or, in some cases, they may think missionary endeavour is hardly worthwhile since (according to some theories) people are going to be swept into the kingdom when Christ comes in some quite different manner to that of prayerful, painstaking missionary endeavour. It is no accident that the French prophets proved an obstacle to the spread of the gospel in the Methodist revival both in England and in New England. It is beyond dispute that Edward Irving poured scorn on the value of missionary endeavour at two large meetings. He had become absorbed in the 'signs'. He was so sure that only catastrophic judgement lay ahead that, in his view, missionary endeavour was futile.[18] Is there not a danger in this direction today? In fact the biggest danger in this connection is the way in which vital differences between Roman Catholic, liberal (or modernistic) and evangelical teachings are constantly being blurred or glossed over. It is certain that Reformed writers whom we have quoted earlier in this chapter would not share the views which we are going on to consider, but it must be asked whether their views do not in fact help to increase the confusion, rather than clarifying the real issues.

Does doctrine no longer matter?

Undoubtedly one of the main ways in which the movement is seen to be manifestly unbiblical is the way in which modernists and Roman Catholics are drawn in and do not cease to be modernists and Roman Catholics. One leader exulted in this in an interview article in a Christian magazine in 1972. He was asked about the wide span of doctrinal conviction in the movement, which embraced 'Roman Catholics or Free Church or liberals', and replied that 'These people are not going to become Evangelicals' and that the movement undoubtedly involved 'Catholics and liberals'.[19] A Methodist charismatic expressed it like this in an article: 'As for the conservative evangelicals and their stand on salvation, let us thank God for them, but realize that, for at least some, their theological stand seems so confined as to exclude them from all that God in this age is seeking to do for them.' After this sweeping dismissal of blessing for evangelicals he went on to write, 'It is amazing for how many different types Baptism in the Spirit is *the* way,' and proceeded to name several individuals who 'are all under this charismatic umbrella'[20] including one who had in the past clearly asserted that all will ultimately be saved and that 'At the very last Love will conquer and save all.'[21] Is the evangelical position moving towards that of the pastor who wrote in a local newsletter. 'Today He is pouring out His Spirit upon the fundamentalists and the modernists', but who gave no real indication that the modernists had now bowed to Scripture and become Christians?[22]

But the really amazing movement is the growth of the charismatic emphasis within large sections of Roman Catholicism. This has been traced to the vision and prophecy of an older Pentecostal, Smith Wrigglesworth, as given to a then young minister in the Assemblies of God who has been nicknamed 'Mr Pentecost'. Another well-known Pentecostal evangelist believed that all this was of God and gave it his blessing.[23] Although a former secretary of the Fountain Trust has occasionally expressed misgivings that Roman Catholics were not moving far enough in the direction of applying Scripture to the life of their churches, he has always been swift to reply to any criticism that he might doubt in any way the credentials of the Roman Catholic charismatics.[24] His firm conviction would seem to be expressed in his book *This is the Day*, published in 1979, where he visualizes three sisters, Evangeline, Charisma and Roma, and says, 'This book is written out of a longing to see these sisters reconciled to each other in the certain knowledge that if they could be brought together untold blessings would follow.'[25]

When there were the two conclaves for the election of Popes John Paul I and II a Baptist charismatic said in an interview, 'It has to be supernatural rather than a natural thing that has happened. That means either supernatural good, or supernatural evil. I've accepted the supernatural good explanation.' He added, with reference to the first election: 'They were saying, "The Holy Spirit has chosen." They called it the Charismatic Conclave.' 'The result told them what kind of Pope the Lord wanted because he immediately brought in a humanity; a humility; and a humour.'[26] When this man died, the Baptist felt 'bereaved of a pope' for the first time in his life, but he was soon consoled as he recognized that John Paul II was the man the Lord really wanted as pope, although John Paul I was needed, however briefly, to prepare the way.

During the interview the Baptist spoke of his numerous contacts, mainly with Roman Catholic charismatics, in largely emotional terms. He told of his challenge to them on their veneration of Mary and of his acceptance of much of their doctrine, saying that 'much' of their 'doctrine is compatible to an evangelical understanding of the Bible. For example – we both still believe in hell.' He expressed the view that among charismatic Catholics belief in purgatory and penance was declining and said that he knew of a group who at one conference were even discussing how to 'reintroduce believers' baptism to Rome'.[27] Like others he linked what the article called 'Catholic Revolution' with the prayer of Pope John XXIII that Roman Catholics would experience a new Pentecost.[28] Paul VI was seen as furthering the process. The Baptist also said, 'But I have had quite a bit of contact with Cardinal Suenens who has been closely involved with the election of the two Popes. (Cardinal Suenens, the Primate of Belgium and Archbishop of Malines – Brussels, has been described as one of today's eminent Christian leaders. He is the author of "A New Pentecost" and a leader of the renewal movement within the Catholic Church.)'[29]

An assessment of two leaders

If we analyse these words we can test the discernment of a charismatic leader who is widely accepted among many sections of the community. We shall concentrate on his view of the present pope and of Cardinal Suenens, with only brief comments on some of his other statements. When he makes the assertion that Roman Catholics believe in hell, he seems unaware of the widespread modernism and even universalism within the church.[30] With regard to the jovial Pope John XXIII, I have sought to assess misplaced Protestant euphoria in an appendix to my book on John Hus, a man who so accurately analysed the evils of the papacy as a system that he was burned at the stake.[31] The unbiblical nature of Paul VI's views can easily be demonstrated and with regard to John Paul I one can only despairingly say that even Hamlet knew that a man 'may smile, and smile, and be a villain'.[32] How undiscerning have some Protestants become? Will a simple smile disarm them and cause them to throw doctrine aside?

But what of John Paul II? Was he a charismatic choice? Norman St John Stevas and Lord Longford in their biographies make no attempt to conceal his deep devotion to Mary. The former tells how when the new pope first appeared he concluded his address with, 'I would like to invite you to join me in professing our faith, our hope and our fidelity to Mary, the Mother of Christ and of the Church, and also to begin again on the road of history and of the Church,' and the latter records that, among his first words at his election, were these: 'I was afraid to accept that responsibility, yet I do so in a spirit of obedience to the Lord and total faithfulness to Mary, our most holy Mother.'[33] The very tours of the pope have frequently expressed his devotion, whether it be to Knock in Ireland, to Lourdes in France or the 'Black Madonna' of Poland.

Space precludes a full analysis of the pope's speeches in England, which at Wembley he described as 'Mary's dowry'. His first sermon was published in full by *The Times*. It was the full-blooded doctrine of baptismal regeneration, the view that we are automatically regenerated if we are baptized as infants. Baptism is 'our new birth in Christ', he affirmed.[34] This is a view that has damned millions. Quite unambiguously and explicitly he urged prayers for the dead in the Falklands conflict. 'In our prayers let us remember the victims of both sides; we pray for the dead, that they may rest in Christ,' he urged.[35] This too is a teaching which has lulled millions to a false sense of security and sapped the urgency of the gospel.(Obviously news of the desire for believers' baptism and abandonment of belief in purgatory had not yet reached St Peter's in Rome.) Speaking to the assembly at Wembley, his address was in far from evangelistic tones: 'As I look at this great assembly I am full of respect for each of you. You are God's sons and daughters; he loves you. I believe in you. I believe in all mankind.'[36] How can this be the utterance of a spokesman of Christ? Christ himself, who loved his hearers with a deep and passionate love, was frank with them. He trusted himself to no man, 'for he knew all men. He did not need man's testimony about man, for he knew what was in a man' (John 2:24,25). He reminded some hearers that, far from being God's children, they were children of the devil (John 8:42-44. See also 1 John 3:1-10). Only those who truly received him and believed on his name were God's children (John 1:12,13; Gal. 3:26-4:7). Not only was the pope not a genuine evangelist, but corruption at the papal court continues unabated. *In God's Name* by David Yallop may not have finally proved that the previous pope was murdered, but it has certainly established the evil nature of many papal transactions and officials and, what is more important, the present pope's acquiescence in much of this, with no attempt at correction or discipline.[37]

But what of the leading spokesman for the cardinals among the charismatics, namely Cardinal Suenens? He has undoubtedly made the movement acceptable and respectable at Rome. He persuaded Pope Paul VI to take an interest in it. That the Roman Catholic delegates at a European charismatic and ecumenical congress at Strasbourg held in May 1982 under the title 'Pentecost over Europe' greatly outnumbered others was largely due to his influence. He has obviously influenced the Baptist charismatic quoted earlier and his persuasive powers are indeed influential on a wide scale. Thus in a Methodist magazine we find an Anglican charismatic referring to him as 'the outstanding and progressive leader of the Roman Catholic Church in Belgium'.[38]

Suenens' book *Ecumenism and Charismatic Renewal* gives the thoughts of this widely regarded leader. He makes it plain that ecumenical advance must involve acceptance of tradition allied to the Word of God and also of the sacramental structure of the church. By the church he means a church 'presided over by the pope'.[39] Those with a charismatic experience are generally 'not referring to a dramatic conversion ... but a new awareness of what the sacrament of Christian initiation had already deposited in us germinally, but now rises to full consciousness'.[40] Therefore, not surprisingly in his view, the baptismal water becomes 'waters of rebirth' and 'children of heaven ... emerge from this sacred font, as from a very pure womb'.[41] Rejecting a testimony of someone who declares that he became a Christian on a certain day, he says that the person was in fact 'sacramentally baptized as an infant and became a Christian from that day'.[42] Since he has written elsewhere that 'To experience communion with the Holy Spirit in union with Mary, we must begin by performing some acts which explicitly direct our attention to her ... We breathe in Mary and breathe out the Spirit', it is not surprising that in this book he sees her not as an ecumenical stumbling-block but as 'a welcoming haven of reconciliation'.[43] Even the appearance of the virgin Mary to Bernadette at Lourdes is accepted as true and what he calls 'proselytism' is excluded by ecumenical aims.[44] Is this a picture of a man who has been renewed by the Holy Spirit, one of the clearest indications of which is whole-hearted adherence to the Word of God? The very thought is preposterous. Can we not legitimately say that there is a strong spirit of delusion abroad?

Views from the popular movement

One has only to survey books like *Catholic Pentecostals* and *The Charismatic Renewal and the Irish Experience* to see that the tongues and the prophecy are only a veneer. Little else has altered. In the former book one testimony specifically records that the person began to pray the rosary, 'a practice I've taken up since baptism in the Spirit'.[45] Another writes as follows: 'Traditional devotions such as those to Mary have become meaningful to us (and I am one who put Mary completely out of the picture many years ago).'[46] In the second book we read the testimony of a priest who declared that after his 'baptism of the Spirit', 'Never before had I such a sense of Mary's role in leading me into the fulness of Christ and the Spirit.'[47] A charismatic archbishop was sure that the papal dogma of infallibility in 1870 was due to the Holy Spirit.[48] Both books follow Suenens in seeing the baptism of the Spirit as merely the renewal of baptismal grace and taking the *ex opere operato* view of baptism; one couple even express their preference for the phrase 'renewing the baptism in the Spirit' rather than 'receiving'.[49] Yet another account can depict the way in which several Roman Catholics were enabled to speak in tongues: 'With other people, the beginning comes quietly, gently and effortlessly; with Tom N., it was as he was finishing his rosary; with Rita M., it was while she was singing a hymn at Mass; with Sister M., it came as she knelt in silent prayer to the Blessed Virgin.'[50] Apparently the 'baptism' leads to a more Marian theology! What kind of baptism is it?

One writer, not a Roman Catholic, nor a professing believer, described a charismatic meeting he attended at Rome. There were no tongues and it was very informal.'A negro rose and, holding his arms above his head, recounted a dream about a person he saw amidst the dark waves at night. It was inconsequential, and he admitted as much by saying, with a slightly apologetic tone: "Well, that was the dream and I wanted to share it." A middle-aged blonde lady stood up, placed her hands above her head and said: "I read the newspapers before coming here. They were full of dreadful news. I said to myself 'why worry?' We all of us love each other. We can live in peace with each other so we must shut out the bad news we read about and be happy in our love of Christ." There were murmurs of approval. What struck me most was the thought that millions of Catholics throughout the world now hold these prayer-meetings regularly.'[51] The movement is spreading. In fact the same writer declares that 'The charismatic movement is distinctly Marian. This movement has grown faster than any within the post-Conciliar Catholic Church and is almost surely the most effective ecumenical phenomenon at the popular level.' And, 'Again, I am aware that the ground is delicate, but I still would not hesitate to place the charismatics on the road to Fatima.'[52] In itself this is alarming enough but there is more to say.

Spurious miracles

We must not raise the question of false miracles. Let us quote some relevant Scriptures. 'At that time if anyone says to you, "Look, here is the Christ!" or "There he is!" do not believe it. For false Christs and false prophets will appear and perform great signs and miracles to deceive even the elect – if that were possible. See, I have told you ahead of time' (Matt. 24:23-25). Obviously these are going to be signs of great subtlety. Even true Christians will be greatly perplexed and almost led astray. The apostle Paul writes in similar vein: 'The coming of the lawless one will be in accordance with the work of Satan displayed in all kinds of counterfeit miracles, signs and wonders, and in every sort of evil that deceives those who are perishing' (2 Thess. 2:10). There are other scriptural passages which bear on this theme (Exod. 7:8-13; 8:6,7,16-19; 9:8-12; Deut. 13:1-5; Rev. 13:11-18; 16:13,14).

Theologians have argued about the question as to whether Satan can actually perform a miracle, or whether he can merely ape with great skill what God himself can do in a perfect and original way. Martin Luther would agree with John Owen in believing that only God can perform a true miracle, but he in no wise underestimates the power and skill and subtlety of the evil one. 'For it must happen that the world is duped and deceived with the name of God. Hence the saying: "All misfortune begins in the name of God". For the devil cannot peddle his lies unless he adorns them with that beloved name.'[53] He pointed out that Rome sought authentication for many of its shrines and doctrines by claiming miracles.[54] According to Gregory the Great one of the hardest trials of the elect in the last great tribulation will be that Antichrist will be able to perform such great miracles that Christian endeavours may appear to be eclipsed.[55] Even if this statement be deemed speculation, the teaching that Satan can perform great signs is not so.

Rome has always believed in miracles of this type. To take but one out of the hundreds of examples that might be adduced, we think of the so-called visions of Bernadette when, over a period of time she reputedly saw Mary, hearing from her lips in the sixteenth vision, 'I am the Immaculate Conception' – words given in 1858 and accepted as confirming the dogma of the immaculate conception of Mary promulgated by Rome some four years earlier, in 1854.[56] Although it is generally contended that few miracles are claimed at Lourdes and the majority of the pilgrims go away unhealed, yet some are accepted as miraculous cures and others who are not officially certified as cured by the authorities yet proclaim that they have received healing. Certainly the church does not discourage, but rather provides for the exhibition of crutches and walking frames discarded by pilgrims in a room near the shrine. But as we think of the words of Luther and Owen about Satan's ability to perform a true miracle, we might profitably recall the comment of Anatole France as he peered into this room. 'What no wooden legs?' he remarked.[57]

Although Percy Dearmer years earlier had dodged the question of why people with amputated limbs were not cured at Lourdes, it is still a relevant question. Satan can go so far and no further. Indeed, admitting for the most part the contrast between biblical miracles and Roman Catholic ones, John Henry Newman, a well-known convert to Rome, surprisingly referred to the latter as 'tentative miracles'.[58] It was an astonishing admission. One modern Roman Catholic in a much-lauded and popular work on healing has even recommended 'that beginners pray for the cure of minor ailments, such as colds', before tackling the bigger illnesses![59] That his own book is very much taken up with 'tentative miracles' (there are large sections on 'inner healing') should not, however, blind us to the fact that the occasional 'striking cures' or 'striking claims' (often heard at a distance of third-hand) do win people's allegiance to false teaching.

For example, what do we make of this from the book *Catholic Pentecostals?* 'At a prayer meeting in South Bend, a priest who was attending his first prayer meeting asked the man next to him where he had learned Greek. Once again the answer was the same – "what Greek?" The priest then told the group that he had distinctly heard the man next to him repeat the opening lines of the "Hail Mary" in Greek during his prayers.' From then on the meeting took a decidedly Marian flavour and although the writer of the account was initially worried by this, he continued, 'We were a little apprehensive that the Spirit of God was not being served when the focus switched from Christ to Mary. But we worrywarts were confounded and joyful to discover that next day was one of the greatest Marian feast days in the liturgical calendar. Our meeting the previous evening had not been a fearful diversion but an occasion. It had been a vigil, a preparation led by the Spirit for the feast that was to follow.'[60]

Robert G. Gromacki has written helpfully and penetratingly on this whole question. He points out how the charismatic movement has the official approval of the church after official investigation and quotes many testimonies from Roman Catholics who have become more devoted to unscriptural Roman dogma after their supposed baptism. 'They also related their charismatic gifts of glossolalia, prophecy and healing to past Roman Catholic miracles and visions,' is a very illuminating comment indeed.[61] Therefore we find a contemporary Roman Catholic author, who will acknowledge no Old Testament miracle as genuine (when Elijah prayed for fire on Mount Carmel, he says, 'It is within credence that he used a burning glass'), who nevertheless treats seriously all the visions of Lourdes and Fatima, even though he candidly acknowledges that, as far as Mary's cult goes, 'As a New Testament character, she never says or does anything to justify her later glorification in the form it takes.'[62] In one remarkable passage he shows how inconsistent Protestants are in their wavering and dithering over whether genuine miracles can still happen and boldly affirms that 'In the Catholic context miracles can still happen.'[63]

Such signs are not confined to Lourdes and one or two isolated places. 'People's Miracle in the Potting Shed', was how *The Times* recently headed a report from Poland. 'Poland is the land of unofficial miracles. Every six weeks or so, the even, languid pace of provincial life is suddenly interrupted by an apparition in a church, a garden or a shed. As the news spreads by word of mouth or in the form of crumpled typewritten testimonies tens of thousands of Poles, many of them lame or blind or despairing, abandon their homes and travel to the scene in packed buses and taxis or piled up in train corridors like Japanese commuters. In Gdansk after martial law was declared a cross was said to be shedding blood, tiny red droplets oozing out of the timber. In a village near Lublin there is a crucifix weeping salt tears. But the most common apparition is that of the Virgin Mary, conjured up in a swirl of fast-moving colourful images or, on a few occasions, appearing in such solid form that she can be touched and rubbed. This week there are two miracles running concurrently, both of them centred on a vision of Mary.'[64] Then details are given of the visions. Even more recently the same paper reported that clergymen were treating seriously a report from Asdee, Co. Derry, that schoolchildren saw two statues move in a church. 'I saw Jesus moving. His hand moved and called me. Then I saw the eyes of the Blessed Virgin move,' reported a seven-year-old girl.[65] Such incidents may be seen as lacking official approval. But Rome has fostered such a climate. However, she is now not alone in this respect. Amazingly it is not that she has a rival but rather an ally.

The Protestant quest for signs

Yes, today Rome has many companions in this quest for confirmatory signs. Among Protestant Pentecostals one claims to have seen a vision of Jesus Christ 900 feet tall. Writes one modern author, 'There are some Charismatics who claim that they have seen the resurrected Lord. D. . . . also believes he has a photograph of God. Another man reported on television that Christ had ridden with him in his car.'[66] While the reader might feel these are just unknown and fringe extremist figures the following paragraph will show that this is not so.

Three of the most widely read authors are well-known Anglican charismatics. Many of the quotations used in this book come from their writings. One records with approval the experience of 'Mr Pentecost' being lifted out of a garden and carried a mile to the bedside of a seriously sick man. He also mentions a mightily used evangelist being lifted 'several feet off the ground in full view of the congregation', although he admits that Satan can also do things like this. Yet he does feel that this was a miracle from God 'simply to rejoice the heart of the people who were listening by showing again how real God is!'[67] He also narrates that when a friend 'visited Indonesia this year he told us that when he asked how many dead had been raised to date, they replied, "We've lost count – besides no one believes us, anyway!"'[68] Another, often quoted as a 'balanced' observer, writes that 'It is said that in the recent Indonesian revival every New Testament miracle has occurred at least once, sometimes on many occasions.'[69] (Why should water ever be turned into wine again? The gospel can only be inaugurated once. It is to this truth that this miracle testifies.) And here is the third writer's uncritical description of one of the first Pentecostal meetings. Parham has been asked to lay hands on Agnes Ozman: 'As he laid hands on her head "a glory fell upon her, a halo seemed to surround her head and face" and she began to speak in tongues. It was 7 p.m. on December 31st, 1900.'[70] He likewise accepts the account that another early leader T.B. Barratt had 'a crown of fire over his head and a cloven tongue as of fire in front of the crown'.[71] Who can fight against such things as this? Perhaps only the Word of God!

Moreover there is no doubt that healings, prophecies and tongues in many people's eyes have given a warrant or authority for schemes or endeavours which otherwise they might have lacked. Thus the authoresses of *Folk Arts and Renewal* describe how they were led to a site in Scotland by prophecy concerning Clyde, which at first they took for a child's name.[72] A Christian newspaper gave a splendid analysis of the book *If my people* when it came out. We quote from the introductory part: '"*If my people*" is the title both of a musical and also of this handbook written by the musical's composers. This paperback lays down their principles concerning national intercession. The whole idea originated in a "prophecy" given on April 30 1974 by the pastor of "the Church on the Way" in Van Nuys, California. On that occasion . . . declared to the assembled church: "This is a day to be marked in the annals of eternity – a great turnabout, a day of enormous consequence".'[73] This would be enough to ensure that many people would automatically accept the whole venture to be from God, yet, as the reviewer pointed out firmly and thoroughly, the whole book was a hotchpotch of largely unbiblical concepts. More recently a report of a meeting conducted by an evangelist showed how people were urged to give extra special attention to the word because of prophetic backing, yet it was also stated that the word was deficient biblically, particularly on the concept of repentance.[74]

The question of healing

The whole question of healing is one that always needs more careful scrutiny than we can give. One contemporary writer can even make this charge: 'It has been revealed that one internationally known charismatic healer uses special mats on the stage. Unbeknown to the sick people who mount the stage to be greeted by this healer, the mats are designed to route tiny electric currents so that each sick person will feel a tingling sensation when the healer's hands touch him. Numerous people then testify to the spiritual "sensation" felt in this healer's presence.'[75] One commentator has warned against the healing miracles of a well-known charismatic leader as being mediumistic rather than Christian. Apparently when asked, 'Isn't it also true that during your television programmes you have sometimes asked the viewers to place a glass of water on the television during the actual broadcast?' the answer was affirmative. He was then asked, 'And isn't it also true that at the end of the programmes you have told the viewers to drink the water if they are seeking healing?' Again the answer was affirmative.[76] Can we believe that he is a true guide in doctrinal matters or that healings produced by these methods are of God?

One lady preacher is much lauded by the charismatics. Her healings (accepted by a wide range of people, from Roman Catholics to a Reformed leader) have led many to accept more readily the unscriptural notion that it is right for a woman to be a minister and to preach, and also to acquiesce in her type of evangelism, with its stress on people being 'slain in the Spirit'.[77] Yet her life story, including the fact that a travelling evangelist divorced his wife to marry her and then was in turn divorced from her, is a hotchpotch.[78] To a Pentecostal friend she expressed the view that, if he were truly anointed, he would feel stronger after the service than before. Yet it is interesting that the admiring biographer who records this mentions later that on another occasion he recalled, 'When she came in I remember her saying to me, "I'm so tired . . . I don't think I can really preach tonight."'[79] We learn from this writer of her new, anointed 'out of the body' detached experience and of the cost in all her services. 'There is a price to pay before I slip into that long white dress and appear on stage,' she softly whispered, 'Consecration.'[80] While she would not blame those not healed for lack of faith and while she said that spiritual healing was more important than physical, she would declare, 'I rebuke that cancer in the mighty Name of Jesus – that asthmatic condition.'[81]

Yet one man, William Nolen, an M.D., has written extensively on her ministry in a book called *Healing: a Doctor in Search of a Miracle* and has concluded from interviews with many people who claimed cures that the so-called facts and statistics of cures or organic diseases simply evaporated under investigation. Moreover there are the many desperately ill patients who are left in despair.[82] She is one who believes that time is running out and that we are near to the rapture as she conceives it. 'There will be miracles that will astound the world,' she announced, commenting on the end times.[83] Significantly after her private audience with Pope Paul VI on 11 October 1972 she said, 'When I met Pope Paul there was a oneness.'[84] Yet so very frequently the cures of this woman have been confidently quoted as God's authentication of her ministry and spiritual stance. This is so common an error.

Wonders, signs, coincidences abound. How one wishes that the lengthy testimony and recantation of Baxter of the Irvingite movement were generally available! He experienced many of these things. In the end he solemnly wrote, 'The whole work is a mimicry of the gifts of the Spirit – the utterances in tongues a mimicry of the gift of tongues – and so of the prophesyings and all the other works of the power. It is Satan as an angel of light, imitating as far as it permitted, the Holy Spirit of God.'[85] The same assessment was given by a Methodist minister more recently, reviewing Pentecostalism in the Caribbean. He warned, 'In fact, if we are not careful Pentecostalism, by its very success, could be the greatest hoax perpetrated by the "Angel of Light".'[86] We do well to remember what Paul said in this connection: 'For such men are false apostles, deceitful workmen, masquerading as apostles of Christ. And no wonder, for Satan himself masquerades as an angel of light. It is not surprising, then, if his servants masquerade as servants of righteousness' (2 Cor. 11:13,14). Both Pentecostalism and Roman Catholicism believe in signs and in new revelations. In some ways the fusion of sections from these two streams is not surprising. (This is not to deny the biblical orthodoxy of some Pentecostals.) Biblical evangelicalism, which stresses the Word alone and believes in the standing miracle of the new birth and in mighty acts of providence, rejects the contemporary signs and revelations as not being from God, however remarkable they might appear to be.

If we are puzzled by the way Roman Catholics can use evangelical language and yet both embrace and abound in unscriptural error, Hugh Farrel, himself a former Roman Catholic, has astutely and helpfully given some background to these matters. Within Rome there are the three levels of pious belief, doctrine and dogma. With regard to pious belief, people may or may not accept the teaching. Doctrine is expected to be believed. Dogma must be believed in peril of mortal sin. Charismatic belief is only pious belief. Belief about the bodily assumption of Mary is dogma! Citing texts which state that when the Holy Spirit comes he will guide into all truth, and noting that Roman Catholic charismatics have not been led deeper into scriptural truth or to reject unscriptural dogma, he reaches the strong conclusion that thousands of charismatic Catholics have not indeed received the Holy Spirit. One wonders whether his assessment is not too sweeping, yet this section has sought to present some of the facts. It is a selection, that must be admitted, but it is a selection that is largely taken from Catholic authors themselves. Dr Farrell obviously sees the work of the Holy Spirit in conversion as a great thorough-going work. He writes, 'My late friend Dr T.C. Hammond of the Irish Church Missions used to make this statement quite often: "It is not difficult to take a man out of Rome, but it is very difficult to take Rome out of the man". But God, through His Holy Spirit can do all things. He can lead Catholics from error to the Truth, but because their church *is* error, He will lead them from that also.'[87] William Ervin, hearing many testimonies of supposedly born-again Roman Catholics was, to say the least, very doubtful of the claims. His convictions were

shared by the editors of *Christian Heritage,* formerly the
Converted Catholic, who did, however, acknowledge that we
cannot finally judge in matters of this kind.[88] All the more
reason why we must view with disquiet the over-ready
acceptance of Roman Catholic charismatics as Christians. I
personally feel that some of them are in fact born again but
this will only be revealed in increasing obedience to the Word
of God, however slow and gradual this process may be.
Obviously many people have been converted from within
Roman Catholicism down the centuries. Luther and Menno
Simons are but two of them. Neither of them instantly left the
Roman Catholic church, but they were increasingly aware of
the great tension between the teaching of Rome and the
teaching of Scripture until they knew that they had reached a
point where they must obey Christ alone, regardless of
consequences. This led them to leave Rome.

But equally dangerous is the appeal from such a widely
regarded figure as Cardinal Suenens that what he terms
'proselytism', and what evangelicals would call 'evangelism',
is to be avoided. Some have heeded him. They have refused to
state doctrines clearly. For example, when among Roman
Catholics, 'Mr Pentecost' was asked what one's attitude to the
virgin Mary should be, 'He replied that she should be obeyed,
but went on to add that Mary said concerning Jesus, "Do
whatever He tells you".'[89] The Methodist charismatic who
describes this episode gives the reply as an example of a 'word
of wisdom'. But surely, a much more appropriate response
would have been to refer them to Luke 8:19-21 or 11:27,28.
The latter reads, 'As Jesus was saying these things, a woman
in the crowd called out, "Blessed is the mother who gave you
birth and nursed you." He replied, "Blessed rather are those
who hear the word of God and obey it."' When we learn that
the same leader has in fact appealed to Roman Catholic
charismatics to stay within their church and that the Full
Gospel Businessmen's group have published in their magazine
testimonies from Roman Catholic charismatics with all these
unscriptural features, we can see that the whole future of the
church in terms of evangelicalism and evangelism is at stake if
ideas of this nature become prevalent.[90] Indeed it is tragic to
read appeals from Spanish and Italian evangelicals who have
much knowledge of Rome at first hand and who are having to

plead that we do not lose sight of the gospel distinctives.[91] What is salvation? What is the gospel? How should it be presented? Our next chapter, which deals with drama, an issue closely bound up with the growth of the charismatic movement, touches on all these questions.

13.
The outward spectacle of drama

Drama groups proliferate

Dance and drama groups of a purportedly Christian character
are now very numerous. At least one church has been sadly
divided over the vital New Testament doctrine of whether to
appoint a choreographer or not. (We all know how frequently
this office is mentioned in the New Testament!) An issue of one
magazine which gave special attention to drama in the church
informed the reader that 'They are springing up everywhere.
There are at least 500 church or Christian-based drama
groups in the U.K. at the moment. Five years ago there were
probably less than half that number.'[1] In keeping with this
emphasis the National Evangelical Anglican Congress at
Nottingham in 1977 featured the group 'Breadrock' as part of
their presentaton of the gospel, and at a meeting of the
Nationwide Initiative in Evangelism also held at Nottingham
in 1980 a newspaper showed the now customary picture of a
group of ladies in long white dresses with the caption 'A dance
group leading worship'.[2] Has not nearly all of this come from
the top? In fact one would surmise that very few drama groups
have sprung up spontaneously from local churches as they
have sought to discover the teaching of God's Word in their
local fellowship together. But they are certainly present in
strength in the various towns now.

Therefore one local newspaper claiming to reflect Christian
viewpoints announced its arrival with a cover page almost
totally given over to pictures of dramatic productions on the
town hall square.[3]When a festival was planned by some for the
town a constant procession of ministers used the Christian
Spokesman column to advocate this type of approach.
'Another lovely feature which is new to many of us is the area

of dance in worship. Some dance is well planned and worked out with great sensitivity.' 'Very soon, Rochdale will be buzzing with Christians celebrating. Music, drama and song are all being used to convey this message of joy and life.' 'Drama has been a traditional part of the Church's presentation of the Christian faith for a very long time.' And, after an appeal to the public to see one of these well-known drama groups, 'If you believe that everything the Church does is humourless, second-rate, archaic and dull then come along and see this group.'[4]

It is because I believe that very important biblical doctrines are at stake that I shall deal with this matter in some detail. Since a most excellent book *Shall we Dance?* has dealt exhaustively with the dance question we shall not discuss this matter here.[5] This book also gives some very helpful coverage of the drama question, but I want to explore this subject from some angles not covered in it. Indeed I hope that the reader will clearly see when we have finished our discussion that the whole question of who Jesus Christ is, the way we view his sinless life and his atoning death, and the very nature of genuine conversion and spiritual delusion are closely bound up with this whole matter. It involves not just how we evangelize but the very survival of the gospel itself. For some individuals it may in fact mean the difference between heaven and hell. I believe it is as important as that.

Flimsy evidence

Despite the irrelevant allusions which people sometimes make to Old Testament ritual, the biblical evidence for drama is very thin; some would say, non-existent. Therefore advocates of drama turn to the dramatic story-telling of Christ himself as he vividly and tellingly used details from everyday life. Christ's use of a coin as a visual aid, his reference to Moses lifting up a bronze serpent, his placing a child in the midst to teach humility and his use of questions have all been used as very tenuous illustrations of the use of drama as practised today.[6] Frequently reference is also made to acts of prophetic symbolism, such as Jeremiah smashing pottery and constructing yokes, or Ezekiel acting out the siege of Jerusalem or mimicking the people going into exile (Jer. 19; 28; Ezek. 4; 12). Considering the fact that these were all solitary, divinely inspired and mostly judgemental acts, there would seem to be no real parallel at all with people gathering as a group to rehearse together to perform sketches of mere human devising which are neither judgemental nor prophetic in any true sense.

The Bible never speaks about the potency of this method of teaching. Characters in Shakespeare do. 'The play's the thing wherein I'll catch the conscience of the King,' declares Hamlet as he prepares to re-enact a scene which will depict the very crime of which his stepfather, the new king, is guilty.[7] Another character in Shakespeare speaks glowingly of the art which seeks 'to hold . . . the mirror up to Nature – to show Virtue her own feature, scorn her own image, and the very age and body of the time his form and pressure'.[8] Evangelicals have always strongly opposed this kind of argument. Sinful human beings are more inclined to laugh and lust when they are shown sin visibly than to reject and shun it. It is particularly interesting that Paul, confronted with the culture-conscious Corinthians, not only refused to pander to their tastes by regaling them with dramatic representations of the gospel on a stage, but deliberately and consciously rejected such methods (1 Cor. 1:20-2:5). If there was any dramatic display it was that of himself and the other apostles who were 'like men condemned to die in the arena . . . made a spectacle to the whole universe, to angels as well as to men' (1 Cor. 4:9).

Drama a good teaching aid?

Because dance and drama are so widespread, we must also examine the practical benefits that are alleged to come from their employment. We find that they are regularly advocated as a good teaching aid. Thus one writer approvingly quotes the verdict that dance and drama can be 'like windows offering a clearer view of God's truth', and also says that they can be used effectively to 'reinforce' the sermon.[9] She further links them with the miracle plays, saying that 'Perhaps it was almost inevitable that truth often became mixed with fable and colourful, if not always accurate, interpretations of the Bible.'[10] Yet she feels that the plays had great potential and were welcomed by the clergy. Another book harks back to the miracle and mystery plays, with their 'comedy, spectacle, pathos, activity, colour and music', and contends that 'The content of the plays imparted a knowledge of biblical material that would otherwise have been inaccessible to the illiterate.'[11] A well-known leader of the 'festivals' where such methods are abundantly used declares that 'The creative arts have a vital part to play in proclaiming the Word which once became flesh. Drama, dance, mime, painting, photography, architecture, tapestry: all of these can tell the glory of God and proclaim his handiwork.'[12] The point at issue here is not whether a Christian should use his artistic gifts for Christ, but that of God-ordained worship.

Yet it was the contention of evangelicals like John Wyclif that miracle plays, far from confirming and illuminating the gospel, obscured it. In the interest of entertainment fidelity to and reverence for Scripture were readily abandoned. Humour came to the forefront. Thus in the story of Noah's flood, which was often depicted, Noah's wife is made into a comic character constantly causing trouble to Noah, her henpecked husband. When the time comes for her to enter the ark, she refuses, because she wants to have another drink with her jolly gossips on the land:

'Here is a bottle of Malmsey good and strong
It will rejoice both heart and tongue
Though Noah think us never so long,
Here will we drink alike.'[13]

Eventually, when she had been dragged kicking and struggling on to the ark, she greets her husband by giving him a clout. It was this non-biblical incident that stuck in people's mind. Chaucer incidentally confirmed this, for when one of his characters alludes to the story it is the farcical aspect that he mentions.

One recent writer has dealt with the parallel argument that pictures in the medieval church were the ignorant layman's book and demolished it with words that are equally applicable to the miracle and mystery plays. After stating that the carver and the sculptor in reality rarely had a teaching aim, he writes, 'If we are to think of the medieval church as a book in which the devout might seek instruction we should envisage a volume made up of pages torn recklessly from a variety of other books and sewn together in no particular order.'[14] Truth and myth, miracle and superstition were all hopelessly jumbled together.

When we turn from the medieval period to the present day, the scene is unchanged. The local Rochdale paper gave the following heading to a letter: 'Godspell lesson in communication for young folk'. This was a reply by a minister to the charge that Godspell was unbiblical and would be likely to confuse and harm people. Next to the minister's letter was a letter from some young people in his church, also defending this musical. In it they wrote, '*Godspell* along with *Jesus Christ Superstar* and others means more to the average young person than the Bible.' The writers then referred to Jesus Christ telling parables and continued, 'We ... believe that when Christ comes again He will tell His stories to the people who need to hear them and we don't think many of these will already be Christians.'[15] The letter displays ignorance about the most basic of Christian truths and envisages the second coming of Christ as giving people a chance to hear the gospel, instead of being the final confirmation of people's choices and division into heaven and hell.

One of the clergymen referred to earlier spoke of the nativity scene as being the one which most of all has been put over to people dramatically. He spoke of this with enthusiastic commendation. It might be assumed from his argument that this is therefore one of the best-known stories in the Bible. I have often tested congregations and groups by asking them if they feel that the following sentence is a succinct summary of events surrounding Christ's birth: 'The three kings came together with the shepherds to worship the baby Jesus in the manger.' When one or two have looked alarmed, a few displayed puzzlement, and most have acquiesced in the suitability of the summary, I then inform them that if we truly follow the biblical account of the nativity there are no less than five errors in that one sentence. Let the readers find them for themselves! Drama introduces new elements and ultimately confuses! The challenging word of one of the prophets is not irrelevant in this case, 'Of what value is an idol, since a man has carved it? Or an image that teaches lies?' (Hab. 2:18.)

Portrayal of Christ

While we are on this subject, we must give special attention to
the fact that where drama is used Christ himself is regularly
portrayed.

In his book *Jesus* Malcolm Muggeridge makes a series of
statements about Christ that demand earnest consideration.
Their implications are tremendous and they bear much
relevance to the whole question of whether Christ should be
portrayed on the stage. In summary Muggeridge alleges that
Christ is inconsistent in his lurid prophecies of the end,
sometimes speaking of it, sometimes enjoining silence. 'On
occasions he would boast of his miraculous cures, and then ask
the person cured under no circumstances to advertise what
had happened. All this is human enough; we are all given to
boasting and self-depreciation . . .' According to him, Christ
occasionally lost his temper and, since Judas betrayed Jesus
with a kiss because he loved him, not because he hated him,
we must assume that Christ was mistaken in his assessment of
Judas. A saying of Christ is 'one of those wild exaggerations to
which he was so humanly prone'. With regard to Gethsemane,
Christ was 'thus indulging himself, for once, most humanly, in
a mood of self-pity'. It is also suggested that Christ will
ultimately save all mankind.[16] Yet, if any one of these statements were true the whole of Christianity would be a gross lie
and there would be no gospel to proclaim. A perfect and
satisfactory atonement demands a perfect sin-bearer. 'But you
know that he appeared so that he might take away our sins. And
in him is no sin' (1 John 3:5; see also 1 Peter 2:22-24; Heb. 7:25-
28). It had to be a spotless lamb that was offered (1 Peter 1:19).
Any sign of temper tantrums, any hint of self-pity and even the
tiniest whiff of pride or boasting, and the whole of the Christian
gospel would lie in ruins. Malcolm Muggeridge has shown by
these statements that he has not understood the gospel.

Yet the whole problem in portraying Christ the God-man is
that he was not merely sinless in a pallid and withdrawn sense,
but that he constantly irradiated goodness and perpetually
mirrored forth the Father. His goodness was not just negative. His
emotions were not weak and thin. 'His heart went out to her' . . .
'Jesus, full of joy through the Holy Spirit' . . . 'Jesus . . .
deeply moved in the spirit and troubled'. . . I have eagerly

desired to eat this Passover with you' . . .'with loud cries and
tears' . . . (Luke 7:13; 10:21; John 11:33; Luke 22:15; Heb.
5:7). All of these expressions indicate the intensity of his
emotions. The words in the Greek are strong words. The word
for 'joy' almost means 'leap for joy', and one of the expressions
for his sorrow is one often used of the shuddering, trembling
motion of a horse neighing.

Not only did Christ have strong emotions, but he also had
different, even contrasting, emotions perfectly blended. Thus
when there was opposition to a sabbath healing we read that
'He looked round at them in anger, and deeply distressed at
their stubborn hearts . . .' (Mark 3:5). Anger with Christ
never spilled over into sinful temper. It was intense but it was
combined with deep grief and sorrow. We see this in the two
temple-cleansing incidents. Both were controlled expressions
of displeasure. Although in the earlier incident he took a whip
and used it on certain animals, and although he scattered
coins, he did not violently unloose the doves, which, unlike the
sheep, could not easily be recovered. Instead he told the sellers
themselves to take them away. As we think of the depth of his
feelings we notice the quotation of Psalm 69:9, then being
fulfilled: 'Zeal for your house will consume me' (John 2:17).
With regard to the second cleansing, we not only see the
deliberateness of the act (he inspected the temple, went and
slept and then came back and cleansed it) but also the
tremendous authority of his person, as it is recorded: 'He
overturned the tables of the money changers and the benches
of those selling doves, and would not allow anyone to carry
merchandise through the temple courts' (Mark 11:11,12,15-
17).

The secular world feels falsely confident in this realm. There
is Dennis Potter's creation of a frenzied Christ tearing into the
sellers in the temple. Dick Lester, wanting an actor to play
Christ, said in 1967 that the actor must be 'fantastic with
marvellous presence and personality' more 'primitive and two-
dimensional' than Renaissance painting. 'The film,' according
to Lester, 'will show Christ as a man who has caught hold of
an idea bigger than he thought it would be, and is frustrated
by the magnitude of the task of trying to convince people of its
truth.'[17] We have quoted these words because ironically they
are an apt description up to a point, not of Christ himself,

but of the task of any who would seek to portray the Saviour. It is they who have caught hold of an idea bigger than they thought it would be. It is they who are frustrated (and defeated) by the magnitude of the task.

Although she went ahead and wrote a cycle of plays on the life of Christ, Dorothy L. Sayers had some awareness of the problem. In the preface to these plays she points out the problem of the dramatist, for the hero is good, which in the world's eyes generally means dull and insipid. Yet in this case the hero is lively and exciting. 'Wherever He went He brought not peace but a sword, and fire in the earth; that is why they killed him. He said surprising things, in language ranging from the loftiest poetry to the most lucid narrative and the raciest repartee.'[18] Consequently there is a massive problem. In another of her works she considers the difficulty of the actor in the role: '"Look," we shall find ourselves saying to him, "if you play the first scene in that stained-glass window way, there'll be an awful jerk when you have to do a quick come-back on hecklers, and insult the Pharisees, and man-handle the traders out of the Temple."'[19]

She is really talking of the impossibility of the task, though she refuses to admit this. Is it therefore surprising that two different reviewers of *The Greatest Story Ever Told*, another attempt to depict the life of Christ on the cinema screen, reaching the same verdict, should say, 'Christ is a withdrawn character' and he has 'a withdrawn expression in the eyes themselves'? One entitled his review, 'The widest and longest story ever told'. Despite all the stress on the exciting potential of this medium, it has all become a bore! When the four main modern 'Christian' drama groups were asked to give a list of 'Dos and Don'ts' to would-be aspirants today, they said, 'Be careful about portraying Jesus. Beware of making him appear to be so soft that he is the least convincing or even the least attractive character on stage.'[20]

With all the warnings and all the care in the world, the task is not only totally impossible; it should not be attempted. Christ was sinless and yet full of life. An actor is sinful. Whether it be a brusque gesture, a harsh tone, a soppy smile, an aloof gaze or a proud glance – that very instant the character of Christ has been not only undermined, but destroyed. The Lord's Day Observance Society got it right when they made their original protest against the series *Man born to be King,* saying that 'To impersonate the Divine Son of God in this way is an act of irreverence bordering on the blasphemous.'[21] I would unhesitatingly say that it always is blasphemous. Later, admitting that the earlier treatment was mild compared with later productions, the Lord's Day Observance Society said that it paved the way for *Jesus Christ Superstar* and more modern distortions.

Another aspect of the inevitable and terrible distortion of the whole gospel story can be seen in connection with the crucifixion. The actual physical sufferings of Christ were awesome, but they were intimately related to his inward agonies. The former cannot properly be depicted in drama, while the latter, the most vital aspect of his atoning death, cannot be shown at all. Take, for example, the terrible banality of these directions: 'The lifting of Jesus on to the cross also needs separate and careful practice so that it does not look too awkward but quiet and reverent.' Was it 'quiet and reverent' when the victim, already nailed to the tree, was dropped into the hole so that he could complain that all his bones were 'out of joint'? (Ps. 22:14.) Stage directions continue: 'The person taking the part of Jesus will need to co-operate in standing on the thighs of his support, but otherwise should let his hands and head flop loosely down.'[22] Does the writer not know that Christ did not flop about pathetically, but 'bowed his head and gave up his spirit', in an act that specifically signified not the pathos of his dying (there was no pathos – this is in the imagination of artists), but the deliberateness, solemnity, finality and triumph of all that he did in his people's stead? Discussing a script on the life of Christ the same person writes, 'Jesus is now nailed to the cross. He could be carried to the wall where the cross is and propped up against it. He should let his head droop down on to his chest, as though dead.'[23] Away with this empty, futile posturing! It has no more Christian significance than the distortions of the Koran on the death of Christ.

Trivialization of momentous issues

All the modern groups, very much like their medieval

counterparts, emphasize humour. Thus a typical comment on
a group is that 'they have become known not only for fast,
imaginative and hilarious sketches . . .'[24] The book on the folk
arts explicitly argues for plenty of comedy: 'Humour aligned
with dramatic action forges a practically irresistible
combination', and 'Humour well-handled makes some types of
correction simple and almost painless.'[25] Whole theologies
underlie these simple statements. Clearly sin is not seen by
these writers as the grim tyrant of biblical terminology.
Therefore they can even go on to say the following: 'Plan the
occasional surprises for children as well. Our family services
are sometimes visited by a gentle clown, costumed in
traditional garb. His amusing antics, all centred on the
teaching theme, captivate the children's attention beyond
their normal rather limited span. "This is the first Sunday wee
Alastair hasn't stayed on the floor playing with the heating
vent," an appreciative grandmother confided after one of our
clown's appearances.'[26]

The Times, under the heading 'Clown priests tumble in and
take a pew', shows how this is catching on, as 'They were
laughing, dancing and rolling in the aisles . . . as Britain's first
Christian clowning course got under way.' Apparently we are
not yet up to the rollicking level of the U.S.A., where there are
now about 3,000 clown ministry groups led by the clergy. One
of the participants of the recent course said that 'Part of what I
hope all this will do is to encourage the Church to make a fool
of itself.'[27] It doesn't seem to have need of much pressure in
that direction if we take these accounts as indicative of a trend!
How can we wonder that in *Godspell* Christ is portrayed as a
clown when others are performing in this manner?

The result of all this is that solemn and great themes
are trivialized. Thus at the Anglican Evangelical Congress
in 1977 the parable about the two houses, which is the
climax of the Sermon on the Mount, is shown by the people
with umbrellas. The momentousness of the issue is lost
sight of. In *Godspell* instead of Christ coming in glory to
sort out the sheep and goats in the final act of judgement,
we have a bumbling clown and a load of braying cattle which
he is pathetically unable to separate and divide, as he goes
along saying, 'Over here matey,' managing to mix up the
directions of heaven and hell. What an unbridgeable gulf

between scenes like this and plain biblical truth!

In 1978 a missionary on furlough attended a conference in which another missionary sought to present a drama as an example of what can now be done to bring the gospel to the unevangelized in a contemporary way. 'The play was performed by local young people and was entitled *The Six who Died*. Having died they appeared before Peter to have their life records processed. The dramatic and emotional final scene depicted five being consigned to hell to the accompaniment of screams of torment etc., while one who had accepted Christ went to heaven. Apart from the heretical notion of Peter dealing with the "records" of men and women after death – perhaps acceptable to some Catholics – what are we to say about "comedy", with or without heresies, to win lost souls for Christ?' runs a perceptive account of this meeting.[28]

In all these three illustrations solemnity had become comedy. Jonathan Edwards frequently writes that Christ, although awesome in his warnings about hell, never attempted to show people what it is actually like by dramatic representation. People may feel that it would be more awesome to do so. The reverse is the case. It ends up by being ridiculous. In the case both of *Godspell* and of the sketch just mentioned we see that the Bible is actually twisted and the story told wrongly. This happens, as it did in the miracle plays, because there are some things which can be told, but which cannot be acted. No one can portray God as Judge. Therefore Peter has to take his place – a role he cannot, of course, in any way properly fulfil. We might incidentally comment that the Bible shows Christ as Judge, rather than God the Father, but to people who have lost all sense of biblical exactitude this is hardly likely to be a serious consideration.

It is not my conviction that there is no place for humour in a pulpit. Anyone preaching on the book of Proverbs or certain other passages of Scripture without bringing in humour has hardly undersood the passage. There is irony in Isaiah. While Elton Trueblood has grossly overstated the case in his book *The Humour of Christ* and seems to write from modernistic presuppositions, it is not departing from the evangelical faith to concede that there is obvious humour in some of the Saviour's sayings.[29] What is so wrong in the modern practice is that humour is not incidental. It is right at the forefront. An advert for a youth meeting in north Yorkshire must be typical of many. It invited: 'Evening programme of drama, dance, comedy and conversation. It will take your breath away.' But will it help to take one's sin away? With the distortion of biblical teaching and the trivializing of solemn themes, this is extremely unlikely.

Hugh Latimer, burned at the stake for his stalwart Protestant faith, was not above using many an ironic sally in the pulpit. But he based his fervent, heartfelt and indubitably serious pleas on the Scripture. William Hubberdyne, a vigorous opponent of Latimer, was an expert mimic and frequently leaped around as he denounced the Reformer. A historian tells us, 'Apparently he danced in the pulpit once too often; one collapsed beneath him and he died of his injuries. The unsympathetic churchwardens commented that they "made their pulpit for preaching, not dancing".'[30] That is what pulpits have always been made for. But even this was not as grim as the story which Luther's colleague Melanchthon relates of the judgement of God upon a company of those who sought to portray Christ's death on the cross. He told how the soldier, coming to the one playing Christ on the cross and intending to pierce a concealed bladder of blood, missed and instead killed him. As the dead actor fell he toppled on a man disguised as a woman underneath the cross and killed him, and in subsequent events the brother of the man first slain revenged himself by killing the man playing the part of the soldier and then was himself hung by order of justice![31]

Getting rid of bodily inhibitions

Next we must review this whole conception of worship with the body. It is incessantly said that Englishmen in general, and conservative evangelicals in particular, and ministers above all, are so staid and inhibited in their emotions and so stilted, stifled and stulted in their bodily movements and expressions that they need release. 'There are those who are very scared of anything moving in a service – either emotionally (such as the sermon), or physically (such as the kiss of peace or a dance)', and clergy, with their 'cerebral

activity', are the worst sinners of all in their aversion to the
language of the body.[32] Thus the same writer informs us that
'Some praise God using the language of the body.'[33] She
recounts how various people found freedom and almost
another dimension of their personality: a woman becoming
tearfully involved in a dramatic portrayal of Jesus and the
lepers; a man learning for the first time the emotional impact
of Christ's death on the cross; people discovering the truth of
Christ's words about making them free by losing their self-
consciousness as they dance.[34] The other tome on this subject
describes how an inhibited lad was made free to move in front
of people without self-consciousness by playing the blind man
in the Gospels. And for people who are uncomfortable with
their bodies, 'Dance provides a vehicle for persons to present
their entire selves to the Lord, as they offer their bodies and all
that they hold – mind, emotions, will, strength, energy.' This
can be done in 'movements which are strong, pulsating,
angular, and painful as well as those which are graceful,
flowing and smooth'.[35]

Yet for one brief moment the former book does suggest that
there might be dangers. 'Does dance and drama encourage
Christians to focus wrongly on the physical?' is asked.
'Perhaps some people are fearful that through watching dance
and drama especially in a church setting, sexual feelings will
be aroused and that does not feel at all right.'[36] This is an
obvious point. But having asked the question, the writer shies
away from any serious answer and in fact argues in ways that
reveal she has little understanding of biblical teaching or of
how even regenerate men can be tempted to view women.
Thus in her book she envisages using all the dramatic
potential of the incident of Jesus and the woman taken in
adultery. Gatherings are to look at this vivid scene.[37] While
she does briefly consider the danger of someone having to play
an adulterous woman, she misses one of the main points of the
whole story.[38] Twice it is said that Christ bent down and wrote
on the ground. The whole group of people gawped and gaped
at the poor cringing woman. Christ would not even look and
add to her embarrassment. Yet audiences are provided with
visual aids that they should never have! Thus elsewhere in her
book she feels able to add to the scene to be enacted about the
prodigal son in this way. 'A girl flaunts in front of him, to the

delight of the group.'[39] One might also ask whether it might not be to the delight of the audience – or are they all so pure and Spirit-filled as to disdain feelings of that sort? One might also take strong exception to the whirling group of women (from the description I assume they are women) supposedly representing the *Holy* Spirit coming at Pentecost.[40] One might recall here that, although a person, the Holy Spirit is represented by oil, a dove, water and wind. He is never symbolized by a man or a woman.) The whole New Testament emphasis is on the silence of women in worship and in particular on the need for modesty in dress and behaviour. How do all these scenes fit in with this biblical demand? By contrast man is repeatedly presented as the one who even needs to make a covenant with his eyes and 'not to look lustfully at a girl' (Job 31:1). (It was one of the most godly of men who had to resolve this.) It is nearly always the man who looks and lusts (Matt. 5:28). This is the biblical emphasis. The woman dresses or behaves provocatively and draws his gaze.

In pictures in brochure after brochure it is the women who lead the dance. 'Oh, but it is all very decent! They wear long dresses,' we are assured. 'I daren't look up,' commented one man, sitting near the platform as they cavorted about in one 'festival'. Who is kidding whom? One wonders at this point whether some men are frightened of restraining their wives, who have wrongfully taken an unbiblical role. Older Christians used to say that the praying knee and the dancing foot rarely belonged together. Have times really changed so drastically? Often the world is better able to see the issues than professing Christians. At a performance of *Godspell,* which has been lauded by many Christians, a reviewer put the issue very clearly: 'Sometimes numbers are in direct contradiction to what the words are saying. "Turn back O Man", theatrically the most irresistible song in the show, delivers its warning against carnal indulgence by sending the most red-hot lady in the troupe through the house, spraying out Mae West invitations as *ad libs* between the lyrics.'[41]

In this whole question of acting the issue of exhibitionism needs facing. Is a young Christian, or indeed any Christian, helped by the publicity, the glare of the footlights and the applause? The writers of the large book on the subject have little reservation about this or about the question of mere men playing Jesus Christ. They describe how in one instance, 'The man who played Jesus was also deeply moved. "I experienced so much compassion for all of you," he shared. "I felt your pain so strongly and wanted to touch each person, to release you from your agony. It changes how I understand the Lord. I know his love on the inside now."'[42] Has he really come to feel like Christ by acting this part? How far are these young people being misled?

Many of the books refer to people being emotionally moved either at watching or participating in some scene from the Gospels, as though this were conclusive proof of the rightness of everything. But one must ask questions even about this. There were women who were emotionally moved at the sight of Christ going to his crucifixion. They shed real tears and exhibited genuine sympathy. In his kind but firm way Christ clearly told them not to weep for him (Luke 23:26-31). He was never, and is never, to be an object of our pity. He does not need our tears and one must say that there are some emotions which do not meet with his approval. Heartfelt grief leading to true repentance, even accompanied by tears, is acceptable to him, but 'worldly sorrow brings death' (2 Cor. 7:10). One recalls the searching and sombre comment of John Owen, who wrote frequently on this kind of theme, addressing himself to those who thought they were Christians because they were moved by some picture or representation of Christ, as he warned, 'An imaginary Christ will effect nothing in the minds of men but an imaginary grace.'[43] At another level, we can at least point out that the word in the New Testament which means 'a dissembler, one who is playing a part, putting on an act' is, of course, the word 'hypocrite'.[44]

Downgrading the Word

Our final comment is on the evident downgrading, or even rejection, of the Word in all this. One of the pioneers of these festivals with dance and drama has been very explicit on this. People 'are satiated with words but hungry for life'. 'Most people today are word resistant.' 'I believe that the church of today needs to think carefully about relevant forms of communication in a world that is increasingly word-resistant.'[45] He is supported by the authors of the large manual, who argue that the influence of T.V. makes 'verbal communication . . . clumsy and wearying'. They complain about a worship 'which is primarily cerebral' or appealing to the mind. Therefore when they give an outline of a specimen service there is inevitably no sermon.[46]

No doubt sermons can be heavy and dull. Leaving the university church after a dull sermon, Lewis Carroll (or Dodgson) offered to lend the preacher an umbrella as it was raining. The loan was refused with the remark, 'No, thanks, I don't mind getting wet; in fact I like getting wet!' To which Dodgson replied, 'You were dry enough in the pulpit this morning!'[47] One description of such a preacher was that he served a good meal on a cold plate. It is a sad description. It may even be an epitaph. But God has appointed preaching. It may seem foolish to the world that some gangly bespectacled elderly male or a small bald-headed individual should stand there in Christ's name and just talk, or even shout, as he expounds the Word. It may be 'foolishness' to the world both as to manner and matter, but it is God's appointed way to save sinners (1 Cor. 1:23). As Paul puts it in Romans, 'How, then, can they call on the one they have not believed in? And how can they believe in the one of whom they have not heard? And how can they hear without someone preaching to them? And how can they preach unless they are sent? As it is written, "How beautiful are the feet of those who bring good news!"' Feet are for bringing the message, not for dancing it. He continues, 'But not all the Israelites accepted the good news. For Isaiah says, "Lord, who has believed our message?" Consequently, faith comes from hearing the message, and the message is heard through the word of Christ' (Rom. 10:14-17).

Every legitimate and God-honouring endeavour must be made to make the message count. Did our Lord tell arresting parables and use vivid speech? We must endeavour to emulate this. Are there in the prophets irony, directness, plainness and cogency? We must seek to echo them. Does the apostle Paul both weep and plead? We must pray for a like frame of mind that we may be urgent and winsome. Well might John Owen tersely refer to 'this sweaty kind of preaching', as he pictures the labours, yearnings and heart-aches that confront the true preacher of Christ's living Word.[48]

It must not be forgotten in all this that the Rome-ward drift is again evident. It was evident as soon as we began to speak about miracle plays. Rome has always preferred drama and shunned true gospel preaching. In *The Mass in Slow Motion* Ronald Knox affirmed that the movements of the priest during mass 'really add up to a kind of dance meant to express a religious idea to you, the spectator'.[49] Rome can readily assimilate drama and dance. She has regularly employed them. What else lies round the corner is tragic to contemplate, as the large book envisages regular pancake suppers, folk evenings and dances. It may seem much more cultured than the old image of the 'pantomime belt', as northern nonconformity was described with its endless pea-and-pie suppers and merry minstrel shows. But it is the old social round in a modern guise. In fact we can enthuse about and participate in anything – other than a devout hearing of the Word of God!

14.
The final verdict

Letting personalities cloud the issue

'But leaving aside these pale pink fellow travellers, Johnny-
come-latelys and theologically boneless wonders whom we
have recently acquired . . .'[1] These words come from one
belonging to the older Pentecostals. He is writing about the
charismatics. There is not always evidence of warm love
between the different sections of the charismatic movement! In
this book I have sought to avoid abusive epithets even where I
have used strong language. Throughout I have not actually
named in the main text living authors with whom I disagree.
One of the reasons is that, sadly, many Christians are unable
to concentrate on a biblical argument when they know the
personalities involved and this book is not meant to be an
argument about different individuals, but a discussion of
biblical principles. Another reason is that among the authors
quoted are some whom I regard as good Christians and, since
in this particular book I have regularly disagreed with them, it
seemed better to identify them in a reference rather than in the
text. Of course, some may be instantly identifiable to
individual readers but this will not be so in the majority of
cases.

I have never held the position that a charismatic cannot be
a Christian whose life is blessed by God. Nor have I ever held
the position that all that is done in churches embracing this
viewpoint is wrong and under God's judgement. There are
individual Pentecostals whose zeal for the Lord puts many of
us to shame. There are charismatic churches where the gospel
is preached and honoured by God. Such should be a challenge
to us all. Nevertheless I have repeatedly argued that the view
that the supernatural and extraordinary gifts of the Spirit are

being restored in our day is unscriptural. Because of this there is always a great danger where this charismatic theology is embraced in a thorough-going way. Wherever there is deviation from scriptural teaching, satanic elements enter, to a greater or lesser degree. Yet it must be recognized that some shrink back from the logic of their own position and, despite appearing in the charismatic camp, in no way embrace a fully charismatic position. Therefore there are those who say that they are persuaded that the gifts have been restored, but who do not believe that God's 'first', namely apostleship, is among them. Others say that they believe that there is prophecy today, but hedge it in with such restrictions that the average person is likely to hear it only on very rare occasions. We may be surprised at the lack of consistency in these positions, but we may also be to some extent grateful and recognize that people like this are more concerned about the central issues of the gospel and are therefore honoured and blessed by God.

Yet, although it is very tempting to evade the issue, in this final section we must face squarely what I have termed 'the satanic element'. Our background text would be the Lord Jesus Christ's vivid portrait of the evil one: 'He was a murderer from the beginning, not holding to the truth, for there is no truth in him. When he lies, he speaks his native language, for he is a liar and the father of lies' (John 8:44). Ultimately Satan wants to destroy churches and people. His consummate deceit in effecting this is underlined by our Lord in phrase after phrase in this description. Other Scriptures support this. We hear of 'the devil's schemes', 'deceiving spirits', 'the serpent's cunning', the fact that 'Satan himself masquerades as an angel of light', 'the work of Satan displayed in all kinds of counterfeit miracles, signs and wonders' and 'Satan, who leads the whole world astray' (Eph. 6:11; 1 Tim. 4:1; 2 Cor. 11:3,14; 2 Thess. 2:9; Rev. 12:9).

The devil seeking to replace God's Word with his own

We saw earlier that Jonathan Edwards was adamant that Satan was active through groups advocating a restoration of the gifts. Edwards believed Satan was desiring to have his word supplant the Word of God. This was indeed the conclusion of William Goode's great and thorough book: 'It is surely a time, then, when, more than ever, we should stand by the acknowledged word of God as our *alone* guide and rule, and hold ourselves aloof from any pretended new revelations, in which we are so likely to be deceived. The latter bears upon the face of it pretensions against which our Lord has especially warned us. The former is, as God himself has assured us, able to make us wise unto salvation, and furnish us for our Christian course *so as to leave nothing wanting* (2 Tim. 3:15-17). Relying on the latter, we are building on a foundation of which comparatively we know nothing; resting *wholly* on the former, we are building on the foundation of the apostles and prophets, Jesus Christ himself being the chief cornerstone.'[2]

Therefore the main contention which I will seek to illustrate in a variety of ways in this final section is that the devil wants to substitute his word for that of God. Sometimes we clearly see that Satan is doing this, for it all seems so obvious. Most Christians recognize the deception. Moses David of the Children of God claimed, 'I was prophesied over many times by many prophets of God, as having been filled with the Holy Ghost from my mother's womb, and many great things were foretold that I would do . . . that I would be like Moses, Jeremiah, Ezekiel, Daniel and even David.'[3] Christians reject this claim, especially in the light of the group's heretical teaching. A little booklet on the rise of Sun Myung Moon and the Moonies relates that 'Among some Pentecostal Christians in the underground church in Pyongyang, there had recently been prophecy of a Korean messiah. So the local populace was fertile ground for this idea.'[4] Yet, extreme though such groups may seem, it must not be forgotten that there are those today who compare themselves with biblical prophets, who believe in new 'revelations' and who are engendering a climate where all kinds of false teachings could readily be accepted. Because this climate is so pervasive and by now almost so 'normal' it may be that many have scarcely noticed it. A writer on this theme can always be accused of taking extreme examples, but many palpably false movements drew in genuine Christians at first. Many temporarily entangled in the Jonestown cult, with its healings, revelations and eventual mass suicide, seem to have been earnest and genuine Christians who were deluded and led astray by the evil one. Firm biblical moorings and a belief that God has furnished a final and all-sufficient Word in Scripture alone is the only real protection and safe guidance that God has provided against deception.

Can it be denied that there are disturbing signs in what are regarded as more orthodox sections of the movement? When we were discussing the meaning of 'the perfection' in 1 Corinthians 13 we looked at the views of a leader of one group. Dismissing the view that 'perfection' is the completed Scriptures he says, 'It assumes that the Bible is "that which is perfect", whereas we know from internal evidence that the Bible is incomplete. There are at least three letters of Paul's missing, besides some works by prophets of the Old Testament. The Bible is not in that sense "perfect" although it is perfect enough for God's purposes by it among men in this age.'[5] What an abysmally low view of Scripture this is! Could not this weak, frustrated God deliver the goods properly? The very fact that Scripture is viewed in this way leaves the door open for the 'revelations' which are needed to supplement its sad incompleteness. These 'revelations' are not likely to be beneficial.

A professor in a university founded by a charismatic declares that 'As christians move more and more into the New Testament world, they will rely less and less on reason and experience as ways of knowing and more and more on pneumatic knowing.' And he then defines this 'pneumatic knowing' as 'a knowing beyond all knowing, a perceiving beyond all perceiving, a certainty beyond all certainty, and understanding beyond all understanding'.[6] According to the writer who supplies these quotations it all sounds like sheer mysticism and is more a twentieth-century version of second-century gnosticism than of biblical Christianity. He is right.

But even in groups where such language is not used there is a decided movement away from the Word of God and a lack of reverence for it as a complete and final authority. This can be seen in the way in which vital passages of Scripture and key phrases are bypassed in book after book. (I would underline this. What I am pinpointing is widespread.) Even the fact that the view of Scripture being the perfection of 1 Corinthians can repeatedly and instantly be dismissed as ludicrous is worrying. I can understand the man who, after weighing the issues, dismisses my interpretation. This is perfectly fair. What is a matter of grave concern is the instant and sarcastic dismissal of the interpretation so ably expounded by such giants as Jonathan Edwards. Likewise we have seen that no detailed attention has been given by charismatics to whole sections of Scripture and that key biblical terms such as 'revelation', 'mystery', 'spirit', 'prophecy', 'apostle' and 'miracle' are never investigated in any depth. Time and time again we meet 'secondary' versions of the biblical norm. Thus we have secondary fallible prophets, secondary tongue-speakers, who do not initially understand what they are saying, and secondary apostles, who lack all the five biblical marks of apostleship. Satan has in fact juggled with the terms, taking us away from strict biblical definition and substituting his own concepts. All distortions of Scripture are satanic. He particularly loves to dilute, distort and deny the Word of God.

So when a writer declares, 'I have not noticed the Pentecostal denominations offering bound volumes of "new Scriptures" for the twentieth century', he is really begging the question.[7] While this may be literally true, can it really be said that 'new revelations' are not being given and acted upon? Was not 'Come Together' sanctioned by a prophecy and thereby automatically validated in many people's minds? Have not particular types of evangelism, deference towards certain figures and unbiblical *rapprochement* between Roman Catholics and Protestants been sanctioned by similar means? Moreover where the Bible is not really properly accepted, the order of priorities is changed and false views begin to gain ground, in some instances dominating entirely. We shall seek to gather together the threads by examining this again with regard to the place of the mind in Christianity, how we use church history, the proper role of leaders, the question of the unity, orthodoxy and discipline of the church and how we assess 'blessing' in the Christian life.

The place of the mind in Christianity

Let us take first *the place of the mind in Christianity*. We have seen the repeated and grave dangers in the movement's failure to take seriously the biblical instruction to worship God with the whole mind. One Reformed writer almost faces this issue but, after arguing that we do need to meet with God with 'the full integration of the individual under fully self-conscious, rational control' and warning against the danger when 'the mind is on vacation', he then says, 'Since the charismatic deliberately chooses glossolalia as a means of expressing adoration and petition on themes he has in mind, but on which he wants to say more to God than he can find words for, it is not quite true to allege that rational control is wholly absent.'[8]

Yet, as discussed in earlier chapters, there is abundant evidence that many in the movement do urge that the mind be made blank as tongue-speaking is sought. It has also been shown how, in face of innumerable false prophecies, there are few really courageous enough to exercise their minds honestly on this question and dig deeper. This is not a peripheral matter. It lies at the heart of the movement. It has always been a central issue. As we have seen, this happened repeatedly in previous centuries. When the prophetess in Flavel's day renounced her 'gift', her followers wished to hush it all up. In the eighteenth century Edwards commented on the enthusiasts' reluctance to look carefully into failed prophecies. A hundred years later, when Baxter recanted and went to Irving, the latter just did not want any searching conversation and fobbed off his earnest entreaties. Likewise the real facts about the countless false prophecies in Pentecostalism at the beginning of the twentieth century have been investigated by very few.

Of this same nature is the widespread reluctance today to analyse closely. Thus in one magazine a reader was quickly pleading with regard to the charismatic movement in the early days of its revival in the 1960s that 'the theologians' might not be permitted to 'analyse it away'.[9] One defence of the founder of Fountain Trust, while rightly deploring sarcastic reactions to his views, just assumed that he must have found something real and therefore it was wrong to challenge it.[10] A pamphlet written by a leader in the north warned critics not to pronounce on a matter in which they have not personally shared. 'Why should a man be given credence if he presumes to speak dogmatically about a gift of the Spirit of which he has no personal functional experience?'[11] Another Fountain Trust writer adopted a very common approach in asserting that

'Years of careful observation, supported by one's own personal struggle in earlier days, have convinced us that the attitude of these brethren towards the Gift of Tongues is a consequence, not of study of the Word of God, but of *fear*.'[12] One charismatic minister actually injected this note into his invitation to meetings at his church, writing, 'You may be uneasy about some, if not all, of the implications of this movement of the Spirit. You may wish that it would go away. You may wish that you could know more about it, without getting involved. Perhaps it is even a threat to you.'[13]

In all these subtle ways the person who wishes to scrutinize carefully by scriptural criteria is being told, 'Hands off!' It is suggested that either he is frightened and reacting out of fear, or he is just without the experience and therefore unqualified to speak, or he is one of the 'dead-letter' men immersed in the minutiae of Scripture but either oblivious of, or hostile to, the great free movement of the Spirit. It can truthfully be said that in many ways I had to fight a big spiritual battle before I was able to give the series of Bible studies which form the basis of the first part of this book. It was no easy task. It was a great consolation to me that a man who initially told me that the Bible studies should not be given was in the end saying, 'Carry on! Carry on!' Fear may not lie only on one side. Many people are fearful of examining carefully an alleged charismatic experience. Some have even been told that it would be a device of the devil if they were to scrutinize or doubt it.

Misuse of history

Secondly, we consider again the *charismatic misuse of history*, taking into account both the remote past and more recent incidents. Why have the views of spiritual giants of the past not been more carefully examined? Why have false views often been ascribed to them? In some cases it has been implied that they were in favour of the restoration of the gifts, when they wrote powerfully and extensively against this position, and in other cases it has been suggested that the issue was not a 'live' one in their day, when in fact they were firmly opposed to the prophets and prophetesses who were their contemporaries. Many Christians today are thus ignorant of the fact that there have been many charismatic movements in the past. Thus even the Religious Affairs Correspondent of *The Times* can write, 'In so far as there is a theory common to the charismatic movement, it is that God has chosen the contemporary age for the first reappearance since New Testament times of the remarkable "gifts of the spirit" said to have occurred then.'[14] While no one is claiming that *every* age has seen claimants to the supernatural gifts (Augustine and Chrysostom knew of no claimants), yet it still remains a fact that not only have there been many charismatic movements, but also that the orthodox stalwarts of the faith were almost invariably of another persuasion. This we have examined in detail.

Similar inaccuracies are rife where more recent incidents are recounted. I once received a magazine reporting a healing, a little later a letter reporting a relapse in the person healed and then the information that death had ensued. As far as I know, the magazine did not give any correction of its earlier claims. At least one magazine did report a correction of its earlier account of a revival in Japan: 'In the May edition . . . we published a report concerning a revival in Japan. We wish forthwith to apologize for the publication of this, as it has since come to our attention that the report is totally incorrect. Further, that the group of people reported on are not Christians at all, but a mixture of Buddhist, Shintoist and Christian beliefs.'[15] This retraction does show commendable honesty and is worthy of praise. But at the same time one wonders how much scrutiny is really given to the reports which many magazines publish if such a 'revival' could be reported in the first place.

Shortly after one minister described in a magazine his experience in exorcising someone in the grip of witchcraft, another minister, also present at some of these meetings, wrote to correct and indeed contradict various details in the report.[16] I personally know that my own version of exorcisms which I have witnessed would be quite different from that of others who were present. Similarly, my assessment of prophecies given within my own area would be very different from that of a whole variety of charismatics of different denominational backgrounds. Yet I would go much further. There have been instances where in investigating such matters I have felt a horror of darkness and blackness quite unique in my experience and again and again words about Satan fashioning himself as an angel of light have come to mind. However, others, some of whom claim the gift of discernment and are engaged in a ministry of exorcism, would see no wrong where I would see hellish confusion. Whether I am right or wrong must be left to the judgement of God. Suffice it to say that I have felt, to use the words of C.S. Lewis uttered in another context, that there are many who 'claim to see fern-seed and can't see an elephant ten yards away in broad daylight'.[17]

A man who has written many books which circulate widely among charismatics spoke at a large gathering in the north of England at which I was present. The message was sensational and not even remotely evangelical or Bible-based. At the close of the meeting there was an appeal. As many young people gathered on the platform the evangelist went round to several, interviewing them with a microphone so that thousands of others listened in. Then, after hearing just a sentence or two from each of them, he pronounced words of a blessing which could only be construed as meaning that these people were saved. One wondered whether the many stories of conversion in the evangelist's books were based on such flimsy counselling. Perhaps not all were, but at least one person in that vast auditorium decided on the evidence of that evening that the exciting and dramatic stories in this person's books could not really be trusted.

I have in fact several times had the experience of listening to speakers of this type and feeling that the central thrust of the gospel was missing. I was therefore fascinated to read the trenchant exposure of the false evangelism often found within the movement as given by Dr Beyerhaus at the conference on evangelism organized by the Billy Graham organization. One wonders what another speaker at the same assembly, who had affirmed, 'I have seen in my own life such great miracles as those described in the Bible,' made of these forthright words from the German theologian, Dr Beyerhaus, as he stated his own reaction to the view that 'signs and miracles' were being restored: *'Firstly,* this concept replaces the biblical hope for the returning Christ by the unbiblical expectation of a second Pentecost. Neither Jesus nor his apostles promised this to the church. *Secondly,* the main evangelistic impact is no longer the convincing force of the Gospel on the conscience of man.

Rather it is the irresistible pull of an anonymously radiating soul-force not entirely different from the demonic spirit force in non-Christian religions.' Then, after referring to pseudo-evangelists, he pleaded that their message be rigorously examined by biblical standards, adding, 'For seldom is Christ as crucified for our sins the centre of their message. Instead the whole emphasis is on the extraordinary gifts ascribed to the Holy Spirit quite apart from the true redemption of the sinner.'[18] Where this kind of thing happens, the devil is seeking to murder the souls of men by distorting and therefore lying about the kernel of the gospel. He hates this message to be proclaimed clearly lest sinners should be saved.

A proper attitude to leadership

Thirdly, we focus on the question of *a proper concept of leadership*. The infidelity to Scripture in the movement is seen in the wrongful deference given to prominent people or to people because, as far as we can tell, they are really Christians and have been mightily used by God. We saw this in the case of Davenport in New England, where critics were warned off because Davenport had been used by God. The following comments by William Goode are helpful: 'And here let it be observed, that we are not, as is common in the supporters of such cases as that we are considering, to argue thus: These persons are evidently pious, and consequently taught of God, and therefore they are right. For even granting that their general conduct is a proof of real piety, and some degree of divine teaching, it does not follow that they have been taught of God in the particular point in question, any more than it follows that the sins into which any of God's servants may at times be betrayed, are agreeable to the will of God, because committed by his servants. Every point that respects doctrine or conduct is to be tried, not by the apparent character of its author, but by the word of God.'[19] Goode also wisely adds elsewhere that there are those who too easily assume that we really know the actual piety of the claimants and who are too forgetful that there may be some workings of satanic pride in even the best of men.[20]

Therefore, although I have admittedly quoted many figures

from the past, I hope that I have not engaged in mere 'name-dropping'. I have not sought to bolster up my own position by just scattering a few big names around, but rather, to the best of my ability, to quote in some detail their expositions of Scripture and to show, as far as possible, that historically their judgement was vindicated. By contrast I feel that wrong use has been made of the name of one leading Christian figure in this connection. Frequently it has been asserted that this man believed in the continuation of the gifts today and the weight of his authority has been given to this viewpoint, yet I have been unable to find any sustained exposition in his writings where on scriptural grounds he maintains this position. In fact a recent review of tapes of sermons by this man simply says that 'The treatment given to prophecy and other gifts is not as detailed as that given to the baptism of the Spirit.'[21] Let the reader consider the treatment by Jonathan Edwards, dealt with in a previous chapter, and he will see that in this case the treatment is meticulously detailed, thorough-going and consistent. Edwards has given us scriptural arguments to persuade us. The contemporary figure has not. His name has merely been used.

It is woefully easy to quote the 'big name' in support of a position without providing real evidence of why the person thought as he did. But it is by biblical evidence alone that the issue is to be decided. This is a typical charismatic error – undue deference to the 'gifted person', even on issues where there are not sufficient grounds for such veneration. A similar danger is excessive or misplaced reliance on elders or charismatically gifted leaders in the locality at the expense of the Word of God. Even the great apostle Paul was no doubt gratified when the noble Bereans checked up on his message and biblical interpretation 'and examined the Scriptures every day to see if what Paul said was true' (Acts 17:11). I would be more than gratified if readers would check my exposition of all the biblical themes. I hope that I have gone through sections of Scripture systematically and not just thrown out casual allusions or told the reader that some other position is 'ridiculous' and hardly worth the trouble of refuting (a very easy way out!).

It is not my intention to disparage the oversight of elders or the balanced judgement of spiritual men, but in this area it seems a somewhat circuitous and often dangerous route when we put undue reliance on them. The great danger is that in the end it becomes not the Bible alone that judges but whichever charismatically gifted man stands at the end of the line. We recall that Irving and others often stressed that it was more a case of sensitivity and 'feeling' rather than solid scriptural criteria. In discussing Irving, Goode thus comments, 'After proving, though in a rather singular way, that the teaching of the Holy Spirit alone affords an adequate security against our being deceived by Satan, he adds, that if persons prophesy "by the Holy Spirit, all others who are partakers of the same Spirit also, will sympathize with those who speak; they will experience this sympathy, not so much by the verbal identity of the things uttered with the written word, although unless they be in such accordance, the spirit which dictates them cannot be divine, as by that secret unction of the Holy One by which they discern all things, and know the voice of the true from the voice of the false Shepherd. Thus the testimony to their own souls will be *independent* and *irrespective* of any forms of the intellect."'[22] The author then indicates his unhappiness with this line of reasoning despite some good things in the statement. The danger is that we will be guided by the 'general feelings' of gifted men. Elders are there to guide. But they must guide in the light of the infallible Word. We must be given clear biblical grounds for following their judgement.

The modernist C.H. Dodd, not unnaturally, could write, 'If the Bible is indeed the "Word of God", it is not so as the "last word",'[23] I would submit that charismatics fall into this same trap, whether they intend it or not. The very view of prophecy held by them, that prophecy needs sifting because it is not the pure Word of God, is a modernistic one. Indeed, the early fathers responded to the view that a man could apparently be motivated one moment by the Holy Spirit and the next by an evil spirit by saying that this was more a mark of possession than piety.[24] Therefore those who have followed carefully the historical section, and seen the catastrophic and sad events that befell genuine Christians who began to trust implicitly in prophetic figures and accept the guidance of apostles, will not readily be silenced when polite scepticism or even laughter greets their warnings about the dangers of the apostles who are growing up in our own midst. It is so easy for Christians to turn aside from the Word of God and yield to 'gifted men'. It has been very common for 'gifted men' (those claiming apostleship in particular) to assume this office quietly and with seeming humility and to end up far differently. To put excessive trust in man is to delight the murderer of souls and to further the lies that he constantly seeks to circulate.

Unity, orthodoxy and discipline in the church

While zeal for dance and drama is another obvious aspect of rejection of biblical teaching and authority, I merely refer to this here to illustrate the fourth aspect of deviation from scriptural truth and ask questions about Christian unity, orthodoxy and discipline. In the book *Praise Him in the Dance* the authoress discusses arrangements for a dramatic/dance presentation to represent the unity of the church and to show the evil of division. Anger, Jealousy, Fear and Pride are dealt with as causes of division at great length.[25] Scripture certainly does challenge us about the terrible dangers in these realms. Yet in significant contrast there is no emphasis on the fact that unity must also be based on truth and that much disunity is caused by error and false teaching. The real doctrinal basis for unity and the major cause of disunity have slipped into the background. One may ask, 'Is this not a theme that could be danced or mimed? Then should a task be undertaken with such a distorting omission?' One might further ask, 'How far is the doctrinal basis for unity even considered important in the authoress's mind?'

A prominent leader in the charismatic movement testified how the Holy Spirit led him alongside ecumenical leaders and how he felt that he must no longer seek to rebuke them for what he 'considered their heresies and false doctrines'.[26] While one can agree that the bitterness of the past should be avoided, ought he to have become a 'theological pacifist'? 'For, as I have often told you before and now say again even with tears, many live as enemies of the cross of Christ,' exclaimed the great apostle (Phil. 3:18). Paul was not bitter or hard. Tears were in his eyes. But he was firm and clear and he exposed false teachers. Dr Martyn Lloyd-Jones quoted the same leader as telling ecumenical leaders in 1964 that doctrine does not matter and 'that what matters is a living experience'. 'That', commented Dr Lloyd-Jones, 'is what they are ready to believe in their bankruptcy. They are ready to listen to a man who can speak in an authoritative manner on the basis of personal experience. Doctrine is being discounted and experience is being exalted at its expense.'[27]

One must also query the stance of another leader of the charismatic movement as we look at the views he recently expressed in an interview about his book *That we may be one*. We read that the basic premise of the book is that, while 'the starting of new churches seems to be the simple answer to spiritual decline in the old churches . . . in the long term it seldom works . . . God's remedy for sin in the camp was never separation or division.'[28] While one would concede that instant separation is seldom the proper remedy and that much must be tolerated if vital doctrine is not affected, yet it still remains a fact that, in certain circumstances, separation is both a biblical remedy and one which has ample historical justification in terms of blessing. The issue is vast and cannot be discussed in detail. Suffice it to say that, at a time when a bishop has been appointed who has denied vital doctrine concerning the virgin birth of Christ and the bodily resurrection, the statements quoted above appear singularly unimpressive. So does the statement by a Reformed writer which was read during the period of controversy within the Church of England over these issues: 'What makes charismatics more demonstrative, however, is not lack of reverence for God, but fulness of happy love for Jesus Christ and Christian people; anyone who has shared in the holy hugging of charismatic congregations or seen charismatic bishops dancing in church, as I have, knows that.'[29] Another Anglican writes with approval of the firm attitude of a bishop: 'One bishop, ministering in our church to a man who confessed pride, said, "Nonsense, you are consumed with fear." He was, and crumpled to the floor.'[30] Yet one wonders where these joyous, courageous bishops have gone during the consecration as bishop of a man who has denied the cardinal articles of the faith. Is it more important to dance around than to make certain that the source of all joy, the doctrine of the glorious bodily resurrection of Christ, is unambiguously safeguarded? Is it more important to deal with the fears of little men than the blasphemies of big ones? Perhaps in the latter case it is right to do both. However, the danger would seem to be once more that people are seeing fern-seed who cannot see an elephant ten yards away.

It may be that the charismatic dancing bishops and the one who exposed the lad's fear may not be in situations involving heresy (if this is so, they cannot be in England) and, should this be the case, I apologize here and now. But there must be no apology for raising the issue of church discipline. Christ himself put it at the forefront of his teaching, mentioning it on one of the two occasions when he gave teaching concerning the church. Paul amplified this. We have his basic teaching in 1 Corinthians 5, but if we compare 1 Timothy 1:18-20 with 2 Timothy 2:17 we see that Hymenaeus was excommunicated ('handed over to Satan') for denial of teaching on the resurrection. Not only have we moved so far from discipline in certain Protestant fellowships, but leaders, with the encouragement of their people, share fellowship with those whose tongue-speaking leads them into deeper devotion to the virgin Mary and to the pope. There are those who, in looking for a spiritual home, are more likely to ask whether tongue-speaking is permitted or encouraged than whether the church is associated in any way with those who deny the deity and bodily resurrection of Christ. Is it not yet again the activity of the enemy of souls, wishing to destroy the church, that brings this about?

The question of blessing

The fifth aspect of biblical denial we examine is the difficult concept of *'blessings'*. Cyril H. Maskey, formerly an apostolic pastor and 'apostle', says that 'The dogmatic denominational presentation of Pentecostalism officially says, "Speaking in tongues is a pivotal doctrine in the Holy Ghost Movement . . . is not only *an* evidence but is *the* Bible evidence of the baptism of the Holy Spirit."' He adds, 'It is further stated that one who has not spoken in tongues does not have the same power for service as one who has.'[31] I have frequently come across this attitude. Better is the attitude of one evangelist who said, 'Don't feel you are superior to anyone else; it is all of grace. I am no better than you are because I speak in tongues, but I am a better Christian than I would have been if I did not speak in tongues.'[32] But although this is much better than the former stance, it still leaves the man who has not spoken in tongues in an inferior position, despite the disclaimer. According to the argument, tongue-speaking is for today and it always brings blessing. The contention of this book is not only that tongue-speaking is not for today, but also that, according to Scripture, even in New Testament times when it was genuinely practised, so far was it from being a test of an advancement in the Christian life, that it was not even a sign of conversion. Just as men may prophesy and never have been truly related to the Saviour ('I *never knew* you. Away from me you evildoers' – Matt. 7:23) so a man speaking even 'in the tongues of men and of angels' without love is worth absolutely nothing (1 Cor. 13:1).

Blessing for the individual is difficult to assess. I personally have witnessed people renounce tongue-speaking (even after publicly claiming great blessing in that area) and, in my view, it is only at that point that they have really begun to be blessed in a striking manner – in several cases developing real gifts of leadership and reliability, and in other cases being equipped to face great trials. The traffic is not all one way! What is rarely realized is that there are many Pentecostals and charismatics who have rethought the whole issue in terms of Scripture, experience and history and have turned their back on the whole futile quest. Declares one former Pentecostal pastor, 'I have heard hundreds of "messages in tongues" and "interpretations". Not one ever added anything of value to the meeting.'[33] Another, renouncing his previous experience, wrote a book *Tongues – to speak or not to speak* and yet another has testified, 'My ministry has been more spiritual and fruitful since I left the Pentecostal church, and I have no desire to ever return.'[34] One of the most moving testimonies in this regard comes from one who spent over twenty years in the Pentecostal atmosphere of the Apostolic Faith Mission, Full Gospel Church and Assemblies of God, attending and assisting in major campaigns by various leaders. He wrote, 'I laid hands on the sick. I rebuked death. I prophesied. I spoke in tongues. I interpreted. I would say now, in all sincerity, that I saw and experienced nothing which would lead me to believe that

Pentecostalism offers anything along the lines of the New Testament Churches' experience.'[35] He acknowledges in a very gracious way that there are many sincere Christians in the movement, but his conclusions and his exposure of the 'faulty doctrinal basis', 'manipulative indoctrination' and 'charged atmosphere' are firm. A former Pentecostal minister has stated that the seeking of these experiences is never 'harmless'.[36]

Blessing for a church is an equally difficult thing to assess. Is a large and full church an indisputable sign of God's blessing? Would a large church with choreographer, dance team, regular prophesying and claims to healing, but which simply grew by drawing in other Christians, necessarily be 'more blessed' than a back-street gospel hall from whose ranks a constant stream of ambassadors for Christ had gone forth to the mission-field? Would a large church which, as a matter of course, had an unorthodox bishop along to take confirmations and which never practised discipline in any meaningful way, but which had its choir, orchestra and weekly 'practice of the gifts' necessarily be 'more blessed' than a smaller group which did take seriously God's call to holiness and purity both in the body of the fellowship and in its teaching ministry? And, of course, the big danger in the view which ties blessing to the presence of the gifts is that eventually one has to ask how many of the gifts are present. Not infrequently the person who left an orthodox church to join a fellowship which has tongue-speaking is soon moving because a mile away there is one which has thrilling prophecies, only to uproot again six months later, drawn by the compelling power of the amazing healings of another assembly in the next town, until won over by the convincing arguments of a house-group complete with apostles! After all, why stay in a church with just some of the gifts if another has more? (Some may even catch on later that Rome has had a much longer claim to apostleship and miracle-working than any of these new upstarts!)

It is sobering to reflect that Christ's penetrating glance obviously must have reversed many superficial human judgements, as he unerringly diagnosed the strength and weakness of the seven churches in Asia Minor. One church, Laodicea, which felt itself to be rich and prospering, was in Christ's sight bankrupt and in dire need. Yet while Ephesus had its problems, it was commended insofar as it could not 'tolerate wicked men' and praised because it had 'tested those who claim to be apostles but are not, and have found them false' (Rev. 2:2). Moreover the warning to Thyatira includes these words, 'Nevertheless, I have this against you: You tolerate that woman Jezebel, who calls herself a prophetess' (Rev. 2:20). Discipline was clearly called for in matters involving the gifts, as in other areas. Interestingly enough, the only two churches to receive unstinted praise were suffering Smyrna and evangelistic Philadelphia. (These may still be the two best qualifications for a church to receive Christ's approval.)

Similar problems of assessment occur whenever we think of God's 'blessing' in answer to prayer. This is not to assume that God never gives remarkable answers to prayer. I am not denying that there may well be a deliverance from the very brink of death, or a healing which astonishes nurses, local practitioners, specialists and even those who have prayed for it. This occurs in both charismatic churches and non-charismatic churches. I have witnessed such where I myself have been involved and would, as far as I am able to judge, attribute the healing to the gracious intervening providence of God in response to prayer. But this is not the issue that we have been considering throughout this book. The question, in the context of the signs, miracles and wonders of the Bible, is simply 'Are there men with apostolic powers who can regularly perform miracles, which are sometimes announced beforehand and are always immediate, complete and lasting?'

There is, of course, a command of Christ to the apostles which, if people were honest, would provide a clear test of many claims: 'Heal the sick, raise the dead, cleanse those who have leprosy, drive out demons' (Matt. 10:8). There are two things here that can be tested clearly. Anyone knows whether a dead corpse has been raised or a leper cleansed. Two are more difficult. Had the cancer already been treated medically? Was the patient already on the mend? Was the paralysis temporary anyway? Was the person actually demon-possessed, or are we merely trusting too implicitly in the diagnosis of the exorcist? It is interesting that the charismatics are not visiting leprosy colonies or the morgues. Can their claims there be tested too easily? Do they prefer to move within less clearly defined borders? (The claims for resurrection are usually from Indonesia – claims rather difficult to investigate!)

I have often used a simple illustration to illustrate this point. A man may say, 'Before I wake up in the morning I invariably dream about fairies. I always open my eyes at exactly 7 a.m. Ten minutes later I always go downstairs to make a cup of tea. Every morning when I go down the stairs I have a feeling of acute nausea.' Now there are two things here which, if you were with the man, you could test quite easily and two other things which are not in the same category. If you were able to observe the man and noted that he snored heavily till 8.30 a.m., whereupon he leaped out of bed, dressed and dashed to work without either a drink or a bite, would you be willing to credit his dreams about fairies and his description of nausea? If a church claims to have people with New Testament gifts of healing such as the apostles and their helpers possessed, but these healers always bypass the spina bifida and mongol child and the person who has lost a limb, and ignore the appeal of the leper overseas or the corpse in the next room, I, for one, am unwilling to believe them.

Throughout this book I have refused to credit many of the claims of charismatics. I do not accept 'secondary' or 'tentative' types of miracle performed by 'secondary' types of apostles among a people who engage in 'secondary' types of prophecy and 'secondary' tongue-speaking. In my view 'secondary' is not even third or fourth-rate. It simply means spurious. The very teachings that flow from many of these groups evidence this. That so many of these prophecies, tongues and revelations have led to the exaltation of dance and drama, to a wrong view of the mind, to so many false predictions (plus an equally worrying refusal to publicize, acknowledge or investigate them), to greater devotion to Mary and zeal for union with Rome, to unbiblical forms of evangelism and counselling, to a carelessness about the purity and discipline of the church, to a downgrading of the major biblical doctrines and emphases and even to false criteria for genuine conversion, is but some of the evidence I have adduced. I have sought throughout to document my case.

The question of the interpretation of 1 Corinthians 13 is not merely theoretical. It is intensely practical. In my view God has now given 'perfection' in the sphere of 'revelation'. He has given a complete Bible. Nothing more is needed. Nothing else is to be heeded. It is when this doctrine is neither believed nor practised that unscriptural views begin to proliferate and even to prevail. The appeal of this book is 'Back to the Word of God'. Our stand must be on this alone. In contrast to all the charismatic movements over the centuries, I believe that there is an immovable Word, which is 'eternal' and which 'stands firm in the heavens' and which is specifically given 'so that the man of God may be thoroughly equipped for every good work' (Ps. 119:89; 2 Timothy 3:17). We end as we began, with the plea from Isaiah: 'To the law and to the testimony! If they do not speak according to this word, they have no light of dawn' (Isa. 8:20).

Appendix
Prophecy in the New Testament

Appendix
Prophecy in the New Testament

The need for a clear test case

It has become widely held by those who follow the views of
Wayne Grudem in *The Gift of Prophecy in 1 Corinthians* that
the Bible itself furnishes evidence for three types of prophets.
Firstly, there are the 'primary' prophets who claim to speak
infallibly in God's name and who, being subject to the stringent
test of Deuteronomy 18:19-22, do emerge as genuine. Secondly,
there are false prophets who, claiming to bring an infallible
message from God, err, undermine the Word of God and lead
people astray. But thirdly, there is also a 'secondary' type of
prophet who does not fit into either of these groups. This
prophet does not claim 'word' authority for his message.
Therefore it can be legitimately accepted as a 'mixture' and the
wheat sifted from the chaff with no undermining of the
prophet's credibility.

Elsewhere I have sought to show that within the pages of
Scripture we do in fact find only two sorts of prophets, and I
have recently sought to give particular attention to the thesis of
Wayne Grudem that we can in fact discover in the Old
Testament evidence for this 'secondary' type of prophet.[1] In my
view, the evidence simply evaporates under careful scrutiny.
Within the whole of his book Grudem does not provide a single
example of actual prophetic speech in the Old Testament
which can be treated as 'secondary'. He simply infers that some
instances (where no content of prophecy is given) belong in this
category. It is an unwarranted inference, as the contexts of
these passages show. For instance, he provides Numbers
11:24-28 as a case of 'secondary' prophecy, whereas verse 17
would lead us to believe that the same Holy Spirit inspired

Eldad, Medad and others as inspired Moses! Another example
which he gives is 1 Samuel 19:24. Yet on this verse Herbert
Carson comments in his recent book, 'The words he spoke were
clearly from the Lord.'[2]

What of the New Testament evidence? In a review of Wayne
Grudem's book Bob Sheehan rightly drew attention to the
pivotal nature of the second prophecy of Agabus in this
connection.[3] While a detailed discussion of this prophecy may
seem to some like taking a sledge-hammer to crack a monkey
nut, or may even seem to be a waste of time when so many other
things demand attention (I have sometimes wondered this
myself!), yet since so many modern writers have alluded to it,
and since it is often brought forward as the clearest New
Testament example of this 'secondary', mixed type of
prophecy, it would seem profitable to look in some detail at it,
and then afterwards to ask some further questions about the
issue of scriptural interpretation and the kind of consequences
that follow from the two divergent views held by evangelicals.
This may lead us to revise our view of whether this is in fact a
trivial matter.

Acts 21:10-14 presents us with a recognized prophetic figure,
tells us the source of his prophecy, gives us details of the actual
content and describes both how it was received and whether it
was in fact fulfilled. One of the largest of the recent works on
the subject of prophecy is *Prophecy in Early Christianity and
the Ancient Mediterranean World* by David E. Aune. 'D. E.
Aune whose work surpasses anything so far written on the
subject,' was the enthusiastic verdict of Max Turner of the
London Bible College.[4] In actual fact the book is full of sheer
modernism. It refers to 'Deutero-Isaiah', sees Daniel as a
compilation of the 'wise', constantly weighs up which sayings of
Christ are authentic and rejects the Pauline authorship of
Ephesians and the Pastorals.[5] Therefore it is not surprising that
the author never really makes clear in his discussion of Acts 21
whether he even believes the incident to be historical or not! In
the end he gingerly drops down from his fence and does say this:
'Yet, in the light of Paul's "disobedience" to the oracle, which is
not regarded by Luke as a violation of the will of God (Acts
21:14), this may be an instance in which prophetic speech is
"evaluated".'[6]

In his book on *New Testament Prophecy,* David Hill, a Reader in Biblical Studies at the University of Sheffield, writes, 'In the case of Agabus, one may be forgiven for wondering if he was not actually trying to cast himself in the role of an Old Testament prophet, but not quite succeeding: for the fact that his word did not strictly come true would have made his prophecy "false" by Old Testament standards.'[7] There is much more in this vein.

Readers of the *Evangelical Times* in April 1986 will have found Wayne Grudem commenting on Paul's response to the prophetic warning in Acts 21:4 as follows: 'He disobeyed it! He would never have done this, if this prophecy had contained God's very words.' He then refers to the prophecy of Agabus as 'a prediction that is nearly correct but not quite. The *Romans* bound Paul (verse 33) and the Jews, rather than delivering him voluntarily, tried to kill him and he had to be rescued by force (verse 32). The prediction was not far off, but it was an inaccuracy in detail that would have called into question the validity of any Old Testament prophecy.'[8]

And Roy Clements, writing in the Scripture Union Daily Bible Reading Notes for January 1985, asks with regard to Acts 21:4, 'Do you think their anticipation of trouble was entirely supernatural?' He then continues, '*Agabus* was a well-accredited prophet of many years' standing. How would you explain the minor differences between the prediction he gives and the fulfilment (27-36)?' and, 'Why do you think Paul was so obstinate in his determination to go to Jerusalem? If a Moses or Jeremiah had told him not to go, would he have felt able to reject their advice?' A big question mark is thus put over the inspiration and the activity of the various prophets. Recently Roy Clements has amplified these comments in a booklet where he writes that 'The details of Paul's arrest, which Agabus the prophet predicts, are wrong in a number of significant respects as a careful reading of later verses shows.'[9]

Roy Clements acknowledges his indebtedness to Wayne Grudem who indeed writes the foreword to his booklet. His views are little more than a summary of those of the American. The same is true of Herbert Carson, who also constantly acknowledges his indebtedness. Here the latter comments on the word of prophecy at Timothy's ordination, of which no details are given in Scripture. 'Once again one is seeing the fact of two levels of prophecy — the infallible biblical oracle and the occasional personal or local message. The former is to be received both "in word and words", the latter "in word only", to use Grudem's useful distinction.'[10] And again, with regard to the second prophecy of Agabus, he writes, 'There is the infallible and universally binding prophecy of Scripture and there is the prophecy that truly reveals something from the Lord but does not have the infallibility of Scripture.'[11] Again Agabus is seen as being mistaken in detail.

It would seem that the book by Wayne Grudem and the booklet by Roy Clements have been strongly recommended at a recently formed conference entitled 'Reformed and Renewed'. Certainly in a session on prophecy at the conference in 1987 Bernard Thompson began by reading the second Agabus prophecy. Then he continued by saying that there were 'two clear kinds of prophecy' — that in the Old Testament which is infallible and that in the New Testament which is 'different'.[12] Without exaggeration one can say that there was no biblical exposition at all in the talk.

Agabus — a truly inspired prophet

It is my considered judgement that it is wrong to regard Agabus as an erring prophet. Such a view has dangerous and far-reaching consequences. I wish to list nine arguments as to why the second Agabus prophecy must be considered God-given and infallible as it is presented to us in Scripture. Not every point is of the same weight but together they form what I would consider an overwhelming case for establishing the fact that New Testament prophecy was just as inspired, infallible and authoritative as Old Testament prophecy.

1.   Agabus had a fine reputation. His track record was excellent. Roy Clements is in fact correct in describing him as 'a well-accredited prophet of many years standing'. In Acts 11:27-8 he is seen as travelling from Jerusalem to Antioch with other prophets. On arrival Agabus is the sole spokesman in the

prediction of the severe and great famine about to 'spread over
the entire Roman world' (verse 28). Luke simply tells us, 'This
happened during the reign of Claudius.' There is evidence also
in other sources of this momentous event. Because of this
prediction, relief was not a belated last-ditch measure but got
under way immediately. Think what a colossal waste of time,
energy and resources there would have been if Agabus had been
wrong. Moreover, consider how the character of the God of
truth would have been dishonoured in the Christian community
and beyond it. But he was not wrong.

2. Agabus was a man who was moved periodically by
overwhelming conviction, at which point the question of
distance or the discomfort of travel were of no consequence.
When he travelled from Jerusalem to Antioch he covered about
200 miles and when he uttered the second prophecy his journey
from Judea to Ptolemais was approximately eighty miles as the
crow flies. Agabus was not a crow. In fact he was a man with a
burden. In his very journeying we have little difficulty in
envisaging him as one of those gaunt, God-impelled figures of
the past, determined to find their man and complete their
mission. On the second occasion one commentator has even
seen his seemingly abrupt entry and confrontation of Paul as an
echo of the dramatic encounters of Old Testament prophets.
Agabus was certainly no lazy layabout with his little 'word from
the Lord'! He was a travelling man impelled by a sense of
mission.

3. His message was in harmony with the other prophetic
utterances spoken by many. In affirming this I am agreeing
with Wayne Grudem that the likely interpretation of verse 4 of
Acts 21 is that these were also prophetic words, and I am
following many commentators who similarly interpret Paul's
word in 20:23 where he asserts, 'I only know that in every city
the Holy Spirit warns me that prison and hardships are facing
me.' Prophecy was evidently not a hit-or-miss affair with some
saying one thing and some saying another. It is true that the
prophets of Tyre would seem to have gone a step further in
urging Paul not to go to Jerusalem, as did the hearers of the
prophecy of Agabus (but not Agabus himself). This is an
important point which must be dealt with but it does not affect

the fact that all the prophets with one voice predicted hardship and suffering. The unanimity was striking. The Holy Spirit does not contradict himself.

4. We also note the clear display of Old Testament symbolism: 'Coming over to us, [Agabus] took Paul's belt, tied his own hands and feet with it, and said...' (21:11). He affirms his identification with Old Testament figures. Commentator after commentator acknowledges this. Even Fairbairn, who argues that not all the symbolic acts (e.g. Isaiah walking naked as recorded in Isaiah 20) were carried out literally, does see that Scripture demands that we affirm that some were. He places the action of Agabus alongside such episodes as 1 Kings 20 and Jeremiah 28 where the symbolism was embodied in definite action.[13] Moreover, as J. A. Motyer points out, this kind of symbolism was more than an attractive visual aid. It implied that the message would definitely be accomplished. The prophet's symbolic action meant God's sure action. Underlining the significance of this the same writer states, 'Prophecy and the prophets form the greatest line of continuity between the Old and New Testament.'[14]

5. Our next point reinforces this argument. Agabus begins his prophecy with the formula, 'the Holy Spirit says'. On this David Hill comments: 'Among the most striking of the phrases characteristic of prophetic speech is the messenger-formula (*Botenformel*), *"tade legei"* ("the words of" or in the NEB "these are the words of..."). Each of the seven letters in Revelation chapters 2-3 begins with these words — found nowhere else in the New Testament except in Acts 21:11, on the lips of Agabus — which often form the Septuagintal rendering of the Hebrew for "Thus says the Lord", and which, functionally, form an exact equivalent to the more frequently used Greek rendering of the Hebrew words, viz. *houtōs legie Kyrios*. This says P. S. Minear is "John's use of an Old Testament formula. The Old Testament prophets had established this formula as the appropriate introduction for God's address to the people...".'[15] Indeed in his larger work on prophecy Wayne Grudem also acknowledges that the phrase used here is very similar to the 'common LXX equivalent' for 'the divine messenger formula used by O.T. prophets'.[16] Of course if we

believe that the Holy Spirit is God, then it is obviously God speaking. This can be recognized without the more complex linguistic argument which is, however, interesting.

6. The Spirit who inspired this message is the 'Spirit of truth' (John 14:17). Scripture shows how much he hates lying, and particularly lying in a Christian context (Acts 5:3, 4). Where people prophesy in his name and do so truly, it is he who inspires the message and who protects the prophecy from start to finish from error. 'For prophecy never had its origin in the will of man, but men spoke from God as they were carried along by the Holy Spirit' (2 Peter 1:21). This is the consistent biblical emphasis. Agabus was prompted and carried along by the Holy Spirit in the same way as other prophets.

7. As in the case of the earlier prophecy of Agabus this is also prediction. It is the 'delayed miracle' so common in Old Testament prophets. Again, J. A. Motyer comments: 'Almost every prophet first appears as a foreteller...'[17] It would of course be quite wrong to limit prophecy to foretelling. Bishop Butler was clearly wrong when he said that 'Prophecy is nothing but the history of events before they come to pass.'[18] None of us wishes to be restricted to such a crudely narrow definition of prophecy, which is indeed wide-ranging and varied both in content and format. Yet the predictive note must not be played down. It is not merely forthtelling. It is often also foretelling.

8. The sequel underlines the power of the prophetic word. When Paul determined to go to Jerusalem notwithstanding, there were deliberate attempts to win round the local Jews, and to head off any likely conflict (verses 20-26). The Christian believers are quite confident that their human strategy will work. 'There are four men with us who have made a vow. Take these men, join in their purification rites and pay their expenses, so that they can have their heads shaved. Then everybody will know there is no truth in these reports about you, but that you yourself are living in obedience to the law' (verses 23-24). Of course the sequel shows that all this was of no avail whatever in preventing the opposition of the Jews to Paul. A tumultuous riot against the apostle broke out within a week of his acquiescing in this stratagem. But the interesting fact is that shrewd local people thought that suffering could be avoided. A

series of prophetic words could not be circumvented so easily.

Was the prophecy fulfilled?

9. More space must be given to our last point for there remains the simple fact that it is true that the Jews did not in person bind Paul. They sought to kill him and the Romans rescued him and bound him. So what do we make of the word of Agabus who proclaimed, 'In this way the Jews of Jerusalem will bind the owner of this belt and *will hand him over to* the Gentiles'? (21:11). Simply what Paul himself made of them. The last chapter of Acts records his arrival in Rome, where summoning the leaders of the Jews he told them why he had come. This is how he puts it: 'My brothers, although I have done nothing wrong against our people or against the customs of our ancestors, I was arrested in Jerusalem *and handed over to* the Romans' (Acts 28:17). He uses exactly the same phrase as Agabus. Now one can be forgiven for assuming that he was not inferring that it was the inhabitants of Malta or even Syria who handed him over. There is only one group who can fill this role. It was undoubtedly the Jews of Jerusalem.

Many have drawn an illustration from the apostolic preaching of the passion narrative where, despite the obvious fact that the Romans actually crucified Christ, Peter can address the listening Jews and say, 'You killed the author of life' (Acts 3:15). Ultimately they were responsible. I believe that there is a similar element in this situation. And yet I feel that we should in fact dig deeper and see that the prophecy has remarkable fulfilment throughout a whole sequence of events from the riot in Jerusalem, right to the close of the book of Acts.

Obviously the Jews did seek to kill Paul during this riot. There were also two later attempts on his life (Acts 23:12; 25:3). When one considers the violent fury of the crowd in the initial attempt, and all the fanaticism and cunning of the later plotting, it is amazing that Paul was not in fact murdered. If he had been, the prophecy would have failed. The very divine protection of his life through the intervention of the Romans in the nick of time at Jerusalem, the role of Paul's nephew and the non-co-operation of Festus with the Jews at a crucial point were all part of the Holy Spirit's implementation of the original prophecy.

Yet what we do see repeatedly throughout these chapters is the Jews from Jerusalem ensuring that Paul remained bound and in the hands of the Romans even when it is quite apparent that the Romans themselves would have been willing to release him. The very fact of his being bound is often stressed. Immediately after the riot he was allowed to address the crowd, and mainly because of the vehement rejection by the Jerusalem Jews of his message, we learn that the Romans 'stretched him out to flog him' until Paul asserted his Roman citizenship. We then read that 'The commander himself was alarmed when he realized that he had put Paul, a Roman citizen, *in chains*' (22:22-29).

When Paul was transferred to Caesarea, the letter of Claudius Lysias to Felix makes it clear that there was 'no charge against him that deserved death or imprisonment' (23:29). It was merely the pressure of the Jews from Jerusalem that prevented his release from captivity. When Tertullus, accompanied by leading ecclesiastics from Jerusalem, arrived to keep up the pressure we learn that 'because Felix wanted to grant a favour to the Jews, he left Paul in prison' (24:27). It was quite unrelenting. The new man Festus was soon confronted by the familiar spectacle of 'the Jews who had come down from Jerusalem' bringing countless false accusations against Paul so that in the end he had to appeal to Caesar and thus remain in bonds (25:7-12).

When Agrippa arrived on his state visit Festus made it abundantly clear that there was no real crime but that *it was solely because of the persistent attacks of the Jews from Jerusalem that the situation was unresolved* (25:15-20). In fact it had reached such a scale that when Paul was brought in he was greeted with these words: 'King Agrippa, and all who are present with us, you see this man! *The whole Jewish community has petitioned me about him in Jerusalem* and here in Caesarea, shouting that he ought not to live any longer' (25:24). Once again Festus acknowledged that Paul was innocent, permitting him to make his great and famous defence which concludes with: 'I pray God that not only you but all who are listening to me today may become what I am, *except for these*

chains' (26:29). It almost seems as though by now the whole
body of Jerusalem Jews was responsible for those chains — a far
more remarkable fulfilment of the prophecy than if four or five
representative figures had trussed him up and passed him over
to the Romans.

Beyond any doubt in the deepest sense it was the Jerusalem
Jews who had put the chains on Paul ('the Jews of Jerusalem will
bind the owner of this belt') and kept them there ('and will hand
him over to the Gentiles'), despite all the knowledge of
successive Roman officials that Paul was a privileged Roman
citizen and was in fact innocent and should be freed. Why
should such a succession of normally powerful and domineering
men be browbeaten in these circumstances by the Jews from
Jerusalem in this way were it not that it had been prophesied?
Indeed Paul refers to all this as he speaks to the Jews from Rome
and sums up the story: '...I was arrested in Jerusalem and
handed over to the Romans. They examined me and wanted to
release me, because I was not guilty of any crime deserving
death. But when the Jews objected, I was compelled to appeal to
Caesar — not that I had any charge to bring against my own
people. For this reason I have asked to see you and talk with
you. It is because of the hope of Israel that *I am bound with this
chain*' (28:17-20). Is the content of this speech and the
concluding reference to the chain purely fortuitous? Of course
not. He was acknowledging the detailed fulfilment of the
prophecy of Agabus.

Prophecy has varied fulfilments

True prophecy was always fulfilled. Sometimes it was very
precise and easy to assess. Paul predicted to the distraught
sailors during the storm that they would land on an island (not a
peninsula), that the ship would be lost (not salvaged) and that
all 276 men would get safely to shore (not 275). Sometimes the
fulfilment was surprising. John the Baptist was the new Elijah
but he was not of course Elijah come back to life (Mal. 4:5-6;
Matt. 11:14; 17:12). A study of the New Testament fulfilment
of Old Testament prophecies would show that they were always
accurate but that there were surprising twists. Patrick

Fairbairn's old book on prophecy is worth almost all the modern ones put together in its discussions of the various types of fulfilment and its deep perception of spiritual issues. For example, his defence of scriptural prophecies about Tyre and Edom against the rationalistic or crassly literalistic critics is well worth reading in this connection.[19]

Yet in these surprising twists there must be no deception or dishonourable 'get out'. For example they are not of the type where the prophets predict the recovery of someone, sometimes with distraught relatives taking comfort from this, and then, when the person dies, there is an instant claim that there was a deeper fulfilment since the person has now fully recovered in heaven![20] Nor are the prophecies like that given through the ministry of the charismatic group who announced a military take-over in 1975 in England after which opportunities for ministry would be curtailed. The alleged fulfilment was that because of rising petrol prices ministry had in fact been curtailed! (It is significant that in this case the group was still trying to say that the original prophecy might in fact come true — later!) By contrast Paul indulged in no explaining away and no verbal somersaults!

As I have shown, Paul confirmed in a totally transparent manner that what Agabus had prophesied had been fulfilled, indeed fulfilled even more thoroughly and profoundly than those who heard and witnessed Agabus' prophecy might have imagined.

It seems somewhat excessively literalistic when we find Herbert Carson in his endeavour to show that Agabus was not fully accurate, writing thus: 'Further, although Paul was bound by the Romans with two chains, Luke notes that his hands were free so that he could use them in his characteristic manner when addressing a public meeting — he "motioned to the crowd" (Acts 21:40).'[21] Do we have to believe that Agabus meant in this case that Paul's hands and feet had to be tied by a struggling group of Jews any more than we have to believe that Jeremiah threatening the Babylonian yoke and himself wearing one meant that ultimately all the Jews of his day would be walking round with literal yokes round their necks? It is surely sufficient to show, as I have done, that Paul was generally in bonds during this period.

Of course there are still problems. Why did Paul disregard the prophecies and particularly the advice that he should not go? (See Acts 21:4.) It is possible to take the view of Calvin that the foreknowledge was inspired but the practical advice was not. (Once again we note that Agabus did not proffer this further advice.) Another view is that even Paul should not have disregarded the Holy Spirit through the prophets and that, though it was God's will that he should eventually go (Acts 20:22), yet the timing was wrong. I incline to the latter view but I state them both.

A critical attitude to Scripture

1.   There are important consequences that flow from all this. The views of Wayne Grudem and those who follow him lead them to criticize the biblical record and a Christian prophet where the biblical record gives us no ground for so doing. Our study of their treatment of the second Agabus prophecy gives clear proof of this. Scripture is made to stand on its head. The obvious reading of the passage is that God is giving to his people a positive example of what is involved in true prophecy. The other view reads it as a warning tract on how prophecy should not be given! This involves the rejection of the genuineness of an introductory formula which is acknowledged as divinely authoritative ('the Holy Spirit says'); the impugning of the authenticity of countless details which indicate continuity between Old and New Testament prophecy (the Greek phrase in the introductory formula, the prophetic symbolism, the whole demeanour and approach of Agabus); and refusal to acknowledge that Paul's own appraisal of the prophecy indicates not a skimpy, partial fulfilment but quite the reverse — a detailed fulfilment over a long period of time against all kinds of odds.

In his explanation of Acts 28:17, I feel that Wayne Grudem does justice neither to the context of this verse (which forms a unit with the three which follow), nor to the content of Acts chapters 21 to 28, nor to the variety of ways in which prophecy can be fulfilled, nor to the way in which Luke expects the ordinary reader to assess Paul's verdict. Grudem writes, 'And in Acts 28:17 *ex Hierosolumon* can hardly be taken to refer to Paul's initial capture by the tribune *in* Jerusalem (21:32-3), but makes much more sense as a reference to his transfer *out of* Jerusalem to Caesarea (23:23ff).'[22] He sees Caesarea as the place of the procurator, who represented Roman rule over Palestine.

In commenting on a difficult verse in Genesis where there are many interpretations, Luther writes, 'I steadfastly follow this rule: the words ought to serve the subject matter and, not conversely, the subject matter the words.'[23] I feel that this comment is relevant here. Also the questions still remain, Who handed over Paul to the Romans, and did Paul envisage the prophecy as having been fulfilled? As I have sought to expound at length the answers seem obvious.

We must also strongly reject Wayne Grudem's attempt to drive a wedge between the prophecy of the Old and New Testaments, except of course in the case of the apostles, whom he acknowledges as legitimate successors to the Old Testament prophets. Max Turner has written, 'The New Testament surely was not claiming that the Old Testament Spirit of prophecy has now returned, but merely to the apostles — thus dividing all other persons or charismata off and levelling them down with the sort of phenomena professed by early Judaism in its consciousness that the Spirit had been withdrawn (Acts 2:17-38). Paul does not say that all New Testament prophets see through a glass darkly while apostles see clearly. The apostles' prophecy, too, is *ek merous* and *en ainigmati* (1 Cor. 13:12).'[24]

Both Herbert Carson and Roy Clements follow Wayne Grudem in his view that the New Testament foundational apostle is the successor to the Old Testament prophet.[25] Both also follow him in seeing 'the inter-testamental period' and 'rabbinic writings' (Clements), or the fact that Paul was 'schooled in rabbinic writings' as providing 'valuable clues' (Carson), to the way words were used in the New Testament.[26] I believe that they have failed to recognize (a) that the rabbinic writers obviously do not claim inspiration by the Holy Spirit, as Wayne Grudem more or less admits,[27] (b) that there is a real theological significance in the prophetic silence in the inter-testamental period (prophecy is only given when

Scripture is being written),[28] and (c) that Paul was supremely 'steeped' in the teaching of the Word of God which is determinative for giving the proper background for his use of words and concepts. In that Word all prophecy, without exception, comes from God (2 Peter 1:21).

Subtle linguistic arguments are being used today to undermine this old orthodoxy. I do not profess to be a skilled linguist myself. Like many men I did Hebrew and Greek at university but now I rely largely on the labours and research of others in this realm. If I have specialized at all, it has been in church history. Yet there is another book on this subject which ought to be given publicity. It is *An Evaluation of Claims to the Charismatic Gifts* by Douglas Judisch, a professor at Concordia Theological Seminary. His book, in my view, shows equal skill in the use of Greek and Hebrew to that of Wayne Grudem, is entirely orthodox in its concept of prophecy and is quite brief (only 96 pages). In a sense I do not think that our opinions on this subject depend on the subtleties of Greek grammar. I rather think that our whole theology is the key factor. In fact, before I read Douglas Judisch I had already reached the same conclusions on the relevance of Old Testament passages like Daniel 9:24-7 and Zechariah 13:2-6 even without his technical know-how. In particular, Judisch powerfully shows that Paul's concept of prophecy was rooted and grounded in the teaching of the Old Testament.

A lack of reverence for the Holy Spirit
2. If all true prophecy originates from God it is inspired by the Holy Spirit. Therefore my next concern must be over the downgrading of the role and power of the Holy Spirit. Both Agabus prophecies are said to be given by the Holy Spirit. Wayne Grudem not only sees the second Agabus prophecy as only partially inspired, but also considerably undermines the status of the first one. He engages in an analysis of the language and commenting on one word suggests that there is 'a rather loose relationship between the Holy Spirit and the prophet, since it allows room for a large degree of personal influence by the speaker himself'. With regard to the word *semainō* (translated 'predict') he argues that 'A degree of imprecision is

also suggested by *semainō,* which is elsewhere used of prophetic speech "that simply gives a vague indication of what was to happen".[29]

Although he refers to a renowned lexicon for this verdict, I would vigorously query the accuracy of all this. If a 'text without a context is a pretext' we ought also to recall that to a considerable degree Greek words must be interpreted within their context. What reader can turn to Acts 11:27-30 and feel that there is any imprecision or vagueness either with regard to Luke's intention to portray Agabus as a prophetic figure, or the prophecy itself, which is crystal clear and of tremendous consequence, or the response (Agabus was heeded and obeyed), or the fulfilment? There was a great famine as predicted. At this rate we shall hardly need the modernist to come along and undermine Scripture! His work will have been done for him.

Another aspect of this is the contrast which Roy Clements makes between Moses and Elijah and poor insignificant, straying Agabus. We recall his rhetorical question, 'Why do you think Paul was so obstinate in his determination to go to Jerusalem? If a Moses or Jeremiah had told him not to go, would he have felt able to reject their advice?' This kind of argument was answered long ago by B. B. Warfield in a discussion, where specifically acknowledging the supremacy of a figure like Moses, he also showed that lesser figures were not less inspired. He wrote, 'We have already been led to note that even on the occasion when Moses is exalted above all other organs of revelation (Num. 12:6ff) in point of dignity and favour, no suggestion whatever is made of any inferiority, in either the directness or the purity of their supernaturalness, attaching to other organs of revelation.'[30] These words are applicable to all attempts to suggest different levels of inspiration because of differences in the stature of prophets. This is to fix our gaze excessively, almost idolatrously, on men, and to withdraw our gaze dangerously, almost irreverently, from the Holy Spirit. To oppose Moses to Agabus is quite unwarranted.

Let us leave the last word under this heading with John Calvin. He puts the issue in true focus, when commenting on the phrase 'the Holy Spirit warns me' in Acts 20:23. '...I do not take this to mean secret oracles, but predictions which he was

hearing everywhere from the prophets. But this statement is of
more value for commending prophecies, than if the very men,
who uttered them, were cited as witnesses. For a word of God
has its authority established in this way, when we acknowledge
that his Spirit is the Author even although men are its
ministers.'[51]

Anti-supernaturalism

3.   This leads on naturally to our next point, which is that
there is an anti-supernaturalism in the view being advocated.
Prophecy is no longer infallible. Yet anyone, from devotees of
the Delphic oracle to modern fortune-tellers, can give words
that are partially true. Indeed some, inspired by the devil, can
be uncannily and persistently accurate. Could we ask Wayne
Grudem whether he feels that the 'slave girl who had a spirit by
which she predicted the future' was not according to his
argument better endowed than Agabus? (See Acts 16:16-18).
Yet this undermining of the supernaturalism of the Bible is not
confined to prophecy. It goes right across the board. In the
realm of healing some speak of 'tentative miracles'. One
modern writer, whose book on healing is a best seller,
recommends that 'beginners pray for the cure of minor
ailments, such as colds' before tackling the bigger illnesses![52] We
also have a new breed of 'apostles' who confessedly perform
none of the great signs and wonders performed by the first
apostles and who have certainly not seen the risen Christ nor
been commissioned by him.

The same thing applies in discussion of tongues. For
example, Wayne Grudem (in a review article to be mentioned
later), can say of a writer that 'He makes some puzzling
statements about speaking in tongues, claiming that the
tongues of Acts 10:46 and 19:6 were intelligible languages...'[53]
It has today become almost common practice to drive a wedge
in this way between the tongues of Pentecost and all other
instances in the New Testament. This enables people to admit
that Pentecost was unique and unrepeatable (I agree in part
with this), and then to argue that the tongues in the rest of the
New Testament like the 'tongues' of today are not recognizable
languages.

Indeed, when you probe behind all the footnotes and all the

technicalities of Wayne Grudem's book you will simply find that the emperor has no clothes on. In other words the evidence evaporates under scrutiny. It is little more than a very elaborate justification of modern error. He more or less admits that his distinction is not an easy one to work out: 'If we assume for a moment that this study is correct in seeing two types of NT prophecy, the one thought to have a divine authority of actual words, and the other only thought to have a [divine] authority of general content, it must still be admitted that such a distinction between types of authority is a fine one, and one which might easily be blurred or forgotten. It would eventually be very easy for more and more Christian prophets, whether for good or ill motives, to begin to claim not only that they had received a "revelation" from God or Christ, but also that they spoke with a divine authority of actual words. This was in fact apparently what happened, at least in Montanism, and probably in many other cases as well.'[34] He then admits that 'A failure on the part of the church itself to distinguish between these two types of prophecy might have been the cause of a total loss of prophecy in the church.'[35] But if the early church, standing so close to events, could not make the distinction, how can we hope to do so more successfully and accurately? The clear teaching of God's Word on the supernaturalness of prophecy and the other gifts has been undermined by his thesis and the result is general confusion.

Standing in judgement on the Word of God
4.   I am aware of Wayne Grudem's assertion that he accepts the infallibility of Scripture and I do not query the sincerity of what he says. Nevertheless I do query whether he and those who support his view have really thought through the implications and consequences of what they are advocating. The view has clear modernistic overtones. Already we have seen this and we shall now see further evidence, for another corollary of the view is that prophetic words from God can be sifted and criticized, indeed should be so treated. It is assumed that prophecy is a mixture and that the good must be sifted from the bad. Two passages, 1 Corinthians 14:29 and 1 Thessalonians 5:19-21, have been used by Wayne Grudem, Peter Lewis and others to justify this procedure. But have these passages been properly

interpreted? And what is the likely effect of this interpretation on the outlook of the believer?

On 1 Corinthians 14:29, Calvin comments, 'But it may seem odd that men are allowed to make judgements concerning the teaching of God, which ought to be established beyond any dispute. My answer to that is that the teaching of God is not subjected to the judgement of men, but their task is simply to judge, by the Spirit of God, whether it is his word which is declared, or whether using this as a pretext, men are wrongly parading what they themselves have made up...'[36] And again, 'What it amounts to, therefore, is that the gift is subjected to examination in this way, that the prophets weigh up what is said to see if it has come from the Spirit of God, *for if it is established that the Spirit is the source of it, there is no need for further perplexity.*'[37]

This, I would submit, is the correct interpretation. There had to be an initial sifting to find out the source. Did the prophecy come from the Holy Spirit or from some other source? If the former, 'there is no need for further perplexity' and it must be accepted totally. If the latter, it must be rejected totally. It was not a call to pick out the good bits from the bad. Therefore, C. J. Ellicott writes that it was a command 'to test the words spoken...whether they really came forth from the Spirit, or were only the imaginings of the speaker's heart'.[38] David Hill, linking the verse with 1 Corinthians 12:10 which refers to those gifted with the ability to distinguish between spirits writes, 'A particular instance of this exercise of this gift of evaluation, in our view, is 1 Corinthians 14:29: there prophecies are tested, weighed, evaluated in order to determine their source of inspiration, their genuine or counterfeit quality.'[39] As it stands, I can accept that statement, though I would apply it in a different way from the writer himself, as will be seen.

It is also interesting to see what many commentators make of 1 Thessalonians 5:21 which, in connection with prophecy, reads, 'Test everything. Hold on to the good.' Repeatedly they say that this is an illustration taken from the testing of metals. It is about choosing the 'genuine as opposed to the counterfeit coin', says Milligan. It means, 'Stick to the true metal; have nothing to do with the false,' argues E. J. Bicknell. True prophecy is 'to be accepted like a coin that is found to be genuine' is the verdict of Hibbert. Leon Morris explains that the verb *dokimazo* was often used of the testing of metals, and that the word used for 'good' particularly means 'that which is good in itself'.[40] The illustration is apt. A coin is either genuine or counterfeit. There is no half-way stage, no percentage of counterfeitness! The same is true of authentic prophecy. This interpretation properly brings these two passages in line with the Old Testament passages on testing prophecy, which indeed never envisage the sifting of the genuine from the false in the prophecies but rather the genuine from the false among the prophets.

In line with his mistaken interpretation of these two passages, Wayne Grudem assumes that, because the setting of 1 Corinthians 14 is the local church assembly and because the prophets were known local figures, there would therefore be little likelihood of false prophets standing up.[41] There are two replies to this. Firstly, there is his own point that from time to time people would be venturing on their first prophecies.[42] The congregation would have no prior knowledge of their proven ability or genuineness. But secondly we need to recall that a genuine prophet told an established congregation with numerous elders that 'Savage wolves will come in among you and will not spare the flock. Even from your own number men will arise and distort the truth in order to draw away disciples after them' (Acts 20:29-30). We never know when Satan is going to seek to introduce his deadly errors. The terrible dangers of false teaching and prophecy are never adequately acknowledged by Wayne Grudem and those who follow him.

What has happened to false prophecy?

5.   This leads on logically to our next point. I would like to know from proponents of the other view whether, except in very rare instances, there can be such a thing as false prophecy. For example, what do they make of the following passage by Roger Day, in *How to Grow Up as a Christian Boy or Girl*? 'When God gives you a message in a meeting or in your family prayer time, such as a prophecy, you'll know deep down in your heart. It may be only a few words but they might be just right for the people who are there. I've heard young people speak a

prophecy from God like: "I love and care for you," and it's really blessed grown-ups... Sometimes the words you get might not be for that meeting. If you're not sure, ask your dad or a leader before you speak out. Then wait for the right meeting and bring your prophecy. Don't worry if you make a mistake. I'm famous for the mistakes I've made in prophecy. I once came up to a microphone in front of 200 people with a prophecy and after two words my mind went blank! But I'm learning that if we're afraid to try, we'll never get anywhere. We often then learn by our mistakes.'[43]

Or there are the words in the address of Bernard Thompson at the Conference of Reformed Charismatics: 'People have a right in open praise and worship to bring a prophetic word that is an encouragement to the flock,' and 'This prophetic word I give is not infallible. I make mistakes. I am not frightened of getting it wrong.'[44] An example he gives is that he accuses a brother of immorality but, finding he is wrong, just seems to laugh it off, adding casually that he is not normally as insensitive as this.

Is it really satisfactory to reply, 'Well, these men are evidently not as serious as others. They are far too glib and superficial?' Is that not too glib and superficial an answer? One man may give dozens of false prophecies and not bat an eyelid or feel a pang of conscience. Another may be in error on only a few details and may mourn and repent earnestly. But is it just a question of the degree of seriousness in the speaker? Or is it the percentage of error? Would a prophecy eighty per cent correct pass muster because seventy-five per cent of truth is the pass mark? Or does the pass mark vary in different congregations in different parts of the country? (I rather think that it might!)

Putting the issue simply, how much would Agabus have had to be wrong to be not just mistaken, and, prophetically speaking, rather too big for his boots, but actually a false prophet? Or is the creature now almost extinct, except perhaps in prophecies which are palpably heretical or totally false? And (has anyone else noticed this?) the definition of true prophecy is actually now the same as the definition of false prophecy in the Old Testament (Deut. 18:20). Satan never did like making frontal attacks when he could squeeze in by the back door. He infiltrates, smuggling in an ounce of poisonous falsehood with a pound of scriptural truth. And what now is to stop him increasing the dose if a percentage of falsehood is permissible?

Acceptance of modernism
6. My next illustration of the decline of clear adherence to Scripture is Wayne Grudem's review of the book on New Testament prophecy by David Hill (published in *Themelios* in January 1982). Undoubtedly this book has some helpful insights. I have quoted some myself. Not unnaturally Wayne Grudem seizes favourably on the emphases which are almost identical with his own position. He mentions with approval the 'error' in the second prophecy of Agabus, the arguments that New Testament prophecy was not infallible, the belief that the apostles are the successors to Old Testament prophets and various points of interpretation with regard to 1 Corinthians 14.

I have myself reviewed the book quite fully elsewhere. I can only give here a synopsis of that review. Firstly, David Hill infers that certain events in the New Testament are not presented accurately. For example, Acts 13 shows how Luke thought Paul might have addressed a synagogue audience, not how he did. Secondly, the Pauline authorship of Ephesians and the Pastorals is denied. Thirdly, various sayings of Jesus are seen as not authentic. On the discourses in the Fourth Gospel he writes that 'These may indeed be homilies composed around sayings of Jesus and presented in the form of a speech by Jesus himself.'[45] Fourthly, authorities like Bultmann and Tillich are praised and evangelicals largely ignored. Fifthly, here is David Hill on the death of Christ: 'Constantly under threat from his opponents he had to reckon with the possibility, even the likelihood, that he would meet the fate of the prophet — persecution and martyrdom.'[46] And on the resurrection, 'What we can say on the basis of authentic sayings of Jesus is this: as a prophet he foresaw his violent death in terms of prophetic martyrdom and probably foresaw his vindication as well in relation to his wider expectation that the consummation of the kingdom was at hand.'[47]

Wayne Grudem alludes to Mr Q and to the undermining of Pauline authorship (without comment) but to nothing else that I have mentioned. Yet although he makes a few criticisms of points of exegesis, he begins his review with the statement, 'This book is a sober and very helpful contribution to the study of New Testament prophecy,' and concludes it in this way: 'Yet the strengths of this book far outweigh its deficiencies. It stands as a valuable contribution to the study of New Testament prophecy.'[48]

It must be conceded that we do not always have the space we would like for reviewing, but I would submit that this is a totally inadequate assessment of a very dangerous book. There are a series of questions which arise. How far are we prepared not only to assert our belief in the authority of Scripture but also to defend it against those who would undermine it and to warn the flock clearly about them? How far is his view on the gift of prophecy, which leads, as I have sought to show, to a critical attitude to parts of Scripture, one which leads to a diminution of firm conviction in other areas? Are the points on which the two writers are in agreement on prophecy of such importance that their disagreements on the reliability of Scripture are peripheral? (I am assuming Wayne Grudem did in fact disagree on this. He did not himself say so.)

I am taking the liberty of giving the closing section of my own review: 'On the question of the modernism we put the issue bluntly. (1) *It is futile* as the following illustration shows. We are reminded of the dilemma of Mr Boffin in *Our Mutual Friend* by Charles Dickens. Upon acquiring wealth, he also acquires Silas Wegg, a "literary man" to read to him. Laboriously Wegg wades through a book on the Roman Empire, Rollin's *Ancient History, The Wars of the Jews* and eventually through Plutarch's *Lives*. Mr Boffin experiences growing perplexity. "What to believe, in the course of his reading, was Mr Boffin's chief literary difficulty indeed: for some time he was divided in his mind between half, all, or none; at length, when he decided, as a moderate man, to compound with half, the question still remained, which half? And that stumbling block he never got over." Are they sure it is the right verse which is authentic?...(2) *It stems from falsehood.* In the open air I used to talk about "satanic euphemisms". I now refer to the "devil's fancy talk". He gets men to refer to shoplifters, light-fingered people, even kleptomaniacs — God calls it stealing. The devil likes talk of Casanovas, having a way with the girls, a bit of a boy — God speaks of adultery. Therefore when Hill suggests that "Luke may well have de-eschatologized and historicized what was originally an eschatological declaration"[49] meaning with regard to the first Agabus prophecy that Luke fitted two totally different things together — some of us who do not move in scholarly circles might feel that it is really being implied that Luke "cooked the books", or more simply, lied. (3) *It is all dishonouring to Christ, God and the Holy Spirit, the author of all Scripture and true prophecy* (2 Peter 1:19-21). Enough said?'

But was anything like enough said in Wayne Grudem's review, which was in fact given considerable space? Equally worrying is the fact that one interpretation of the second Agabus prophecy which he sets down together with three others is this: 'Luke has confused either the prophecy, or the introductory formula, or the subsequent narrative about the capture of Paul.'[50] This is the first explanation of the passage he gives and although ultimately he opts for another explanation, he does add that 'Others, however, may find one of the first three more acceptable.'[51] Is it in any way acceptable to an evangelical understanding of Scripture that Luke is confused and therefore, to put it bluntly, inaccurate? I feel that the confusion and inaccuracy lie elsewhere and that with regard to the inerrancy of Scripture it is a most dangerous confusion.

Conclusion
Herbert Carson, writing at length and in strong terms of certain arguments of those who believe that the perfection in 1 Corinthians 13 is completed Scripture says, 'This certainly is novel doctrine coming from those who wax eloquent in face of the contention that there are two levels of prophecy.'[52] Later, where he is again discussing the subject of two levels of prophecy, he pleads that Christians be allowed to 'discuss the subject without being accused of incipient liberalism or some subtle attempt to undermine the canon of Scripture'.[53] As one who has profited considerably from books by Herbert Carson I am sure he does seek to adhere to the Word of God. Yet I have not been able to work out the full logic of many of his own comments. For example, he is one of the few writers contending for the gifts today who is prepared to state, after alluding to Deuteronomy 18:19-22, that 'The death sentence then to be

carried out points with solemnity to an equivalent church decision now, namely, suspension from fellowship, and from the Lord's table, and the discrediting of the one who laid claim to a God-given knowledge of the future.' This would include anyone 'whose prediction is falsified by the events'. The context of this is a discussion of false predictions for recovery of the sick. He reiterates this later, again referring to Deuteronomy 18 and the penalty of stoning, and saying, 'In a day when predictive utterances have been all too lightly given this is a very sobering reminder that the subsequent proof that they are unfounded brings great spiritual peril.'[54] Again, writing of the Holy Spirit, he says, 'It can be concluded that he must be utterly consistent in his speaking. There is no possibility of contradiction.'[55] Yet later still he refers to the clear predictions of Agabus, argues that he is partially wrong and sees him as a pattern for such mixed prophecy today! It is difficult to sort all this out.

My plea is that the issues really be sorted out and the consequences clearly faced. Both sides on certain occasions have made references to 'liberalism'. Long before I wrote anything on this matter Peter Lewis was arguing that, if we believe certain gifts have ceased, 'we have come close to reasoning like liberals, have argued like Catholics and entrenched ourselves behind a new dispensationalism'.[56] Dr Martyn Lloyd-Jones writes similarly: 'It seems that this idea that these things belong only to the New Testament period and have nothing to do with us is really guilty of the error known as "higher criticism".'[57]

The position of Dr Martyn Lloyd-Jones is strange. I certainly cannot summon him to support my position. But surely neither can those who take the view that there are two levels of prophecy. His general view is that while the gifts may sometimes be bestowed today they are always 'perfect'. Thus the healing is instantaneous, complete and without relapse. Similarly the prophecy is always accurate. Thus he refers to the 'accurate, literal prophecies of things that subsequently took place' by Alexander Peden and others.[58] This is not the view of those who follow Wayne Grudem.

Acknowledging that charges of incipient modernism have been made by both sides the question still remains: where does the truth of the matter lie? In both cases is it the pot calling the kettle black? My submission is that the view that prophecy is a mixed business and yet is valid is modernistic even though some of its proponents are not themselves modernists. It contradicts the Old Testament teaching that there are only two types of prophet. It turns the second prophecy of Agabus upside down and leads men to become critics of Scripture where there is no ground for doing this. It downgrades the supernaturalism in all prophecy and in a real measure plays down the role of the Holy Spirit, who is always the Spirit of truth. It leads to some strange alliances (the need for support from Hill and Aune), and some even stranger views of prophecy (Roger Day and Bernard Thompson). It rarely treats error in this realm with utter seriousness.

Let me quote John Bunyan in one of his comments about how we should deal with Scripture. He wrote, 'Also, truths are often delivered to us, like wheat in full ears, to the end we should rub them out before we eat them, and take pains about them, before we have the comfort of them.'[59] Bunyan meant by 'rub out' that we should get to the kernel and feed. The trouble today is that there are those who would 'rub out' or erase truths of Scripture to accommodate modern error. My plea is that we both retain the original meaning of Bunyan and adhere to the old orthodoxy on this question of prophecy.

Listen again to John Owen's categorical reply to a writer of the past who held the view that prophecy was a 'mixed phenomenon'. He wrote, 'That men receiving any revelation from God had always an assurance that such it was, to me seems most certain; neither could I ever approve the note of Gregory on Ezekiel 1 — namely, "That prophets being accustomed to prophesying, did oftentimes speak of their own spirit, supposing that it proceeded from the Spirit of prophecy." What is this but to question the truth of all prophetical revelations, and to shake the faith that is built upon it?' He adds, 'But that any true prophet should not know a true revelation from a motion of their own hearts wants not much of blasphemy.'[60]

Notes

Notes

When a book is mentioned for the first time the title will be given in full. After this the book will be referred to by the author's name unless otherwise stated. Q = 'quoted in'.

Chapter 1
1. *Buzz* magazine, November 1982. See front cover.
2. 'David Wilkerson's Vision of Doomsday' as quoted in magazine of Leeds City Evangelical Church, November 1974. I actually heard this prophecy being given. Details of Jeanne Dixon and her prophecies can be found in Hal Lindsey, *Satan is alive and well on Planet Earth*, Lakeland, 1973, pp.114-128, and Merrill F. Unger, *Demons in the World Today*, Tyndale House Publishers, Wheaton, Illinois, 1972, pp.68-71.
3. Q. Donald Coggan, *Stewards of Grace*, Hodder, 1963, p.79.
4. H.H. Rowley, *The Servant of the Lord*, Lutterworth Press, 1952, p.126.
5. See article on this cartoon in *The Times*, 1 May 1984.
6. Q. Thomas Brooks, *Works*, Banner of Truth, 1980, Vol.VI, p.83.
7. John Owen, *Works*, Banner of Truth, 1972, Vol.III, p.145.
8. Charles Wesley in the hymn 'Let earth and heaven combine'.
9. Q. O.T. Allis, *The Unity of Isaiah*, Tyndale Press, 1951, p.3.
10. Viscount Mackintosh, *By Faith and Work*, Hutchinson, 1967, p.151.
11. Colin Morris, *The Hour after Midnight*, Longmans, Green and Co. Ltd. 1961, p.96.
12. John Wesley, *Fifty-Three Sermons*, Wesleyan-Methodist Book-Room, p.462. (Henceforth referred to as 'Wesley, *Sermons*'.)
13. Compare E.M.B. Green, *The Authority of Scripture*, Falcon Booklet, 1963, p.30, with the same writer's book, *To Corinth with Love*, Hodder, as quoted in *Buzz* magazine, November 1982, pp.39-41. See my article on the historicity of Jonah in the *Evangelical Times*, October 1977.
14. W. Keble Martin, *Over the Hills*, Michael Joseph, 1968, p.95.
15. Q. Theo Laetsch, *Bible Commentary on Jeremiah*, Concordia Publishing House, 1965, p.201.
16. William Gurnall, *The Christian in Complete Armour*, Banner of Truth, 1974, Vol.I, p.98.

Chapter 2

1. Donald Bridge and David Phypers, *Spiritual Gifts and the Church*, I.V.P., 1973, p.41.
2. As above, p.64.
3. Michael Griffiths, *Cinderella's Betrothal Gifts*, O.M.F. 1979, p.30.
4. Keith Mason, *Some Prophets . . . All Prophesy*, (pamphlet), p.2.
5. Sylvia Macey, *Dunamis* magazine, April 1973, p.4.
6. Ross Peart in article entitled 'The Church – A Prophet-Making Organisation' in *Sound of Revival* magazine, Summer 1984, p.19. The very title of this article reflects a far from biblical theology although it does perhaps tell the truth!
7. Clifford Hill, *The Day Comes*, Fount Paperbacks, 1982, p.25. Also see introduction.
8. Dennis and Rita Bennett, *The Holy Spirit and You*, Coverdale House, 1973, p.106.
9. Review by Owen Milton of *Keep in Step with the Spirit* in *The Evangelical Magazine of Wales*, August/September 1984, p.22.
10. J.I. Packer, *Keep in Step with the Spirit*, I.V.P. 1984, p.215.
11. As above, p.216.
12. As above, p.217.
13. Peter Lewis, *Evangelical Times*, March 1981, p.17. See also Michael Harper, *Prophecy*, (Pamphlet) 1964, p.11. (Henceforth referred to as 'Harper, *Prophecy*'.)
14. Arnold Bittlinger, *Gifts and Graces – a commentary on 1 Corinthians 12-14*, Hodder, 1973, p.111.
15. Griffiths, p.31.
16. Ross Peart in *Sound of Revival* magazine, Summer 1984, p.18.
17. J. Rodman Williams Q. John F. MacArthur, *The Charismatics*, Lamp Press, 1979, pp.20f.
18. David Wilkerson, Q. magazine of Leeds City Evangelical Church, November 1974.
19. David J. du Plessis Q. Walter J. Chantry, *Signs of the Apostles*, Banner of Truth, 1976, pp.24f. Michael Harper tells how a reporter described him in this way in *As at the Beginning*, Hodder, 1967, p.54. (Henceforth referred to as 'Harper, *Beginning*'.)He offers no criticism of this description.
20. Bill and Gloria Gaither Q. MacArthur, p.15.
21. Bennett, p.110.
22. Green in excerpt in *Buzz*, November 1982, p.41.
23. As above.
24. Sylvia Macey, *Dunamis* magazine, April 1973, p.5.
25. David Watson, *One in the Spirit*, Hodder, 1973, p.90.
26. Bennett, p.108.
27. Harper, *Prophecy*, p.26.
28. Adelaide College lecture sheet, *The person and work of the Holy Spirit*, Lecture No.7, 'The Gifts of the Spirit', p.3.
29. *Teamwork* magazine, August 1973, p.7.
30. Prayer Letter No.78 of the Come Back to God Campaign.
31. Maynard James, *I Believe in the Holy Ghost*, Oliphants, 1969, p.114.

32. Mason, p.5.
33. Story related in Kilian McDonnell, *Catholic Pentecostalism: Problems in Evaluation,* Dove Publications, Q. Alec Taylor in an article 'Prophets in the First and Twentieth Centuries', *Peace and Truth* magazine, 1979, No.2, p.13. I am much indebted to articles by Mr Taylor.
34. Leith Samuel, *Speaking in Tongues,* Christian Literature Crusade, (booklet) p.14.
35. David Watson in *The Times,* 3 October 1983.
36. David Watson, *Fear No Evil,* Hodder, 1984, pp.25 and 87f. See also pp.50-7, 157f and 169f.
37. Review of above book by H.M. Carson in *Evangelical Times,* July 1984, p.17.
38. Packer, p.216.
39. Edinburgh Youth Outreach, October Prayer Letter, 1974. This was a conference at which Michael Harper spoke.
40. Q. *Peace and Truth* magazine, 1979, No.2, p.13.
41. As above.
42. Mason, p.3.
43. Ross Peart in *Sound of Revival* magazine, Summer 1984, p.18.
44. Derek Prince in *Revival* magazine, September/October 1981, p.4.
45. Sylvia Macey in *Dunamis* magazine, April 1973, p.5.
46. W.R. Davies in *Dunamis* magazine, October 1973, p.12.
47. David Mansell as interviewed in *Buzz* magazine, November 1982, p.38.
48. Bridge and Phypers p.64. Cf. Bennett p.107.
49. David Mansell as quoted by Brian Beevers in an article entitled 'The Restoration Movement' in *Reformation Today* magazine, November/December 1984, p.46. A very long excerpt from the message is given here.
50. As above, p.48. The criticisms of Brian Beevers are excellent. He has been very helpful in providing information. (The stand of the magazine *Reformation Today,* on this issue has been consistent from its inception.)
51. Bittlinger, p.112. For similar views see also J.A. Schep, *Spirit Baptism and Tongue Speaking According to Scripture,* Fountain Trust, 1970, p.132, and G.W. North, *Spiritual Life and Spiritual Gifts,* Pamphlet, 1978, pp.53f.
52. Green in excerpt in *Buzz* magazine, November 1982, p.41.
53. *Buzz* magazine, November 1982, p.39.
54. See Bridge and Phypers p.65, Mason p.6, and James p.119.
55. Bridge and Phypers state this, p.42. North p.60 and Harper *Prophecy* p.8 deny it.
56. D. Martyn Lloyd-Jones, *The Supernatural in Medicine,*C.M.F. 1971, pp.10-11.

Chapter 3.

1. D. Martyn Lloyd-Jones, as quoted on the cover of the book by James.
2. See North, pp.66-8.
3. Watson, pp.95ff; Larry Christenson, *Speaking in Tongues a gift for the Body of Christ,* Fountain Trust, 1970, pp.16-20; Alexander Tee, *Speaking with*

Tongues, (leaflet); Michael Harper, *Life in the Holy Spirit*, Fountain Trust, 1973, pp.1-17. (Henceforth referred to as Harper, *Life*.)

4. Harper, *Life* p.9.
5. Christenson, p.12.
6. Watson, p.93. See also Bridge and Phypers, pp.71f.
7. Matthew Henry, *One Volume Commentary*, Broad Oak Edition. Part II. p.438. I cannot accept the view of John Stott that Paul wrote with irony here. See John R.W. Stott, *Baptism and Fullness*, I.V.P. 1979, p.115. Nevertheless this is an excellent booklet.
8. See, for example, Christenson, pp.13 and 23; Harper, *Life* pp.8-12; Bittlinger, pp.99-106; Watson, pp.93-97; Griffiths, pp.57-63 and James, pp.119f. The latter simply speaks of 'this mysterious gift'!
9. Leonard J. Coppes, *Whatever Happened to Biblical Tongues?* Pilgrim, New Jersey, 1977, p.56.
10. Merrill F. Unger, *New Testament Teaching on Tongues*, Kregel Publications, 1974, p.110.
    11. Charles Hodge, *A Commentary on 1 and 2 Corinthians*, Banner of Truth, 1978, p.280.
12. Matthew Henry, Part II, p.619.
13. Jamieson, Fausset and Brown, *Commentary on the Whole Bible*, Zondervan, 1978, p.1218.
14. Hodge, p.249.
15. Matthew Poole, *A Commentary on the Holy Bible*, Banner of Truth, 1979, Vol.III, p.587.
16. W.G. Putman, *The New Bible Dictionary*, I.V.P. 1962, p.1287.
17. MacArthur, p.160.
18. Griffiths, p.64.
19. William Goode, *The modern claims to the possession of the extraordinary gifts of the Spirit stated and examined and compared with the most remarkable cases of similar kind that have occurred in the Christian Church: with some general observations on the subject*, J. Hatchard and Son, 1834, p.60.
20. For this section I am particularly indebted to Gordon H. Clark, *1 Corinthians – a Contemporary Commentary*, Presbyterian and Reformed, 1975.
21. Matthew Henry, Part II, p.619.
22. John Wesley, *Explanatory Notes on the New Testament*, Epworth Press, 1958, p.629.
23. Hodge, p.288.
24. Poole, p.589.
25. Wesley, p.629.
26. Wesley, p.630.
27. Peter Lewis in *Evangelical Times*, February 1981, p.13.
28. Letter in *Evangelical Times*, October 1983, p.11.
29. W.M. Capper and D. Johnson, *Arthur Rendle Short, Surgeon and Christian*, I.V.F. 1955, p.103.
30. Q. George F. Willison, *Saints and Stranger*, Heinemann, 1966, p.189.
31. John Wesley, *Journal*, edited by Nehemiah Curnock, Epworth Press, 1938, Vol.VI. p.182. (Henceforth referred to as Wesley, *Journal*.)
32. Q. in James S. Stewart, *Preaching*, Hodder, 1955, p.132.

33. Wesley, *Journal*, Vol.VII, p.255.
34. Q. Dewey M. Beegle, *God's Word into English*, Eerdmans, 1960, p.134.

Chapter 4
1. *The Times*, 9 April 1980.
2. Blaise Pascal, *Pensées*, Penguin Books, 1975, p.95.
3. *Sword and Trowel* magazine, January/February 1981, p.9.
4. Q. J. Paul Taylor, *Goodly Heritage*, Light and Life Press, p.58.
5. Frank Bartleman as quoted in Frederick Dale Bruner, *A Theology of the Holy Spirit*, Eerdmans, 1976, p.120.
6. Harper, *Beginning*, p.110.
7. In order the references are: Bennett, p.69; Edward Swindale in *Dunamis* magazine, January 1973. p.7; Tom Stuckey in *Dunamis* magazine, July 1973. p.11; Schep p.107; Bennett p.60; and letter from the Rock Church, Garston, Liverpool, as quoted in *Peace and Truth* magazine, 1981 no.1, p.10.
8. *Belonging to an Anointed Body*, the commitment class notes of Church House, Bradford, p.17. (Henceforth referred to as *Belonging*.)
9. As above, pp.15 and 16.
10. Roger Salisbury, *The Holy Spirit Experience*, Lutterworth Press, 1973, pp.65f.
11. As quoted in *Peace and Truth*, 1979, No.1, p.11.
12. Bennett, p.69.
13. As above, p.70.
14. Christenson, p.20.
15. Harper, *Life*, p.11.
16. Bittlinger, p.102.
17. *The Times*, 15 April 1978.
18. Wong Ming-Dao, *A Stone Made Smooth*, Mayflower Christian Books, 1981, p.65.
19. Q. review of his book *Though I spoke with other tongues* in *Evangelical Times*, August 1970, p.13.
20. Quoted in *Peace and Truth*, 1979, No.1, p.12. See also Bennett, p.90; North, p.76; and Packer, p.212.
21. Alec Taylor in *Peace and Truth*, 1981, no.1, p.12.
22. The references are from Norman Hillyer in *The New Bible Commentary Revised*, I.V.P., 1970, p.1069; Donald Gee Q. *The Monthly Record of the Free Church of Scotland*, June 1982, p.124; Watson p.94; Robert V. Morris Q. MacArthur p.156; another testimony Q. MacArthur p.174; as above; North, p.71; Goldingay Q. Griffiths, p.61; and Bennett, p.66.
23. Packer, p.183. See also pp.207 and 211.
24. As above, p.280.
25. As above, p.187.
26. As above, p.177, 209, 210, 224.
27. A. Morgan Derham in *Christian Update* magazine, Issue No.4, p.41.
28. Bob Horne in *Evangelical Times*, August 1984, p.21.
29. Donald MacLeod in *The Monthly Record of the Free Church of Scotland*,

November 1984, pp.249-50.
30. See Schep, pp.103-5, Bennett, pp.92-4; and James, p.119.
31. See, for example, discussions in Donald W. Burdick, *Tongues – to speak or not to speak,* Moody, 1978, pp.60-67, and Robert G. Gromacki, *The Modern Tongues Movement,* Presbyterian and Reformed, 1972, pp.56,66 and 102.
32. Wong Ming-Dao, p.83.
33. Gromacki, p.67.
34. A.A. Hoekema, *What about Tongue Speaking?* Paternoster, 1976, p.132 note 20.
35. As above, p.133.
36. See W.H.T. Richards, *Charismatic Movement in the Historic Churches,* Ambassador Productions 1972, p.11.
37. *The Supernatural,* Viewpoint No.25, I.S.C.F., p.9.

Chapter 5
1. Lloyd-Jones, p.10.
2. Harper, *Prophecy,* pp.8f. See also Bridge and Phypers, pp.28f.
3. D.G. Lillie, *Tongues Under Fire,* Fountain Trust, 1966, pp.10-11.
4. Schep, p.123. See also p.131.
5. Letter in *Evangelical Times,* October 1983, p.11.
6. Lindsey, p.137.
7. North, p.62.
8. Wesley, p.623.
9. John MacLeod in an article 'The Cessation of the Charismatic Gifts with the Apostolic Age' in *The Baptism of the Spirit and the Charismatic Gifts,* B.E.C., p.37.
10. Douglas Judisch, *An Evaluation of Claims to the Charismatic Gifts,* Baker Biblical Monograph, 1978, p.83.
11. Bridge and Phypers, p.29.
12. Schep, pp.124f.
13. Unger, p.97.
14. Judisch, pp.50f.
15. Q. Pascal, p.104.
16. James Moffat, *Commentary on 1 Corinthians,* Hodder, 1959, p.201.
17. Peter Naylor in an article 'The New Testament understanding of the Meaning of the Charismatic Gifts' in B.E.C. report, p.54.
18. Bittlinger, p.95. Also see Joseph Dillow, *Speaking in Tongues – Seven Crucial Questions,* Zondervan, 1980, pp.122-124.
19. Harper, *Prophecy,* pp.8f. See also Watson, p.79.
20. George Smeaton, *The Doctrine of the Holy Spirit,* Banner of Truth, 1961, p.140.
21. Paul Noble in an article 'Does Revelation Continue Today?' in *Reformation Today,* March/April 1984, p.27.
22. Q. Chantry, pp.141f.
23. Judisch, pp.32f. See also Dillow, p.144.
24. Q. Chantry, p.36.
25. Jamieson, Fausset and Brown, p.1217.
26. A.W. Pink, *Divine Healing,* Evangelical Press. p.21.

Chapter 6
1. Peter Lewis in *Evangelical Times,* March 1981, p.17.
2. Peter Lewis in *Evangelical Times,* November 1981, p.15.
3. As above.
4. Mike Wood in *Metro Extra,* 1 October 1982.
5. Q. *The Times,* 13 December 1973.
6. Leon Morris, *Ministers of God,* I.V.F., 1964, pp.42f.
7. As above, p.43.
8. As above, p.44.
9. As above, p.45.
10. Ray Gaydon in a tape message on apostleship.
11. Q. Morris p.49.
12. See Henry Bettenson, ed. and trans., *The Early Church Fathers,* Oxford University Press, 1978, p.46.
13. Q. W.J. Grier, *The Momentous Event,* Banner of Truth, 1970, p.47.
14. See Wilbur M. Smith, *Israeli/Arab Conflict and the Bible,* Regal Book, 1967, p.23, and John F. Walvoord with John E. Walvoord, *Armageddon,* Zondervan, 1974, p.28.
15. C.H. Spurgeon, *New Park Street Pulpit,* Vol.II. p.97.
16. Owen, vol.IV. pp.448f.
17. Stephen Short in *The Witness* magazine, January 1966.
18. Vincent Taylor Q. Bittlinger, p.67.
19. Tape message of Ray Gaydon.
20. *New Bible Dictonary,* p.50.
21. Q. John Stott, *The Preacher's Portrait,* Tyndale, 1961, p.12.
22. W. Hendriksen, *Commentary on 1 and 2 Timothy and Titus,* Banner of Truth, 1957, pp.49-51.
23. F.F. Bruce, *The Book of Acts,* Marshall, Morgan and Scott, 1962, p.287, note 6.
24. James B. Hurley, *Man and Woman in Biblical Perspective,* I.V.P., 1981, pp.121f.
25. Q. Frank Colquhoun, *What is Apostolic Succession?* Crusade Reprint, 1960, p.2.
26. *The Times,* 29 May 1982.
27. *The Times,* 31 May 1982.
28. *The Times,* 8 June 1982.
29. Q. Morris p.39, note 1.
30. John Wesley, *Letters,* ed. John Telford, Epworth Press, 1931, Vol.VII, p.31. (Henceforth referred to as Wesley, *Letters.*)
31. Martin Luther, *Selections from his writings,* Anchor Books, 1961, p.325. (Henceforth referred to as Luther, *Selections.*)
32. *The Times,* 31 May 1982.
33. Article in *The Connexion* magazine, January 1981.
34. See *Evangelical Times,* April 1976, p.13.
35. Q. article by Ronald M. Enroth entitled *The Power Abusers.*
36. *Belonging,* p.26.
37. As above, p.25 and 32f.
38. Harper on Ortiz in *Crusade,* March 1976, p.30.
39. Brian Hewitt quoting Derek Prince in article in *Redemption Tidings*

magazine, 21 February 1980.
40. *Redemption Tidings,* 7 March 1980.
41. Six articles by Colin Duriex, *CWN Series,* 19 February 1982–26 March 1982.
42. D. Martyn Lloyd-Jones, *Christian Unity: An exposition of Ephesians 4:1 to 16.* Banner of Truth, 1980, p.186. Compare the title on the book advertising his tape ministry, 'D. Martyn Lloyd-Jones, Apostle and Prophet of the 20th century'.
43. Selwyn Hughes, *Discovering your place in the body of Christ,* Crusade Publications, 1975, p.13.
44. Griffiths, p.24.
45. As above.
46. Letter in *Evangelical Times,* October 1983, p.11.

Chapter 7
1. B.B. Warfield, *Counterfeit Miracles,* Banner of Truth, 1972, p.10.
2. Bettenson, p.51.
3. J.B. Lightfoot, *The Apostolic Fathers,* MacMillan and Co, 1893, p.435.
4. See Eusebius, *The History of the Church,* Penguin Classics, 1983, p.151.
5. *The Ante-Nicene Apostolic Fathers,* Eerdmans, 1969, Vol.I, p.240. (Henceforth referred to as *Ante-Nicene Fathers.*)
6. As above, p.243.
7. As above, p.407.
8. As above, p.409.
9. Warfield, p.25. See p.240 for similar verdict of Schaff.
10. *Ante-Nicene Fathers,* Vol.I, pp.409 and 531.
11. Hoekema, p.14. See Eusebius, pp.209f.
12. *Ante-Nicene Fathers,* Vol.I, p.429.
13. Q. Robert M. Grant, *Augustus to Constantine,* Collins, 1970, p.160.
14. As above.
15. Eusebius, p.218.
16. Q. Grant, p.159.
17. Eusebius, p.220.
18. Eusebius, p.221.
19. Eusebius, p.223.
20. Eusebius, p.222.
21. Q. Goode p.113.
22. Bettenson, p.133.
23. As above.
24. As above, p.132.
25. *Ante-Nicene Fathers,* Vol.III, Eerdmans, 1968, pp.446f.
26. As above, p.188.
27. Q. Goode, pp.114f.
28. *Nicene and Post-Nicene Fathers, First Series,* Eerdmans, 1969, Vol.XII, p.168. (Henceforth referred to as *Post-Nicene Fathers.*)
29. *Ante-Nicene Fathers,* Eerdmans, Vol.IV, p.443.
30. Q. Goode, pp.8f.
31. *Post-Nicene Fathers,* Eerdmans, 1956, Vol.VII, pp.497f.

32. As above, p.172.
33. Q. Goode, pp.66f.
34. Q. Goode, p.67.
35. Q. Goode, p.73.
36. Q. Goode, p.129. See also pp.139-143.
37. Q. Goode, p.132.
38. Q. Goode, p.135.
39. Victor Budgen, *On Fire for God – The Story of John Hus*, Evangelical Press, 1983, pp.39, 76-80, 291-3.
40. Luther, *Works*, Fortress Press, Philadelphia, Vol.24, p.413, and Luther, *Selections*, p.456.
41. Luther, *Works*, Vol.24, pp.366ff.
42. Martin Luther, *Commentary on Galatians*, 1956, p.34.
43. *Luther's Letters of Spiritual Counsel*, Vol.XVIII of Library of Christian Classics, S.C.M. 1955, p.308. (Henceforth referred to as Luther, *Letters*.)
44. See E.G. Rupp, *Patterns of Reformation*, Epworth Press 1969, pp.100, 112, 186, 202 and 215, and Roland H. Bainton, *Here I stand*, Mentor Book, 1959, p.204.
45. Q. Goode, pp.156f.
46. Luther, *Works*, Vol.48, pp.365f.
47. Q. Goode, pp.157f.
48. Q. Goode, p.158.
49. Luther, *Works*, Vol.40, pp.50,53,55,59.
50. As above, p.70.
51. As above, p.83.
52. Martin Luther, *The Bondage of the Will*, James Clarke and Co. 1957, p.111.
53. Luther, *Selections*, p.38.
54. See Bridge and Phypers, pp.37f. and Bittlinger, p.68.
55. John Calvin, *Institutes of the Christian Religion*, James Clarke and Co. 1957, Vol.II, p.319. (Henceforth referred to as Calvin, *Institutes*.)
56. As above, p.318.
57. As above, p.319.
58. As above, p.637.
59. Calvin, *Institutes*, Vol.I, p.8.
60. Calvin, *Commentary on 1 Corinthians*, pp.291,292.
61. Q. Goode, p.64.
62. Q. Goode, p.62.
63. Q. Goode, p.64.
64. *Spiritual and Anabaptist Writers*, Vol.XXV of Library of Christian Classics, S.C.M. 1957, p.210. (Henceforth referred to as *Anabaptist Writers*.)
65. As above, p.212.
66. As above.
67. Q. James M. Stayer, *Anabaptists and the Sword*, Coronado Press, 1973, p.223.
68. *Anabaptist Writers*, p.216.
69. Menno Simons, *Complete Writings*, Herald Press, Scottdale, 1966, p.547.
70. As above, p.310. See also pp.218f.

Chapter 8
1.   Owen, Vol.III, p.30.
2.   See Antonia Fraser, *Cromwell Our Chief of Men,* Weidenfeld and Nicolson, 1974, p.277.
3.   As above, p.486.
4.   Owen, Vol.IX, p.197. See note 1.
5.   Richard Sibbes, *Works,* Banner of Truth, 1977, Vol.V, p.129.
6.   Thomas Watson, *A Body of Divinity,* Banner of Truth, 1960, p.21.
7.   Thomas Manton, *The Complete Works,* Maranatha Publications, Vol.XVII, p.359.
8.   Thomas Goodwin, *Works,* Edinburgh, James Nichol, Vol.I, p.10.
9.   Owen, Vol.IV, p.439.
10. Owen, Vol.XVI, pp.34f.
11. As above.
12. John Flavel, *Works,* Banner of Truth, 1982, Vol.I, p.507.
13. John Bunyan, *Works,* Baker Book House, 1977, Vol.III, p.467.
14. As above, p.417.
15. As above, pp.418f.
16. Flavel, Vol.III, p.482.
17. As above, p.483.
18. As above, p.484.
19. As above.
20. Gurnall, Part I, p.284.
21. As above, Part II, p.203.
22. As above, pp.203f.
23. As above, pp.204f.
24. As above, p.205.
25. Owen, Vol.IV, p.148. See also pp.134,451-453 and Vol.III, pp.130f.
26. Owen, Vol.III, p.130.
27. Owen, Vol.XIII, p.30.
28. As above, pp.31-33.
29. As above, p.32. See also Vol.VII, p.92.
30. Owen, Vol.III, p.13.
31. Brooks, Vol.II, p.519.
32. Brooks, Vol.III, p.263.
33. As above, p.287.
34. Flavel, Vol.II, p.308. See also Vol.V, p.434.
35. See, for example, Flavel Vol.II, p.331; Owen, Vol.VII, p.32; and Bunyan, Vol.I, pp.285, 373, 385.
36. Brooks, Vol.IV, p.92.
37. Flavel, Vol.III, p.82.
38. Bunyan, Vol.II, p.201.
39. As above, p.134.
40. Owen, Vol.II, p.257.
41. Bunyan, Vol.II, p.76.
42. Flavel, Vol.III, p.76.
43. Flavel, Vol.I, p.132.
44. Flavel, Vol.III, p.554.
45. Brooks, Vol.IV, p.216.

46. Brooks, Vol.V, p.428.
47. William Greenhill, *An Exposition of the prophet Ezekiel*, James Nichol, 1863, p.96.
48. Owen, Vol.IV, pp.453-475.
49. Owen, Vol.III, p.35. See also IV, p.472.
50. Flavel, Vol.V, pp.511-2.
51. See Bunyan, Vol.III, pp.710 and 718.
52. Bunyan, Vol.I, p.632
53. Owen, Vol.XIII, p.35.
54. Brooks, Vol.I, pp.419-21.
55. Owen, Vol.I, pp.376f.
56. Bunyan, Vol.II, p.24.
57. Bunyan, Vol.III, p.231.
58. As above, p.551.
59. Gurnall, Part II, p.93.
60. Sibbes, Vol.II, p.296.
61. Flavel, Vol.II, pp.353 and 361. See also pp.347-9 and Vol.I, p.136.
62. Bunyan, Vol.I, p.247.
63. Gurnall, Part II, p.215.
64. Watson, p.55. See also p.155.
65. Thomas Adams, *Works,* James Nichol, 1861, Vol.III, p.170.
66. Bunyan, Vol.I, p.27.
67. Flavel, Vol.III, p.58.
68. As above, pp.67f. See also Vol.I, pp.389f and Bunyan Vol.III, p.605.
69. Owen, Vol.VI, p.14.
70. Flavel, Vol.III, pp.462f.

Chapter 9
1. Charles Tylor, *The Huguenots in the Seventeenth Century*, Simpkin, Marshall, Hamilton, Kent and Co. 1892, pp.256f.
2. As above, p.258.
3. As above, p.260.
4. Charles Tylor, *The Camisards*, Simpkin, Marshall, Hamilton, Kent and Co., 1893, p.66. (Henceforth referred to as *Camisards*.)
5. As above, pp.74,82 and 84.
6. Q. as above, p.99.
7. Q. as above, pp.109-111.
8. Q. J.E.C. Harrison, *The Second Coming. Popular Millenarianism 1780-1850*, Routledge and Kegan Paul, 1979, p.27.
9. As above, p.234, note 50.
10. Wesley, *Journal*, Vol.III, p.490. See Harper, *As at the Beginning*, pp.19f.
11. Q. Goode, p.171.
12. Q. Goode, p.175.
13. Q. Goode, p.177.
14. Q. Goode, p.179.
15. Q. Harrison, p.25.
16. Q. Harrison, p.26.
17. Q. Goode, p.184.

18. As above.
19. Q. Goode, p.186.
20. Q. Goode, p.188.
21. Q. Walter Wilson, *The Life and Times of Daniel Defoe*, Hurst, Chance and Co. 1830. Vol.III, p.20.
22. Q. Wilson, pp.20f.
23. Q. Wilson, p.21.
24. Q. *Camisards*, p.227.
25. *Camisards*, pp.231f.
26. Q *Camisards*, p.237.
27. Q. *Camisards*, p.238.
28. Q. *Camisards*, p.243.
29. Q. *Camisards*, p.242.
30. Wesley, *Journal*, Vol.II, p.136.
31. As above, pp.136f.
32. As above, p.137.
33. As above, p.215.
34. As above.
35. As above, p.226.
36. As above.
37. Charles Wesley, *Journal*, Baker Book House, 1980, Vol.I, p.138. (Henceforth referred to as 'Charles Wesley'.)
38. As above.
39. As above, p.152.
40. As above, p.153.
41. As above.
42. As above, p.168.
43. Charles Wesley, Vol.II, p.52.
44. As above, p.55.
45. Warfield, pp.128 and 129.
46. John Wesley, *Works*, James Mason, London, 1829 Vol.VII, pp.26-7. Unfortunately these words are quoted in the Mormon leaflet *The Falling Away and Restoration of the Gospel of Jesus Christ Foretold*.
47. Wesley, *Journal*, Vol.III, pp.53f.
48. As above, p.148.
49. As above, p.239.
50. Wesley, *Journal*, Vol.V, p.11.
51. Wesley, *Journal*, Vol.IV, p.539. See pp.535f and Wesley, *Letters* Vol.IV, pp.202f, 205 and 206.
52. Wesley, *Journal*, Vol.V, p.9.
53. Wesley, *Journal*, Vol.VII, p.459.
54. Wesley, *Sermons*, p.41.
55. As above, p.143.
56. As above, p.525.
57. As above, p.527.
58. Wesley, *Journal*, Vol.VII, p.153.
59. Wesley, *Letters*, Vol.IV, p.122.
60. Q. Arnold Dallimore, *George Whitefield*, Banner of Truth, 1970, Vol.I, p.327.

61. As above.
62. As above, p.328.
63. George Whitefield, *Journals*, Banner of Truth, 1960, p.442.
64. Q. D.M. Lloyd-Jones, *Exposition of Romans 8:5-17*, Banner of Truth, 1974, p.332.
65. George Whitefield, *Letters*, Banner of Truth, 1976, p.50.
66. As above, p.51.
67. As above.

Chapter 10
1.   Jonathan Edwards, *Works*, Banner of Truth, 1974, Vol.I, p.378. (Unless otherwise stated all the references in this chapter will be to this two-volume work.)
2.   Joseph Tracy, *The Great Awakening*, Banner of Truth, 1976, p.326.
3.   As above, pp.146 and 176.
4.   As above, p.205.
5.   As above, p.234.
6.   As above, p.245.
7.   As above.
8.   As above, p.250.
9.   As above, p.241.
10. Vol.I, p.363.
11. Vol.II, p.274.
12. Vol.I, p.lxxxiv.
13. As above.
14. Vol.I, p.xcix.
15. See the flyleaf.
16. D. Martyn Lloyd-Jones, article on 'Jonathan Edwards' in *The Puritan Experiment in the New World*, Westminster Conference Papers, 1976, p.109.
17. Vol.I, p.369.
18. Vol.II, p.261.
19. Vol.I, p.408.
20. Vol.I, p.587.
21. Vol.I, p.396.
22. Vol.I, p.398.
23. Vol.I, p.431.
24. Vol.I, p.282.
25. Vol.II, p.158.
26. Vol.I, p.281.
27. Vol.II, p.958.
28. Jonathan Edwards, *Charity and its Fruits*, Banner of Truth, pp.29-30.
29. Vol.II, p.274.
30. Vol.II, p.275.
31. Vol.II, p.274.
32. Vol.II, p.800.
33. Vol.I, p.617.
34. Vol.II, p.520.

35. Vol.II, p.86.
36. Vol.II, pp.160 and 162.
37. Vol.I, p.609.
38. Vol.II, p.474.
39. Vol.I, p.268. See also pp.251, 254, 287, and 405.
40. Vol.I, p.272.
41. Vol.I, pp.404f.
42. Vol.I, p.258.
43. Vol.II, p.451.
44. Q *Increasing in the Knowledge of God*, Puritan Papers, 1960, p.20. Dr Packer gives no reference for this intriguing comment!
45. Vol.I, p.478. See also pp.412 and 417 and Vol.II, p.859.
46. Vol.I, p.278. See also p.411.
47. Vol.I, p.406.
48. Vol.II, p.274.
49. Vol.I, p.404.
50. Vol.II, p.275.
51. Vol.I, p.404.
52. Vol.I, p.248.
53. Vol.I, p.379.
54. Vol.I, p.577 and II, p.563.
55. Vol.II, p.70 and I, p.268 note.
56. Vol.I, p.404.
57. Vol.II, p.269.
58. Vol.II, p.268.
59. Vol.II, p.265.

Chapter 11
1. Q. Arnold Dallimore, *The Life of Edward Irving*, Banner of Truth, 1983, p.175.
2. See Dallimore, pp.137-140, 158f and Goode, pp.24f.
3. Q. Goode, pp.38f.
4. Q. Goode, p.22. See Dallimore, pp.116f and 155f.
5. Q. Goode, p.34.
6. Q. Goode, p.23. See also pp.29, 41f, 132-5.
7. See Goode, pp.28-33 and Dallimore, pp.147 and 153.
8. Q. Goode, p.11. See pp.11-14 and Dallimore, p.58.
9. Q. Goode, p.39.
10. Q. Goode, p.48f.
11. Q. Dallimore, p.156.
12. Letter in *Evangelical Times*, October 1983, p.11.
13. W.R. Davies, in *Dunamis*, April 1974, p.8.
14. C.H. Spurgeon, *New Park Street Pulpit*, Vol.IV, p.207. All the following references to Spurgeon are from the original New Park Street and Metropolitan Pulpit Volumes. Just the volume and page number will be given.
15. XVIII, p.185. See also X, p.542, XVII, p.178, XVIII, p.626, XXIII, p.471 and L, p.195.

16. XXX, P.11. See also p.225.
17. X, p.542.
18. XII, pp.692f.
19. XI, pp.32f.
20. XXXVII, p.45.
21. XXX, p.386.
22. Harper, *Beginning,* p.25. See also Bruner, pp.48f.
23. G. H. Lang, *The Earlier History of the Tongues Movement,* Raven Publishing Co. (n.d.) p.5. (Henceforth referred to as Lang)
24. Lang, p.63, See also pp.74f.
25. G.H. Lang, *The Churches of God,* Paternoster, 1959, pp.126f.
26. Bruner, p.118.
27. Q. Bruner, p.120.
28. Q. Lang, p.16.
29. Q. Bruner, p.100.
30. Q. Bruner, p.123.
31. Q. Bruner, p.124.
32. Lang, pp.28-30.
33. Q. Lang, p.10.
34. Q. Lang, p.59.
35. Q. Lang, p.60.
36. Q. Lang, p.61.
37. Q. Lang, p.20.
38. Q. Lang, p.77.
39. Q. Lang, pp.20f.
40. Q. Lang, p.22.
41. Q. Lang, p.42.
42. Q. Lang, p.44.
43. Q. Lang, p.37.
44. Q. Lang, p.23.
45. Q. Bruner, p.125.
46. Q. Agnus Hall, *Strange Cults,* Aldus Books, 1976, p.19.
47. See MacArthur, p.215.
48. Q. Lang, p.57.
49. Q. Lang, p.62.
50. Q. Lang, p.61.
51. Lang, p.63.
52. Q. Lang, p.64.
53. Lang, p.50.
54. As above, pp.40f.
55. As above, pp.25f.
56. As above, p.58.
57. As above, p.18.
58. Q. Lang, p.41.
59. See Lang, pp.14f.
60. See Lang, p.24.
61. Q. Lang, p.39.
62. Lang, p.49.
63. See Lang, p.73.

64. Goode p.iv.
65. Harper, *Beginning*, p.100.
66. As above, p.101. I feel also that the quotation from Owen given by Dr Packer at the close of his book (see p.251) is hardly justified in view of the author's trivial treatment of the gifts and hardly just in view of Owen's exhaustive analysis. I feel moreover that it is a quotation taken somewhat out of context.
67. As above, p.111.
68. In Carl Brumback, *What meaneth this?* Stanley H. Frodsham, *With Signs Following*, John L. Sherrill, *They speak with other Tongues*, (see Hoekema, p.17 note 17) and Keith Mason, *New Languages*, p.12.
69. Christenson, p.31.
70. Harper, *Beginning*, p.20. No reference is given by Harper but the passage can be consulted in Luther, *Letters*, p.52.
71. John Knox, *The History of the Reformation in Scotland*, Banner of Truth, 1982, p.277. see note 1. See also p.251.
72. See Thomas M'Crie, *The Life of John Knox*, Free Presbyterian Publications, 1976, pp.282-5.
73. Letter in *Evangelical Times*, October 1983, p.11.
74. Robert Woodrow, *A history of the Sufferings of the Church of Scotland from the Restoration to the Revolution*, Glasgow, 1830, Vol.IV, p.396.
75. As above, pp.396ff.
76. See Alexander Smellie, *Men of the Covenant*, Banner of Truth, 1960, pp.406ff.
77. John Kennedy, *The Days of the Fathers in Ross-shire*,Christian Focus Publications, 1979, pp.90, 141,156f., 187 and 209.
78. Leslie Davison as quoted in William R. Davies and Ross Peart, *The Charismatic Movement and Methodism*, Methodist Home Mission, 1973, p.2.
79. Charles Clarke on 'John Wesley's Charismatic Ministry' in *Sound of Revival*, magazine, April 1975, pp.3-7.
80. Bennett p.65. See also Harper, *Beginning*, p.21, where a diary reference from an early Methodist preacher Thomas Walsh is given which is by no means a clear reference to tongue-speaking!

Chapter 12
1. Philip Hughes Q. *Crusade*, February 1964, p.13.
2. Norman Grubb, *Once Caught, No Escape*, Lutterworth, 1969, pp.196f. See also pp.83-89.
3. Rex Gardner in *Crusade*, June 1974, p.7.
4. Letters in *Crusade* magazine, August 1974, p.3. See also p.4.
5. Lloyd-Jones, *The Supernatural in Medicine*, p.12. See also pp.10f.
6. Peter Lewis in *Evangelical Times*, August 1980, p.13.
7. Peter Lewis in *Evangelical Times*, February 1981, pp.12f.
8. Q. Bruner p.28.
9. As above. See also Gromacki, p.102.
10. Lillie, pp.15f.
11. Q. *Crusade* magazine, March 1976, p.29.

12. Peter Lewis in *Evangelical Times,* November 1981, p.15.
13. Lloyd-Jones, *The Supernatural in Medicine,* pp.23f.
14. Billy Graham, *The Holy Spirit,* Hodder, p.178.
15. Judisch, p.16.
16. See Goode, p.273.
17. Q. Goode, p.192.
18. See Dallimore, pp.48f and 61f.
19. Michael Harper in *Crusade* magazine, May 1972, p.23.
20. Ross Peart in *Methodist Recorder,* 2 August 1973.
21. See essay by Lord MacLeod in *Is there a Life After Death?* Arthur James, 1960, pp.100-101, where he says, 'But because Love is the final reality I am glad that Christ in 1 Corinthians 13, reveals Himself, makes it clear that at the very last Love will conquer and save all – that "Love may be everything to everyone".'
22. Church Newsletter of United Apostolic Faith Church, Scarborough, Ontario, Canada. May 1973.
23. Harper, *Beginning,* pp.51-3.
24. Letter to *The Times,* 7 August 1974. See also *Crusade,* January 1975, p.21.
25. See the back cover of the book.
26. David Pawson in *Buzz,* December 1978, p.7.
27. As above, pp.4-9.
28. As above, p.4. See also Dennis Bennett, *Nine O'Clock in the Morning,* Kingsway Publications, 1979, p.226.
29. As above, p.5.
30. See H.M. Carson, *Rome and Reunion,* (pamphlet) p.13. Or better still a symposium by leading Roman Catholics in England where modernism, undermining of Scripture, denial of hell are all apparent. Michael de la Bedoyere ed., *The Future of Catholic Christianity,* Penguin Books, 1968, especially see pp.20f, 23, 35 (note 1), 46, 61f, 65 (note 1), 82 (note 1), 89, 135, 206, 247-50, 256.
31. *On Fire for God,* pp.287f.
32. On Paul VI see Roy MacGregor-Hastie, *Pope Paul VI,* A Four Square Book, 1966 and John Clancy, *Apostle for Our Times, Pope Paul VI,* Collins, 1964. The reference from *Hamlet* is from Act 1, scene 5.
33. Norman St John Stevas, *Pope John Paul II,* Faber and Faber, 1982, p.90. See also p.92, and Lord Longford, *Pope John Paul II,* Michael Joseph/Rainbird, 1982, p.10. See also pp.40, 66, 84 and 120.
34. *The Times,* 29 May 1982.
35. As above.
36. *The Times,* 31 May 1982.
37. See David Yallop, *In God's Name,* Jonathan Cape, 1984, especially pp.262, 290f and 307. For a view of the bargaining and scheming behind the papal elections see the book by the Jesuit Malachi Martin, *The Final Conclave,* Corgi Books.
38. Harper in *The Kingdom Overseas* magazine, October 1973, p.9.
39. Cardinal Suenens, *Ecumenism and Charismatic Renewal,* Darton, Longman and Todd, 1979, p.41. See also p.12.
40. As above, p.29.

41. As above, p.41.
42. As above, p.47.
43. As above, p.80 and as Q.   *Peace and Truth*, 1981, No.1, p.13.
44. As above, p.58.
45. Kevin and Dorothy Ranaghan, *Catholic Pentecostals*, Paulist Press Deus Books, 1969, p.68.
46. As above, p.87.
47. Thomas Flynn, *The Charismatic Renewal and the Irish Experience*, Hodder, 1974, p.92.
48. As above, p.129.
49. Ranaghan, p.151.
50. Edward D. O'Connor, *The Pentecostal Movement in the Catholic Church*, Ave Maria Press, 1971, p.128.
51. Peter Nichols, *The Pope's Divisions – The Roman Catholic Church Today*, Faber and Faber, 1981, pp.201f.
52. As above, p.200f.
53. Luther, *Works*, Vol.24, p.64. See also Owen, Vol.XIII, p.34 and Bunyan, Vol.II, p.76.
54. Luther, as above, p.74.
55. Richard Chenevix Trench, *Notes on the Miracles of Our Lord*, London, 1886, p.26 (note 1).
56. Patrick Marnham, *Lourdes*, Granada, 1981, p.27.
57. Q. above work, p.120.
58. Warfield, p.49. See also pp.53-4 and 283f.
59. Francis McNutt, *Healing*, Bantam Books, 1979, p.115.
60. Ranaghan, p.178.
61. Gromacki, p.156.
62. Geoffrey Ashe, *Miracles*, Sphere Books (Abacus), 1979, pp.41 and 78. See also pp.32, 35, 38-9, 77 and on Lourdes and Fatima pp.100-123.
63. As above, p.65.
64. *The Times*, 22 June 1984.
65. *The Times*, 18 February 1985.
66. See Peter Masters, *The Charismatic Phenomenon*, (booklet) p.19 and MacArthur, p.59.
67. Bennett, pp.126-130. See also Ashe, pp.66f on levitation.
68. Bennett, p.137.
69. Watson, p.90.
70. Harper, *Beginning*, p.27.
71. As above, p.32.
72. Patricia Beal and Martha Keys, *The Folk Arts in Renewal*, Hodder, 1980, pp.58f.
73. See review by Malcolm Watts in *Evangelical Times*, February 1976, pp.14,15.
74. See *Evangelical Times*, January 1982, pp.8, 9.
75. Masters, p.2.
76. See Kurt Koch, *Occult Bondage and Deliverance*, Evangelization Publishers, p.55.
77. See MacNutt pp.14 and 131f and Lloyd-Jones *(The Supernatural in Medicine)* pp.7 and 21. Dr Lloyd-Jones is cautious in his assessment. He

by no means believes that striking cures validate a woman being a minister! There are many helpful points in his booklet.

78. See Helen Kooiman Hosier, *Kathryn Kuhlman*, Lakeland, 1977, pp.55f.
79. As above, p.98. See also pp.74f.
80. As above, p.91. See also pp.78f.
81. As above, pp.110-112. See also pp.66f and 102f.
82. MacArthur, pp.136-41.
83. Hosier, p.47.
84. As above, p.118.
85. Q. Goode, pp.41f.
86. See William W. Watty in article in *Kingdom Overseas* magazine, October 1973, pp.17f.
87. *Sword and Trowel*, December 1982, p.18.
88. Gromacki, p.159.
89. See W.R. Davies on David du Plessis, *Dunamis*, October 1973, p.9.
90. Gromacki, pp.156 and 160.
91. See, for example, appeal from Spanish Evangelical Alliance in *Evangelical Times*, April 1980 pp.8f and also attitude of Italian Evangelical Alliance in *Evangelical Times*, May 1980, p.9.

Chapter 13

1. *Crusade* magazine, April 1981, p.27.
2. *Evangelical Times*, November 1980, p.6.
3. *GrapeVine*. First issue of local newspaper.
4. Mike Wood, Peter Simpson and Andrew Howell on 10 January, 25 February, and 1 March 1980 in *Rochdale Observer*.
5. See Brian Edwards, *Shall we Dance?* Evangelical Press, 1984, especially pp.3ff. and 54-67.
6. Beall and Barker, pp.31f and Anne Long, *Praise Him in the Dance*, Hodder, 1976, pp.21f.
7. Q. Robert L. Short, *The Parables of Peanuts*, Fontana, 1969, p.12.
8. Q. above book, p.32.
9. Long, pp.24 and 74f.
10. As above, p.23.
11. Beall and Barker, p.33.
12. David Watson, Q. Beall and Barker, p.48.
13. Marjorie Rowling, *Everyday Life in Medieval Times*, Carousel Book, 1973, p.77.
14. Derek Wilson, *The People and the Book*, Barrie and Jenkins, 1976, p.7.
15. Letter in *Rochdale Observer*, 5 March 1983.
16. Malcolm Muggeridge, *Jesus*, Collins, 1975, pp.92, 102, 119, 139ff, 146, 161.
17. *The Guardian*, 26 September 1967.
18. Dorothy L. Sayers, *The Man Born to be King*, Gollancz, 1943, p.26.
19. Dorothy L. Sayers, *Unpopular Opinions*, London, 1946, p.21.
20. *Crusade*, April 1981, p.30.
21. Q. Janet Hitchman, *Such a Strange Lady – a biography of Dorothy L. Sayers*, New English Library, 1965, p.154.

22. Long, p.146.
23. As above, p.166.
24. *Crusade*, April 1981, p.28.
25. Beall and Barker, pp.46,47.
26. As above, p.130.
27. *The Times*, 20 August 1983.
28. Newspaper of European Missionary Fellowhip, Ocotber/December
29. See Elton Trueblood, *The Humour of Christ*, Libra Book, 1965.
30. Wilson, p.82.
31. Flavel, Vol.VI, p.379.
32. Long, pp.25 and 48. It is noteworthy that Dr Packer's book uses this kind of language. See pp.229 and 231-2. In the former passage he says, 'Glossolalia prayer may help to free up and warm some cerebral people . . .'
33. Long, p.24.
34. As above, pp.29, 46 and 119.
35. Beall and Barker, pp.251f. See also pp.77 and 101.
36. Long, pp.26f.
37. Long, pp.28f and 174f.
38. As above.
39. As above, p.158.
40. As above, pp.90 and 179.
41. *The Times*, 24 June 1981.
42. Beall and Barker, p.80.
43. Owen, Vol.I, p.393. In this volume he turns again and again to this theme. See also pp.141-3, 159f, 244, 290.
44. See William Barclay, *A New Testament Wordbook*, S.C.M. 1959, p.57.
45. David Watson in *Crusade* magazine, May 1980, pp.43 and 44 and also in *Rochdale Observer*, 8 March 1980.
46. Beall and Barker, pp.95, 76, 124.
47. Florence Becker Lennon, *Lewis Carroll*, Cassell and Co. 1947, p.170.
48. Owen, Vol.VII, p.93.
49. Quoted in article by John Marshall, 'Dance and Drama in Worship and Evangelism – a Contemporary Problem' in *Banner of Truth* magazine, July 1978, p.20.

Chapter 14
1. Letter in *Crusade*, December 1974, p.13.
2. Goode, p.290.
3. Q. *Crusade* magazine, April 1973, p.5.
4. J. Isamu Yamamota, *The Moon Doctrine*, Intervarsity (USA), 1980, p.4.
5. North, p.62.
6. Charles Farah of Oral Roberts University Q. MacArthur pp.32f.
7. Peter Lewis in *Evangelical Times*, March 1981, p.17.
8. Packer, p.224.
9. Letter in *Crusade*, April 1964, p.32.
10. Letter in defence of Michael Harper in *Crusade*, September 1972, p.32.

11. North, p.54.
12. Lillie, p.42.
13. Circular letter from John Ward, November 1973.
14. Clifford Longley in *The Times,* September 14, 1981.
15. *Revival* magazine, August 1973, p.2.
16. See *Crusade* magazine, June 1974 pp.34-7 and *Crusade,* August 1974, p.12.
17. C.S. Lewis, *Fern-seed and Elephants,* Fontana, 1978, p.111.
18. *Let the Earth hear His Voice,* pp.39 and 300f.
19. Goode, p.232.
20. As above, pp.247 and 252.
21. Peter Lewis in *Evangelical Times,* December 1984, p.21.
22. Goode, pp.45f.
23. Q. MacArthur, p.32.
24. Goode, p.286.
25. Long, pp.104-109, 162-169.
26. David du Plessis Q. Chantry p.43.
27. *Crusade* magazine, July 1964, p.5.
28. Interview with Michael Harper in *Today,* March 1984, p.31.
29. Packer, p.186.
30. Michael Green as Q. *Buzz,* November 1982, p.41.
31. Q. Leon Morris, *Spirit of the Living God,* I.V.F., 1960, p.64, note 3.
32. Dr Eldon Wilsdon Q. *Methodist Recorder,* 2 May 1974.
33. George E. Gardiner, *The Corinthian Catastrophe,* Kregel, 1977. p.53.
34. Q. Hoekema, p.134.
35. Ken Haarnhof in *Reformation Today,* October/November 1973, p.20.
36. Q. Gardiner, p.55.

Appendix

1. See Chapter 1 and a leaflet containing a review of the books by Wayne Grudem and David Hill.
2. H. M. Carson, *Spiritual Gifts for Today? Evangelical and Charismatic Come Together,* Kingsway Publications 1987, p. 161.
3. See Review in *Banner of Truth* Magazine, December 1985 and especially p. 23. Don Carson in *Showing the Spirit. A Theological Exposition of 1 Corinthians 12-14* (Baker Book House 1987) pp.97f also draws attention to this text. He supports the position of Wayne Grudem with some reservations. His book is very disappointing and his view of tongues, in its failure to grapple with the point that they are real languages, and theologically significant as such, verges on the weird. See especially pp.82-7.
4. Article 'Spiritual Gifts Then and Now' by Max Turner in *'Vox Evangelica'* Vol. XV. 1985, p. 10.
5. David E. Aune, *Prophecy in Early Christianity and the Ancient Mediterranean World,* Eerdmans 1983, pp. 96, 111, 163, 178, 184, 248.
6. As above, p. 264. See also p. 263.

7. David Hill, *New Testament Prophecy*, Marshall, Morgan & Scott. 1985, pp. 107-8.
8. Article in *Evangelical Times*, April 1986.
9. Roy Clements, *Word and Spirit*, UCCF Booklet, 1986, p. 26.
10. Carson, p. 165.
11. As above, p. 173ff.
12. Bernard Thompson, tape *Speaking the prophetic word into people's lives.*
13. Patrick Fairbairn, *Prophecy*, Baker Book House. Reprint 1976, pp. 113, 117-8, 501-9.
14. *The New Bible Dictionary.* Edited by J. D. Douglas, IVF 1962, p. 1044. See also p. 1040.
15. Hill, p. 77. David Aune writes, 'Early Christians characteristically claimed divine authority for their message, and there is no reason to regard the claims of Agabus (Acts 21:11) or Ignatius of Antioch (Philad. 7:1) as in any way inferior to John the prophet' (p. 208). Just prior to this he alludes to the striking claim of Revelation 22:10-11. See also Aune pp. 328-9 for a discussion of 'messenger formulas'.
16. Wayne Grudem, *The Gift of Prophecy in 1 Corinthians*, University Press of America. 1982, p. 79.
17. *New Bible Dictionary*, p. 1038.
18. Quoted in Fairbairn, p. 80.
19. Fairbairn, pp. 212-9. See also pp. 79, 98 and 159ff.
20. See chapter 10, pp. 166 and chapter 11, pp. 190-191, where I give two examples of this kind of false prophecy.
21. Carson, p. 174.
22. Grudem, p. 80.
23. Luther, *Lectures on Genesis*, Vol. II. Concordia Publishing House. 1960, p. 137.
24. Turner, p. 16.
25. Carson, p. 164; Clements, pp. 22f.
26. Clements, p. 22; Carson, p. 162.
27. Grudem, pp. 21-33.
28. See George Smeaton, *The Doctrine of the Holy Spirit*, Banner of Truth 1961, p. 140.
29. Grudem, p. 76. Aune in a complicated discussion seems to feel that Agabus was wrong and that Luke has tampered with the evidence. 'Luke has, in effect, removed the eschatological features of the prediction of Agabus' (p. 265). See later for similar views of Hill.
30. B. B. Warfield, *Biblical Foundations*, Tyndale. 1958, p. 26. (See also p. 24.) Actually Numbers 11:24-30 is one of the passages used by Wayne Grudem to prove a secondary type of prophecy. See Grudem pp. 36f and 151 note 65.
31. Calvin on *Acts 14-28;* Oliver and Boyd, 1966, pp. 178f.
32. McNutt, *Healing*, p. 115.
33. *Themelios*, January 1982, p. 26.
34. Grudem, p. 111.

35. As above, p. 112.
36. Calvin on *1 Corinthians*. Oliver and Boyd. 1960, p. 302.
37. As above, p. 304.
38. C. J. Ellicott on *1 Corinthians*, Longmans. 1887, p. 279.
39. Hill. p. 134. David Aune writes, 'W. Grudem "A response to Gerhard Dautzenberg", pp. 256-8 is unnecessarily sceptical about the connection between 1 Corinthians 12:10 and 14:29' (p. 411, note 185).
40. Milligan on *1 Thessalonians*, MacMillan. 1908, p. 76; E. J. Bicknell on *1Thessalonians*, Metheuen, 1932, p. 63; Hibbert on *1 Thessalonians*, Moody, 1971, p. 248; Leon Morris on *1 and 2 Thessalonians*, Tyndale. 1956, p. 106.
41. Grudem, p. 63
42. As above, pp. 231, 261.
43. Roger Day, *How to Grow Up as a Christian Boy or Girl*, pp. 51f.
44. Tape of Bernard Thompson.
45. Hill, p. 169.
46. As above, p. 61.
47. As above, p. 62.
48. *Themelios*, January 1982, pp. 25 and 26.
49. Hill, p. 107.
50. Grudem, p. 81.
51. As above, p. 82.
52. Carson, p. 48. I think I am the one to whom he refers in this paragraph. My own position has always been that a study of prophecy rather than a particular interpretation of 1 Corinthians is the key question with regard to the gifts. This is why in this book I quite deliberately deal with prophecy first. See also my comment in a review of two books by Dr Martyn Lloyd-Jones: 'On prophecy he is particularly disappointing because of the brevity of his treatment. This, Judisch...would emphasize, is the lead-in to the gifts (and I would agree)...' See Review article in *Reformation Today*, 92, p. 29.
53. Carson, p. 158.
54. As above, pp. 97, 160.
55. As above, p. 24.
56. Peter Lewis, article in *Evangelical Times*, February 1981, p. 13.
57. Martyn Lloyd-Jones, *Prove All Things*, Kingsway, 1985, p. 43. In my review (see note 52) I have sought to reply to this. See also what I have written on pp. 55-60 and 141-2.
58. As above, p. 45. See also p. 88.
59. *Works of Bunyan*. Baker Book House. 1977. Vol. II, p. 3.
60. Owen, *Vol XIII*, p. 30.